W9-BUE-910

Edwin K. Gedney

The Deviant Child in the Classroom

The Deviant Child
in the Classroom

GARTH J. BLACKHAM

Arizona State University

Wadsworth Publishing Company, Inc., Belmont, California

4 5 6 7 8 9 10   74 73 72 71 70

To
My parents, wife, and children—
all of whom have taught me
the importance of love and
the desire to care.

L. C. Cat. Card No. 67–14243

Printed in the United States of America

Preface

Five to ten percent of the children in an average classroom today have emotional or adjustment problems. These children provide the major focus of this book—a distillation of more that a decade of work with deviant children, their parents, teachers, counselors, school administrators, and others who were intimately involved in helping the deviant child at school.

The children in this group are in conflict with themselves or others to the extent that they are unable to mobilize enough of their resources to become productive, satisfied learners. While they are not so ill as to be considered "severely disturbed," these children do need careful consideration and skillful handling to prevent them from becoming personal and academic failures.

This book is addressed to teachers—in training and in practice, and to counselors, school administrators, and others interested in children with problems. With this audience in mind, three major objectives have directed the writing: (1) to provide sufficient theory to enable the reader to understand the bases of deviant behavior; (2) to describe and explain the underlying dynamics of behavior deviations that occur frequently in the regular classroom; (3) to provide the helping person with specific and practical methods for working with and handling the deviant child at school.

Chapters 1, 2, and 3 are basically theoretical and lay the foundation for understanding the bases of maladaptive or deviant behavior patterns. Chapter 1 describes the emergence of personality, the significance of various levels of mental life, the nature of conflict, and the ways in which the developing person learns to cope with conflict. In Chapter 2, the importance of socialization and psychosexual stages, as they affect the child, is discussed. The effects of certain types of parent-child relationships and parent problems in creating difficulties in children are the major themes in Chapter 3.

Methods, techniques, and *practical* approaches, which can be effectively utilized in obtaining diagnostic information about children, are considered in Chapter 4.

Chapter 5 delves into the development and meaning of maladaptive behavior. It provides a broad perspective on the nature, dynamics, and developmental progression of a range of deviant behavior patterns.

The remaining chapters are addressed primarily to teachers. Chapter 6 emphasizes the ways in which a school's philosophy, organization, curriculum, and socio-cultural setting can either support or hamper the teacher in his efforts to help the deviant child.

Chapter 7 was written after a study of the types of classroom problems that teachers constantly reported as causing them difficulty. This chapter suggests approaches for dealing with these common problems in the classroom.

Chapters 8 through 11 are concerned with specific types of deviant behavior patterns in children. Each chapter gives the reader an understanding of the dynamics of specific maladaptive patterns and provides explicit suggestions for assisting the child. The concluding chapter summarizes and synthesizes the significant ideas discussed in various chapters throughout the book. In the final pages, those principles that have valuable applications in working with the deviant child are concisely stated. My hope is that the reader will find the book helpful in his work with the deviant child and that the child will, as a result, become a healthier and happier person.

ACKNOWLEDGMENTS

I am indebted to a number of people who have been instrumental in the creation of this book. Although it is difficult to know all of the sources from which one's thinking has been stimulated, in the formulation and writing of the manuscript the ideas of Freud and other psychoanalytic theorists and the pioneering and creative work of Fritz Redl, David Wineman, and S. R. Slavson have all had significant impact. For permission to paraphrase from the identified works listed below, I wish to thank the following: The Macmillan Company, for *The Aggressive Child* by Fritz Redl and David Wineman; Harcourt, Brace & World, for *Mental Hygiene in Teaching*, 2nd ed., by Fritz Redl and William Wattenberg; Harper & Row, for *Motivation and Personality* by Abraham Maslow; Columbia University Press, for *Child Psychotherapy* by S. R. Slavson.

For typing the manuscript at various stages, I express sincere appreciation to my wife (Sharon), Miss Nancy Magro, Mrs. Dorothy Doyle, and Mrs. Linda Burke. Deep appreciation is also expressed to Dr. Duane Manning for his constant encouragement. A word of thanks is also due Robert Gold for his work on the index. Finally, sincere thanks are expressed to Wadsworth Publishing Company for technical assistance with the final manuscript as well as for its publication.

Garth J. Blackham

Contents

12

Psychosocial growth. Parent influences and the child. Understanding the child. The facilitating potential of a school. The deviant child: Some generalizations.

The Deviant Child in the Classroom

CHAPTER ONE

The Developing Person: Basic Psychological Concepts and Processes

The task of educating children has become one of the significant challenges of the twentieth century—not only because of the international situation and the high premium placed on "brains" but also because we realize how crucial healthy personality is in the achievement of important educational aims.

Research in child development has illuminated the importance of the "whole child." However, children do not grow up "whole" unless they feel at home with themselves and with the people around them. Children who are burdened with anxiety and self-doubt cannot commit themselves wholeheartedly to learning but must exhaust their energies in fighting the private battle that rages within themselves. The upset child strives continually to satisfy his needs and to resolve his conflicts. He demands to be heard and consequently affects the entire classroom. In every classroom (of, say, thirty children), there are probably three or four children whose behavior deviates to a significant degree. In addition, there are many other children with less visible problems who need special help and skilled handling. The teacher must build on the basic structure which the child brings with him to school. It is imperative, therefore, that teachers gain insight into behavior and emotional problems and learn to deal with those forces that affect a child's behavior.

Human behavior is so complex that no pretense is made here to construct an encompassing theory of behavior. Rather, a set of concepts has been selected that will help to explain the behavior deviations of children. In this and the following two chapters, a theoretical framework is developed to lay the foundations for a more meaningful understanding of behavior.

SURVIVAL: THE BASIC TASK

The most basic urge of the new-born infant is survival (13). Yet, being human, he is more helpless than other mammals and is, therefore, notoriously ill-equipped to meet his basic needs. At birth he is capable of responding only in a general and undifferentiated way; however, he is equipped with the drives or impulses to satisfy his unlearned organic needs—for food, oxygen, water, elimination, and rest. In addition, the infant needs to experience his environment through the senses and to reduce or relieve tension through muscular activity.

The bodily processes through which the infant's survival needs are met involve three openings, or orifices: mouth, rectum, and genitals. Food is taken in through the mouth, and waste products are excreted through the rectum. Sexual activity provides a means by which the species is perpetuated. Through these processes the energy for sustaining life is generated, and these life-preserving functions are ensured because each provides intense pleasure. The discomfort arising from hunger and the pleasure associated with its relief assure the intake of food by the organism. Similarly, discomfort in delaying defecation produces tension, but relief of tension and a sensation of pleasure occur after successful defecation (13). Because these erogenous zones (orifices) provide pleasure and the means for survival, they are immediately important to the infant and his parents. These zones are also

very important in the psychological development of the child.

As the infant attempts to meet his organic needs, his behavior vacillates between excitation and relaxation (3). Because the infant is helpless, dependent on others for his care and survival, and has an inadequately developed apparatus for dealing with tension, flooding of the organism by excitement creates marked threats to his survival. He tends to avoid such a state of unmastered excitement during this early period as well as in the future. One of the basic aims and necessary accomplishments of the infant, then—if he is to survive—is to reduce excessive, unpleasant tension.

The tendency of the body to compensate for changes and to maintain a constant, optimal level of tension has been referred to as *homeostasis* (2). The principle of homeostasis is useful in explaining both psychological and physiological processes of the body. Just as the body reacts with various mechanisms to reduce excessive physical tension, so does the individual react with distinctive mechanisms to reduce excessive psychological tension.

In addition to the automatic operation of homeostatic mechanisms within him, the infant needs adults around him if he is to survive. Because he is helpless and dependent on others, he soon learns to attach significance to those who care for him. As he experiences feelings of acceptance and nurture, his tensions are reduced and a feeling of well-being ensues. Thus, he learns to value love, to attach significance to those who give it, and, later, to seek it for its own sake. And, as he matures, he comes more and more to recognize that satisfaction of his needs rests on the activities and efforts of others. He begins to attend to the world around him. As he does, certain functions and structures begin to develop (10).

A PSYCHOANALYTIC LOOK AT PERSONALITY STRUCTURE

Psychoanalytic theory divides the personality into three major divisions or functionally related processes: *the id, the ego, and the superego* (6, 8). These divisions are not to be regarded as structural entities of the brain but as useful concepts that help us understand mental phenomena and behavior. How does each division of the personality develop? What functions does each perform, and what is the significance of each in the developing child?

The Id

At birth, the *id*, or the "it" (as it is translated in English to mean), comprises the total personality structure. The ego and the superego are later differentiated from it. The id, which is totally unconscious, is the source of basic drives and the reservoir of psychic energy (1, 8).

The id drives, or impulses, constantly strive for discharge, for gratification, and for reduction of accumulated tension. The functioning of the id can be inferred, though not directly observed, by an infant's behavior, which is a continuous struggle to seek gratification, to reduce painful tension, and to enhance comfort. In the infant, the id drives know no limits except those imposed by external reality (8).

The infant, however, cannot continue to be directed by the subjective demands and strivings of the id. Limits are imposed upon his unrestrained impulses and pleasure seeking, and he is forced to begin his adjustment to reality.

The Ego

The *ego*, or the "I," is not totally unconscious. It does, however, deal at the unconscious level with the impulses originating in the id. The ego gradually comes into existence as the person develops a concept of himself. So it may be said that the ego (and the self system of which it is a part) is a result of one's maturation and his interaction with his environment.

The *self* first begins to emerge from one's feelings and sensations, which give a sense of "being." Then, as the organism matures, perceptions and images are formed that help the developing person differentiate the "me" from the "not me." The concept of self is further crystallized as the child is responded to as an entity, is called by name, and is related to, either positively or negatively, by those in his immediate environment (14).

Until the developing person has a concept of himself—a system of feelings, attitudes, desires and images that he recognizes as part of himself—he has no particular need to perpetuate his self system. With one's awareness of being a self or a person, the task of maintaining, regulating, and inhibiting the self in order to survive becomes clearly established. It is then that the executive functions of the self system —the ego functions—are established.

The ego is the mediator between the demands of the id and reality and, as such, performs a reality-testing function. Reality testing refers to one's ability to distinguish between what is "self" and what is not "self" (1). It is one's capacity to check his perceptions, sensations, memories, thought, desires, judgment, and actions to make certain they are consistent with external reality (14). Furthermore, reality testing is the process by which the ego weighs external reality against id impulses to determine which impulses will be satisfied, when they will be gratified, or if they must be modified or given up (6, 8). In addition to serving two masters, the id and the real world, the ego must reckon with the superego. The ego also functions as the mediator between the demands of the id and the superego.

The ego, then, performs some highly significant functions, and its effectiveness is crucial in the development of a healthy personality. Let us examine more specifically how the ego develops and how distortions and defects in the ego may occur.

According to Slavson (13), there are four conditions that weaken ego: (a) the thwarting or frustration of the drives for independence or selfhood; (b) ambivalence or inconsistent relationships with parents; (c) identification with inadequate, unstable parents; and (d) interpersonal relationships that induce fear, guilt, and neurotic conflicts.

During the first five or six years (the crucial years of ego development), the child's experiences are influenced and determined primarily by his parents. Consequently, ego development is very closely related to the emerging relationships between parent and child. The personalities and temperaments of the parents, the manner in which they attend to and nurture the child, and the ways in which they cope with life's tasks present models for imitation by the child. Parents tend to produce children with personality characteristics similar to their own. If the parents are affectionate, consistent, and reasonable in handling the child and in setting limits for him, he will desire to *identify* with them—that is, to imitate their behavior and to incorporate within himself their attitudes, values, standards, and ways of reacting. If they have healthy, stable personalities, the child's identification with his parents will probably provide him with an adequate, effective ego structure. On the other hand, a child may identify with parents out of frustration or fear, to protect or defend himself. But in so doing, the child will lose much of his autonomy and selfhood. Such parental identification (as a protective device) is not conducive to healthy personality development or effective ego functioning.

Excessive parental indulgence inhibits proper development of a child's ego. Overindulgence encourages self-centeredness and impairs the development of self-regulation and control. If ego development had been properly understood, the "permissive theory" would not have been perpetuated so long and so loudly. Complete permissiveness provides a magnificent field day for the id, makes it difficult for the child to develop self-control, creates self-centeredness, and produces excessive anxiety.

However, severe discipline and excessive demands for conformity also weaken the ego. In this instance, too much, as well as indiscriminate, submission is induced in the child, autonomy is impaired, and self-control is inappropriate, since the child can feel safe only when he severely restricts all impulses (13); thus, his ego is deprived of the opportunity to test reality. To develop an adequate ego structure the child must have the opportunity to distinguish the rational from the wishful and to make decisions based on his distinctions.

The child must also have the opportunity to test his developing skills and master his environment in an atmosphere that is safe and consistent with his level of development. A two-year-old, who is just learning to eat with a spoon and drink from a glass, cannot be expected to exhibit all the niceties of dinner-table etiquette. A three-year-old cannot be expected to keep his hands off the decorative things around the home. If rigid discipline is enforced in such matters, reality is stacked against him, not graded for him. Demands for learning, conformity, and control must be well within the capacity of the child to perform.

At the same time, the child needs to have appropriate limits set for him during the time he is learning to inhibit and regulate his behavior. External limits and controls are necessary to keep him safe from physical dangers and bodily injury; they protect the child from his own impulses while he is learning self-control, which emerges gradually. Moreover, appropriate limits on behavior protect the child from the anxiety that inevitably arises when he is uncertain about others' expectations of him.

The Superego

The inner representation of the traditional moral, cultural, and ethical standards of society is contained in the *superego*. Since it is the division of the personality specifically concerned with moral standards, the superego is popularly referred to as the conscience. However, unlike the conscience, the punitive function of the superego is unconscious. Because this aspect of the superego is unconscious, we are unable to control its activities; we simply experience its operation.

The superego performs several important functions. Among these functions are the following (1, 6, 8):

1. It serves as a "watchdog"—approving or disapproving a person's wishes and actions. In other words, it acts to inhibit the impulses of the id.

2. By inducing feelings of guilt or remorse, it punishes the person and demands repentance for wrong doing.

3. It enhances a person's self-esteem, in reward for submission to its forces. Resistance to its forces usually results in feelings of remorse or unworthiness; that is, there may be a loss of self-esteem for the performance of actions inconsistent with the incorporated values of the superego.

4. It strives for perfection.

Like the ego, of which it is said to be an outgrowth, the superego develops as a result of the child's identification with, and incorporation of, the prohibitions, standards, and values of the parents during his formative years. The standard view holds that the introjection (the taking in or inception) of prohibitions and standards is influenced primarily by the child's fear of punishment and loss of affection. This view gives undue emphasis to the importance of punishment in superego development. An affectional bond must first be established between parent and child before values and standards are introjected. Thus, parental love, the prospect of losing it, and discipline are all influential in the development of the superego.

With the establishment of the superego at about five or six years of age, the child has internalized prohibitions against unacceptable impulses. When he is faced with impulses that are unacceptable, the anxiety he experiences is internal rather than external. In other words, when the child does something contrary to the code of the superego, he experiences guilt. The guilt feelings initiate a desire for punishment so that these feelings will be alleviated or terminated. For now the feelings of guilt induced for disobeying the superego are similar to the anxiety experienced earlier when the child disobeyed the commands of his parents. Thus, the child's self-esteem and feelings of guilt depend upon his doing or not doing the right thing (5).

Molding of the superego, then, is intimately involved in the child's relationship with his parents. The parent in whom he has the greatest investment (or who is most significant to his survival) will tend to be the one who interacts most frequently with and controls the child. Thus, dominating mothers often assume a disproportionate role in the superego development of the child.

The general pattern of demands and restrictions in the family also has a marked impact. If both parents are strict and punish the child severely for the expression of most impulses, the child is likely to have a tyrannical superego. His behavior, indeed his life, will be characterized by a rather rigid moral code. Unfortunately, little can be done consciously by the person to alter these superego demands.

The development of the superego, then, is of crucial significance in the personality development of the child. A child's superego structure has much to do with his emotional health, the pleasure and happiness he experiences in life, and, ultimately, the superego model to which he will subject his own children.

LEVELS OF MENTAL LIFE

The activities of the mind (the mental life) operate at several levels of awareness. Conscious mental activity is only a part of one's total mental life. Psychoanalytic theory postulates three major levels of mental life: (a) the conscious, (b) the preconscious, and (c) the unconscious (7, 8).

The Conscious Level

The *conscious* level of mental life consists of those mental experiences that one is aware of in the present, here and now. Conscious mental activity is comprised of sensations or thoughts arising from one's reactions to his environment and from that part of the unconscious mental activity that enters consciousness. This activity, arising from the unconscious, often assumes a symbolic disguise and (not being understood by the person) may seem strange, unusual, or even frightening, depending upon its unconscious meaning.

Conscious mental processes are generally susceptible to control by the individual. That is, by effort or force of will, one is able to concentrate his attention on one thing or deliberately think of other things. Thus, we can readily examine the content of our consciousness, and we can report what is "on our minds" and "what we are thinking."

The Preconscious Level

The *preconscious* level of mental activity is much like the conscious, differing primarily in the degree to which it is accessible.

Effort is required for one to bring contents of the preconscious to consciousness. Preconscious mental activity may be considered as the background of consciousness and is not instantly available for inspection. In everyday language, people often refer to preconscious processes when they indicate that what they are attempting to remember is "right on the tip of my tongue."

The Unconscious Level

The third level of mental life, the *unconscious*, consists of mental processes that may affect one's attitudes and behavior but do not reach his level of awareness. One part of the unconscious consists of needs, wishes, and thoughts that have never been conceptualized or consciously experienced. The other part consists of thoughts or mental experiences that were at one time conscious but, because of threat or anxiety, were forced back to the unconscious level (7, 8).

How do we know that the unconscious exists? Five lines of evidence are generally cited to confirm its existence. First, individuals receiving psychotherapy are able to recall forgotten or repressed conflicts. Second, a person under hypnosis, told to perform an act at a later time, will perform that act without conscious recognition of the request. Third, studies of dreams indicate that they are conscious representations of unconscious material too threatening to the individual to be dealt with. Fourth, "slips of the tongue," or parapraxes, are believed to be indications of inner conflicts that "seep out" in a disguised form. Fifth, sudden ideas or solutions to problems often seem to be the result of unconscious activities (7, 11).

Unconscious impulses are constantly striving for discharge. However, since the ego maintains constant vigil against expression of forbidden desires and wishes, these impulses must seek expression by substitute or indirect routes. For instance, a child with unconscious hostility for his parents may not express it directly to them, for fear of losing their love, but may vent a great deal of anger toward other people who are symbols of authority. The child may recognize that this anger is unreasonable, but he will not recognize that it is displaced; that the anger he feels is really for his parents. As a matter of fact, when such hostility is unconscious, the child will surely deny its existence if he is faced with this interpretation.

Unconscious processes play a very important role in the lives of all people. Of course, the exact contribution is dependent upon the circumstances of one's early life and the interpersonal relationships one has experienced. Certainly, a person whose early experiences made it necessary for him to inhibit feelings and impulses will resort to repression as a method of dealing with life. Thus, unconscious processes in the life of such a person will assume a very prominent role.

CONFLICT

Obviously, a child's need to satisfy all of his desires is likely to conflict with the needs of others. This is particularly true when parents begin to mold him in ways that seem desirable. The child learns that cooperation, conformity, and the absence of aggression are likely to be rewarded by parental approval. Yet, parents often do not meet his needs, or even sense his needs, at times when he seeks gratification. He gets angry, bites, hits, and cries, but he strongly feels the displeasure of his parents for such actions. Being dependent upon his parents and needing their approval, his own negative impulses frighten him because they threaten his security. Thus, he experiences a state of conflict.

Conflict arises when impulses encounter tendencies that prevent their necessary discharge. Essentially, this involves conflict between impulses of the id and counter forces of the ego, the former seeking gratification and the latter preventing expression of impulses which are not in harmony with the demands of reality. The ego, determining that certain impulses are threatening to its survival, turns against them (5).

Conflict is not unnatural. Everyone has conflict to a greater or lesser degree. However, some conflicts have a particularly detrimental effect on one's emotional well-being. Conscious conflicts rarely result in severe emotional disturbance; but unconscious conflicts frequently do. Conscious conflicts are usually the result of a striving for two desirable but opposing goals, and both goals are consciously recognized as such. However, the attainment of one rules out the possibility of the other. In unconscious conflicts, we have said that impulses of the id strive for expression while the counter forces of the ego (and sometimes superego) prevent such discharge. When conflict is unconscious, one does not know the nature of the impulses that are striving to be expressed and cannot, therefore, resolve the conflict directly.

ANXIETY

When impulses strive for gratification that may lead to punishment, loss of love, or loss of self-esteem, a state of *anxiety* or tension is produced in the individual. Since the child has earlier learned to avoid anxiety, the anxiety acts as a signal to warn the individual that his security and survival are in jeopardy. Anxiety is to be distinguished from fear in that fear is conscious and can generally be related to an object, situation, or event. Anxiety is a rather vague, disorganized, fearful reaction that rarely can be related to any object or event. In other words, it is usually unconscious.

Anxiety is an inclusive term, then, that refers to unconscious fear of experiencing a traumatic or psychologically painful state. Guilt and shame, being variants of anxiety, are also psychologically painful and tend to be avoided. These feelings also impel one toward some kind of defensive action. If one experiences too much anxiety, the ego is overwhelmed. When this happens, the capacity of the ego to perform inhibiting, regulating, and integrating functions is diminished or lost. Impulses break through, and the ability to test reality appropriately is greatly impaired. The excessively anxious person cannot perform his accustomed tasks adequately. In school an excessively anxious child may be hyperactive or unable to concentrate; in general, he does not perform in ways consistent with his abilities.

COPING BEHAVIOR: MECHANISMS OF DEFENSE

It is now clear why painful psychological states (anxiety) activate the ego to put into operation mechanisms of defense. Psychological defenses are unconscious means of dealing with anxiety arising from unacceptable impulses that seek expression or conflicts that cannot be resolved. Thus, by warding off an impulse that is dangerous (one that creates guilt, fear, depression, etc.) psychological balance is maintained.

Because all people experience conflict and anxiety, all people employ mechanisms of defense. The utilization of psychological defenses is not necessarily abnormal. However, the severity of the internal conflict, between impulses and the anxiety associated with them, determines how extensively one must defend. When impulses must be blocked constantly to avoid the anxiety associated with punishment, loss of love, or loss of self-esteem, defensive behavior becomes excessive. Much energy is expended in such defensive struggle, making it impossible for one to direct his energy to more constructive purposes. Behavior becomes rigid and loses its adaptability.

Consequently, whenever stimuli (both internal and external) tempt expression of unacceptable impulses, one's defenses attempt to ward off the stimuli (as well as the painful anxiety they generate). Psychological defenses, then, accomplish three major purposes: (a) block dangerous impulses, (b) ward off reality aspects that tempt impulsive expression, and (c) reduce excessive tension. However, in extreme instances, one may distort or misperceive the external world to avoid personal threat. If the personal threat is severe, one may even develop delusions and hallucinations to avoid conflict between inner impulses and external reality.

Fenichel (5) has suggested two major types of defenses: (a) successful defenses which achieve a termination of that which is warded off, and (b) unsuccessful defenses which require continuous, repetitive effort to prevent expression of the warded-off impulses. Pathological defenses are of the second type; impulses are not appropriately discharged and *remain* to influence behavior actively.

Sublimation

Perhaps the only successful defense (mentioned above) is *sublimation*. Sublimation means that one form of gratification, usually an unacceptable one, is given up for a more socially approved type of satisfaction. That is, the original impulse alters its form of expression. A child who exhibits marked aggressiveness in his social interaction may redirect such actions and energies into being a good football player or boxer. A man who experiences difficulties with his aggressive impulses may become a policeman and apprehend or punish those who break the law.

Inasmuch as sublimation represents surrender of an unacceptable form of gratification for an acceptable one, it is to be encouraged. However, this is not as easily done as it may appear. The ways in which children consistently behave have a past history of strong reinforcement. Typical behavior represents a compromise between opposing goals. Therefore, it is strenuously resistant to change. Children do not readily sublimate strongly reinforced drives simply because suggestions are made to do so. The new type of satisfaction must be sufficiently gratifying to warrant the change.

It would appear that the minimum prerequisite for encouraging sublimation in a child is identification with a warm, accepting person who provides an acceptable model. As the child actively strives to be like the other person, he also adopts the more acceptable form of gratification.

Denial

The person who develops the capacity to sublimate objectionable impulses is very fortunate. Actually, however, relatively few people are this fortunate. More pathological defenses are perhaps the rule rather than the exception. *Denial* is one such defense. Although denial may not *necessarily* be pathological, when used excessively or exclusively it may become so.

Denial is the tendency to explain away or to refuse to acknowledge the existence of certain facts, disturbing external realities, or inner problems. This defense is likely to be one of the first a child employs to avoid recognition of unpleasant experiences or facts. Denial appears early as a defense and is related to the child's immaturity and underdeveloped ego. However, as his perception, memory, and logical reasoning improve, he finds it increasingly difficult to deny reality.

Children use denial very frequently to avoid recognizing their own inadequacies or failures. Those children who habitually stretch the truth or refuse to admit their involvement in a situation, even when they have been caught "red handed," are making use of denial as a defense. A steadfast refusal to admit the truth can often be traced to parental training methods that were unusually strict or harsh.

Adults as well as children often use this denial mechanism to cope with life's problems. For example, parents of a retarded child frequently utilize denial to avoid recognition or acceptance of the child's mental limitations. Similarly, denial may be used by the person who has difficulty in accepting, or refuses to accept, the death of another to whom he is very much attached emotionally. Furthermore, some people will deny feelings of anger by becoming intensely affable and ingratiating. Indeed, it is not at all uncommon to see people deny any feeling that is socially disapproved.

Individuals who are excessively cheerful or attempt to keep things "light" are often defensively protecting themselves against depressive trends. Such people tend to avoid taking things seriously and look at life through "rose-colored glasses." As a matter of fact, they will go to great lengths to avoid anything that is unpleasant or depressive.

Denial, like any other defense, can perform a stabilizing personality function by delaying recognition of a problem or threat until one is emotionally able to deal with it. This is true of the person who has difficulty in accepting the loss of a loved one. His temporary refusal to face reality indicates that his emotional equilibrium has been disturbed and he needs time to adjust to the reality. It is of very little value to chastise him or to "humor" him out of the particular behavior. Excessive or exclusive use of denial is abnormal and a danger signal, suggesting the need for professional assistance.

Repression

This defense is purposeful but unconscious forgetting; it is one's refusal to recognize inner impulses or external situations that may punish or tempt him (5). Repression differs from suppression, which is one's conscious recognition of his attempts to inhibit expression of certain impulses or feelings. In a sense, repression represents a more decisive and thorough attempt to remove threatening events from consciousness than does denial or suppression.

As Fenichel (5) has indicated, repression is often the defensive action of one who simply forgets a name or a plan of action. Careful analysis of such instances reveals that the forgotten name or intent is associated with some objectionable motive or impulse. By forgetting, the person does not have to deal with the objectionable impulse or the anxiety that expression of it would produce.

Repression, then, may prevent an individual from seeing something right before his eyes or may distort perceptions arising from the sense organs in other ways. In a similar manner, dangerous ideas or memories of traumatic experiences may be repressed to avoid experiencing the pain associated with the original, frightening events. If the anxiety associated with the original, traumatic episodes is severe, one may block out all memories that are connected with the earlier events. Thus, repression can effect massive blocking out of early experience (9). It is understandable why people who rely excessively on repression tend to be quite unreflective. The simple act of thinking may provoke the return of repressed material.

As new experiences occur which relate to previously repressed ones, conflict is produced. The conflict occurs because the new events provide outlets for old repressions. The ego attempts to prevent such substitute discharges, but is not always successful. For instance, a repressed attitude or feeling toward a parent may be displaced (transferred) to another person who symbolizes the authority of the parent, but the irrational nature and intensity of feelings which are often expressed betray the repression.

Inasmuch as repressed material continues to exist in the unconscious and constantly strives for expression in some form, one must expend energy to maintain the repression. The expenditure of energy to maintain repression is observed in the neurotic who complains of chronic fatigue. So much energy is used in maintaining the repression that little remains to be used for more productive, creative enterprises (5).

A good example of repression is that of siblings who have been reared in a home where extreme demands are placed on loving each other. When such emphasis is placed on loving, the child inhibits natural feelings of hostility. Overtly, interaction between the siblings may be characterized by kindness and devotion, and unacceptable anger is repressed. However, anger will continually seek discharge, and it may be expressed in the form of dreams (12). Repression, then, keeps out of consciousness thoughts and feelings (representative of impulses) which threaten an individual. If used to an excessive degree, repression may lead to very serious difficulties.

Reaction Formation

In order to maintain an established repression, a person may develop a reaction formation. Reaction formation is a defensive operation in which an unacceptable attitude or feeling is first repressed and then its opposite is given conscious expression. For instance, a mother who unconsciously hates her child may express excessive affection to ensure the repression of her hatred (5). Similarly, some mothers who are very overprotective may actually be disguising real feelings of dislike or hostility for the child.

In everyday life there are many instances when one assumes attitudes contrary to his real feelings. For example, a child who feels impelled to violate a norm or taboo may bolster his controls against such impulses by being excessively conforming. A child who unconsciously wishes to be bad may assume the opposite attitude and become a model of virtue and righteousness (12). The person with the saccharine personality may actually be harboring contrary impulses against which he is defending.

When a person develops a reaction formation, a lasting change in the personality occurs. Therefore, when he faces dangerous impulses, he need not develop a new defense mechanism to deal with the threat. His personality reacts as if the danger were constantly present, and he remains in a state of readiness to meet the intrusion of threatening impulses (5).

Projection

This defense is a means of coping with conflict by avoiding blame or responsibility—by attributing one's own unacceptable impulses to someone or something else. In *projection*, we relieve anxiety originating from a conflict in ourselves by attributing the cause of the conflict to the external world.

Essentially, projection consists of changing the subject or object of a feeling which actually exists in oneself. When it takes the form of exchanging the subject for the object, the feeling "I hate you" is changed to "You hate me." When one subject is substituted for another subject (with the object staying the same), the formulation becomes "He is punishing me" instead of "I am punishing myself." Using this transfer of feelings, one objectifies internal threats by placing them outside himself. Another example of the use of projection is the person with difficulty in handling his own aggressive or sexual impulses, who relieves his anxiety by attributing the aggressive and sexual impulses to other people (9).

This defensive behavior is often used by children. Those who constantly tattle are really projecting onto someone else their own desire to break rules. Or a child may expect a teacher to behave toward him with the same hatred or contempt which he feels toward others. In much the same way, a teacher may be spurned by a child to whom he has demonstrated much interest and friendship because he interprets the display of friendship as an attempt to trick him. In this instance, he is projecting onto the teacher his own wish to deceive (12).

Projection, then, may provide a partial resolution for conflicts that rage inside. It helps to diminish the anxiety a person feels from internal impulses that are threatening or highly conflicting. Moreover, it provides a convenient excuse for expressing one's true feelings. For instance, if a person believes he is hated or persecuted, he may feel justified (thereby reducing his guilt) in attacking his imaginary enemies. At the same time, by construing his actions as a defense against his enemies, he is able, also, to gratify his hostile impulses (9).

As is true of other defenses, projection becomes an indication of severe disturbance when used excessively or carried to extreme. It is expressed in its more serious form by the individual who believes he is constantly being persecuted. If there is no basis in reality for these feelings of persecution, the individual may be exhibiting paranoid trends. This condition is serious and requires expert help.

Rationalization

One way of dealing with (or explaining away) a conflict is through *rationalization*. This defense allows one to make a socially acceptable excuse for actions or behavior that are not entirely acceptable to ourselves or others. Rationalization is used to gain approval from others, to avoid the pangs of conscience, and to prevent loss of self-esteem. It is a frequently used mechanism and can be regularly observed in almost all people. Indeed, it is rare to find anyone who does not occasionally make acceptable excuses for deficiencies in himself or his actions.

Any situation that requires performance beyond a person's mental or physical capabilities or requires excessive control of basic drives fosters the use of rationalization. School curricula that are out of harmony with a child's developing capacities and needs may often lead to much excuse making or avoidance on the part of the pupil. Similarly, classroom discipline that is too harsh may prompt children to give many excuses for their rebellious or defiant behavior. As a matter of fact, if a number of children use this defense in the classroom, it is usually an indication that changes in expectations or method of teaching should be considered.

Displacement

The term *displacement* implies the discharge of an unconscious impulse by shifting from the original object to a substitute. Displacement is related to repression in that feelings which are associated with repressed experiences are transferred to persons or situations where one feels safer in expressing such feelings. For instance, a child who has repressed hatred for his father may transfer these feelings to others who symbolize authority, or he may symbolically disguise his hatred by strongly rebelling against the conventions of society, even to breaking the law. In this instance, the child is quite unaware of his need to rebel against symbols of authority.

Inasmuch as teachers are symbols of authority in our culture, they may become the object of displaced feelings from youngsters who have been reared in very authoritarian homes. Since such displacements are not uncommon (particularly in adolescents), it is important for teachers to recognize that feelings expressed in this way are symbolic and not directed toward them personally.

However, it is well to recognize also that children may become the objects of displacement by the teacher. A teacher may, for example, transfer feelings generated in other life circumstances to children. This becomes especially evident when a teacher tends to persecute an individual child to an unreasonable degree. Upon investigation one may find that the child's actions or behavior do not warrant the wrath expressed by the teacher toward the child.

Displacement can also be seen in the actions of groups. For instance, minority groups may become the object of displacement of feelings by secret societies. Similarly, displacement of feeling was apparent in the destruction that took place in many cities after the allied victory in World War II (12).

The use of displacement is not abnormal unless used to an excessive degree. Like the other coping behaviors, it may have a stabilizing function and provide relief from stress or extreme pressure.

Compensation

It is relatively common for an individual to seek gratification in one phase of life that cannot be achieved in another. Inadequacies or failures in academic performance may be offset by energetic application to athletics, where success is more easily assured. These coping efforts are referred to as *compensation*.

The use of compensation can be very helpful to a child, especially the child with a handicap that prevents normal participation in activities. A crippled boy who cannot participate in baseball may compensate for the handicap by mastering the rules of the game and performing the role of umpire. In this way he is able to participate in group activity and make a contribution that is valued by the group.

A teacher may make a valuable contribution to a child who has limitations or handicaps by encouraging acceptable compensation. The stimulation of acceptable compensatory activities helps a child maintain stability and protect his self-esteem which deficiencies usually impair. As a matter of fact, such guidance may stimulate in a child satisfying lifetime hobbies or professional pursuits.

There are times, however, when compensation is not entirely healthy. The nature of the conflicts that motivate compensation may be so serious that the child uses this defense in the extreme. For instance, when a child repeatedly sacrifices relationships with others for study, to maintain top academic rank, he is not adjusting satisfactorily. Obviously, he is over-compensating for inadequacies or lack of gratification in other areas of living. Such a child may need professional assistance. This extreme use of compensation often leads to the development of a personality that is too strongly skewed in one direction. Thus, the individual shuts himself off from the types of interpersonal relationships and satisfactions that are necessary for a well-balanced and emotionally gratifying adulthood.

Regression

There are times in the life of a child when he may attempt to cope with frustration or stress by reverting to behavior that is immature or childish. When he does so, he is defending himself by the use of *regression*.

Regression, then, is one's tendency to return to habits previously associated with a period during which he felt more secure. A child may revert to regressive behavior when he is hesitant about accepting newer modes of satisfaction, or when he is expected to perform on a more mature level. This hesitancy to grow may often result from the parents' tendency to keep the child infantile.

Regressive behavior in children is not infrequent. It is often seen when one sibling feels he has been replaced in the affections of the parents by another. Such is the case at the birth of a new baby. In this instance, the regressive symptom may be bed-wetting or the desire to be fed from a bottle. Adolescents, frightened by the prospect of growing up, may resort to immature forms of speech. Teachers of high school students should not be surprised to observe girls who at one moment are sophisticated adults and at the next moment are pouting childishly as a result of being corrected (12).

As is true of other defenses, regression has its serious aspects. If it is an habitual and frequent response to frustration or problem situations, it is not healthy. Regression in its most extreme form is seen in psychotic behavior. A regressed psychotic may, at some stages of his illness, revert to behavior characteristic of a two- or three-year-old child. Regression of this extreme type is unusual and is characteristic only of severe emotional disturbances.

Regression has its more normal and useful aspects. One's ability to regress when the reality of a situation demands can be adaptive. For instance, an adult's capacity to regress in order to join in the fun of children's games is a distinct asset. It brings one closer to children and promotes good, wholesome relationships.

Compulsive Activity

The word *compulsion* as used in psychopathology means that one is irresistibly driven toward the performance of some irrational act. Thus, *compulsive activity* is the performance of certain acts as a way of coping with both internal and external demands and conflicts.

This defense is useful in coping with conflicts because it keeps one from thinking about his problems. It is obvious that a person has little time to dwell on his problems if he is busily engaged in activities requiring every minute of the waking day. There are many examples of this defense in operation in everyday life. For example, the disappointed lover may become involved with frequent pleasure-seeking activities to avoid thinking about his disappointments. Similarly, unhappy, deprived children often persist in seeking pleasures such as attending parties, movies, and amusement parks (12).

Dollard and Miller (4) present the case of a woman who had two main symptoms: (a) agoraphobia or fear of open spaces and, (b) compulsive counting of breaths or heartbeats. Among other things, analysis revealed that both symptoms were related to her intense need to defend herself against her sexual impulses. Her fear of being on the street was related to the possibility of being sexually tempted. Thus, by her avoidance of the street, she did not have to deal with the anxiety and guilt that sexual temptation would produce.

Of importance to our present analysis is the woman's second major symptom—compulsive counting of breaths and heartbeats. Analysis revealed that her compulsive counting tended to keep "sexy thoughts" out of mind. Obviously, the counting of breaths and heartbeats is such an absorbing activity that the woman hardly had time to think about anything else.

In everyday life compulsive activity occurs frequently, although it is not as extreme as in the above case. Some people, faced with conflict, will immerse themselves in activity to avoid direct dealing with a conflict. This is often the case when a person suffers a collapse as a result of "overwork." It can often be demonstrated that the collapse is not basically the result of overwork. Rather, the overwork is symptomatic of a more basic motivation—a need to avoid thinking about certain problems or conflicts.

The mechanisms of defense discussed in this chapter do not, of course, exhaust all the ways in which individuals cope with conflicts or problems. However, the mechanisms that have been discussed are relatively common and are inclusive enough for one to understand better a wide range of coping behavior.

The concepts introduced in this chapter provide us with the background for a deeper and more meaningful look at children's behavior. In the next two chapters, the basic conceptual framework will be utilized for further elaboration.

References

1. Brenner, C. *An elementary textbook of psychoanalysis.* Garden City: Doubleday Anchor Books, 1957.

2. Cannon, W. B. *The wisdom of the body.* New York: W. W. Norton, 1932.

3. Coville, W. J., Costello, T. W., and Rouke, F. L. *Abnormal psychology.* New York: Barnes and Noble, 1960.

4. Dollard, J., and Miller, N. *Personality and psychotherapy.* New York: McGraw-Hill, 1950.

5. Fenichel, O. *The psychoanalytic theory of neurosis.* New York: W. W. Norton, 1945.

6. Freud, S. *New introductory lectures on psychoanalysis.* Translated by W. J. H. Sprott. New York: W. W. Norton, 1933.

7. Freud, S. *Collected papers.* Translated by Joan Riviere. Vol. 4 (1925). London: The Hogarth Press, 1956.

8. Freud, S. *The complete psychological works of Sigmund Freud.* Translated by J. Strachey. Vol. 19 (1923–1925). *The ego and the id and other works.* London: The Hogarth Press, 1961.

9. Hall, C. *A primer of Freudian psychology.* New York: Mentor Books, 1954.

10. Hall, C., and Lindzey, G. *Theories of personality.* New York: John Wiley and Sons, 1957.

11. Hutt, M., and Gibby, R. *Patterns of abnormal behavior.* Boston: Allyn and Bacon, 1957.

12. Redl, F., and Wattenberg, W. *Mental hygiene in teaching,* 2nd ed. New York: Harcourt, Brace and Co., 1959.

13. Slavson, S. R. *Child psychotherapy.* New York: Columbia University Press, 1952.

14. Thorne, F. *Personality: A clinical eclectic viewpoint.* Brandon, Vermont: Journal of Clinical Psychology, 1961.

CHAPTER TWO

The Developing Person:
Stages of Psychosocial Growth

No mention has yet been made of the biological and genetic contributions to development. This is not an oversight but a matter of delimitation and emphasis. Our chief focus is on the psychological structure and development of the individual. Hereditary traits make the task of survival either more or less difficult, depending upon the traits the organism has inherited. Also, because of one's inherited body structure, he may be predisposed to certain behavior; however, even with a given constitution, one's development is dependent upon his training and the relationships he experiences. Therefore, in this chapter our focus will be on the psychosocial stages of development.

CRUCIAL ASPECTS OF THE SOCIALIZATION PROCESS

Before discussing the specific psychosocial stages of development, we need to explore, in general terms, some significant aspects of *the socialization process*—the process by which a child learns to behave appropriately in his culture. In other words, socialization is the process of learning whereby one develops human traits and behavior that conform to the societal code in which he lives (18).

The process of socialization is long and tedious, since the child experiences it from birth. Because his potential for learning is great, he can move in an infinite number of directions. Yet, the type of person he can become is greatly restricted by the culture in which he grows. For example, he must learn to communicate in a specified language, obtain food in a prescribed way, and conform to the social behavior of his culture.

The importance of the socialization process hardly needs emphasis; however, dramatic illustrations of its impact occur when an individual has been denied this process through isolation. In 1920 two Hindu children, Amala and Kamala (ages 1½ and 8 respectively), were found in a wolf's den in India and placed in an orphanage. Details of their life with the wolves are not known, but the fascinating accounts of their behavior at the orphanage reveal the importance of human contact and socialization (19). Amala died soon after discovery and placement in the orphanage. Kamala, about whom most of the observations are made, manifested most interesting behavior. She had a fine appetite for raw meat and ate in the manner of a wolf. She seemed unaffected by changes in temperature, had a remarkable olfactory sense, and restricted her speech to grunts and howls. Kamala walked on all fours, being physically unable to stand erect. She exhibited her first real tears at the death of Amala.

The process of changing from wolf-like to human behavior was difficult and long for Kamala. She avoided human contact, tore off her clothing, and displayed aggressive reactions by biting and scratching. It was a year and a half before she learned to hold a bowl in her hands while eating rice, eighteen months before she learned to stand erect, and four years before she acquired a vocabulary of a few words. However, even though she was extremely slow in acquiring human traits, she did achieve a minimum amount of socialization.

Why did Kamala take so long to learn relatively simple functions? Was she mentally retarded, as some have speculated? Or did she miss crucial opportunities to learn at a time when certain responses and functions would have been ready for development?

The hypothesis is gaining credence that timing is crucial in the process of socialization. That is, each level of development has a time when it can be learned most effectively by the individual. If the time or opportunity for learning is missed, that particular process is less quickly learned at a later time, and, in addition, learning of subsequent processes will be retarded. For instance, Lorenz (12) has suggested that goslings become *imprinted* (response fixated) to their mother and follow after her according to a specified pattern soon after birth. However, when goslings are removed from their nest soon after birth and do not have the opportunity to see the mother, they can become conditioned to follow their keeper. This and other studies with birds suggest that imprinting or fixation of similar responses occurs within a relatively short time after birth.

Of course, goslings or geese are not human beings, and overgeneralization is always a danger. Goldfarb (9), however, did some studies of the effects of environmental impoverishment on learning; his results suggest that similar generalizations might also apply to human beings. He compared the development of two groups of children: (a) children reared three years in an institution and then placed in foster homes, and (b) children who had lived from early infancy in foster homes. He found that even though the mothers of the institution-reared group were superior in intelligence to the natural mothers of the children in the foster-home group, the foster-home children were superior (in later childhood) in school achievement and had better ability to conceptualize. In the institution-reared group, there seemed to be an absence of ordinary inhibitions, an excessive and continuous demand for affection, "emotional imperviousness and superficiality of relationship," and an impaired capacity for typical tension or anxiety reactions.

Goldfarb's studies indicate that the type and timing of socialization experiences do have crucial effects on the developing personality of the young child.

Goals of Socialization and Development

The society, culture, or subculture in which the child lives affects his development in many ways. However, two particular forms of influence seem most basic. First, a particular society has certain goals and commonly shared value orientations for socializing children; second, child-rearing methods are employed that help children learn to behave in ways consistent with these goals (13). These two basic influences determine the manner in which a child's primary needs are met and the type of secondary needs he learns, which later motivate his behavior. In our society, for example, getting along with others, being self-reliant, achieving material success, and adhering to a puritanical code seem to be excessively emphasized. To the degree that the child in our society achieves these goals, he is presumed to have been successfully socialized (13).

Acquiring this behavior (and other human traits as well) is not readily achieved, however. As McCandless (15) has pointed out, our failures in socialization are quite impressive. The incidence of psychosis, delinquency, crime, narcotic and alcoholic addiction, and homosexuality in the United States equals or surpasses Western European, Eastern, and even so-called primitive cultures.

Are these failures in socialization necessary? What is wrong with the way we rear our children in the United States? Is something amiss with our goals? Obviously, there are no simple answers to these questions. However, we should begin to realize that we will continue to have failures in socialization as long as we subject children to goals, standards, and expectations that are contrary to their developmental pattern. Children trained to inhibit their aggression excessively will probably not be victorious in the competitive struggle that our economy demands. They cannot be reared to overconform without giving up a good deal of their autonomy. Children cannot be barraged with massive doses of "the academics" at four, five, and six without looking longingly back in their adult years to the childhood they have missed. The goals, processes, and instruments of socialization are crucial indeed.

Identification

Identification, a term we used (see p. 6) to explain the process by which the child internalizes his superego, is an essential mechanism of socialization. According to McCandless (15), the term *identification* may refer to modeling or copying, acceptance or affiliation with a person or group of which an individual feels a part—toward which he feels empathy, closeness, or loyalty. Mussen, Conger, and Kagan (16) define it as the process through which the child thinks, feels, and behaves as if the attributes of another individual or group are possessed by him. Our use of the term will be similar to this latter definition; however, in the interest of preciseness, we may define identification as the process by which a person incorporates or assumes the attributes, standards, and behavior of another individual.

The Freudians have elaborated the concept of identification, suggesting four types (10): (a) narcissistic identification, (b) goal-oriented identification, (c) object-loss identification, and (d) identification with the prohibitions of an authority figure (identification with the aggressor). In narcissistic identification one identifies with someone who resembles oneself. Quite literally, a person attaches himself to an object that mirrors himself. This attachment is in reality self-love, or identification with one's self. It does not involve incorporation of the attributes of another because the person already has the characteristics himself.

Goal-oriented identification is a result of frustration or anxiety. One person imitates the behavior of another because the imitated person has achieved a goal that the imitator wishes to achieve. For example, an adolescent girl may yearn for the popularity of a certain actress. By imitating this actress's behavior (talk, walk, and gestures) she hopes to achieve the same goal—popularity.

The third type, object-loss identification, is not uncommon. It occurs when a person is unable to possess a desired object or has lost the object. He attempts to secure or regain the object by trying to make himself exactly like the object. For instance, a child who has been rejected by his parents may attempt to regain parental love by rigidly behaving in accordance with parental expectations. Thus, he restores the lost object by incorporating its

attributes as part of his personality.

The fourth type—identification with the prohibitions of an authority figure—is different from object-loss identification in that the person identifies with the *prohibitions* of someone who is *present*. Thus, a child may avoid punishment by conforming to the demands of a "potential enemy." Identification of this kind is presumed to play a significant part in the development of the superego.

Although these four types of identification can often be seen clinically, many clinicians disagree with the Freudian concept. Many also disagree with the classical Freudian explanation of how identification occurs. This explanation is intimately related to one's psychosexual development and to his relationships with his parents, particularly during the Oedipus conflict. This concept will be discussed in detail later in this chapter, under *Psychosexual Stages of Development.*

A second theory, the *social-learning* theory, has also been advanced to explain identification (15). According to this view, identification proceeds satisfactorily and the child learns to assume sex-appropriate behavior when the parent of the same sex is loving and rewarding to the child. The boy does not necessarily give up his identification with his mother to move toward his father. The mother, by virtue of loving both father and son and desiring the son to be like the father, facilitates the process of identification.

The *power* theory of identification argues that identification takes place with the father (in the boy's case) because he is powerful. That is, the boy models his behavior after his father because the father is an effective punisher as well as a source of reward. According to this view, the threat of the father's power is just as important in the identification process as his reward value.

Although we do not know precisely how identification develops, we do know that boys tend to identify more completely with loving, powerful fathers than with rejecting, punishing ones, and identification is especially facilitated when love is emphasized and power is used wisely and benevolently. Identification for girls is more complex, although it is probable that similar factors are significant determinants in the process. However, girls apparently do not require as strong an identification with the same-sexed parent in order to be considered adjusted (15).

Stokes (17) has drawn attention to the fact that identification is significantly influenced when (a) social pressures encourage the child to identify with his own sex; (b) the model is affectionate and gratifies the needs of the child; (c) there is clarity in the role the model provides; and (d) the child has the capacity to be like the model or person with whom identification is attempted.

Now that some of the theories regarding the identification process have been discussed, the significance of the process in socialization and personality development can be clearly established. The crucial role that identification plays in the development of the superego has been noted. It is well to underline the fact that identification is primarily responsible for the incorporation of standards, values, and prohibitions in the child. Difficulties in the identification process usually lead to distorted, inadequate, or inappropriate value systems in later life. And, since identification significantly determines the behavior and roles the child learns

to assume, difficulties in this process lead to problems in establishing heterosexual relationships and in performing sex-appropriate roles. Obviously, the best way to learn how to act like a male is to have a strong identification with an adequate, loving father. Similarly, to perform the future role of husband and father, the most crucial preparation is through appropriate identification with both mother and father.

Children who experience difficulty in making sex-appropriate identifications generally have difficulty assuming proper sex roles. Boys who overidentify with their mothers tend to be effeminate. They also have difficulty with the masculine role and with establishing heterosexual relationships. If they marry, they tend to select somewhat masculine women for their mates. In many cases, cross-identification (identification with the opposite-sexed parent) is instrumental in the development of homosexuality.

Girls who have difficulty in making sex-appropriate identification have similar troubles. They tend to have problems in assuming feminine roles, relating to men, and being adequate mothers. During adolescence, their difficulties may be revealed by their tomboyish interests and excessive participation in masculine activities. Even in married life, their strong masculine orientation may lead them to dethrone the man or become highly competitive with him.

It seems likely that the identification process plays a significant part in practically all instances of social learning (3). For example, the child's acquisition of language probably is determined to some degree by an adequate identification with a nurturing parent model. Furthermore, identification probably continues to play a significant role in personality refinement as long as a person remains open and receptive to change. Indeed, the individual's self-concept is constantly changing as a result of this process.

The Self-Concept

Very important in a child's development, and primarily a product of social learning, is his self-concept—the manner in which he characteristically views and evaluates himself, or feels about himself. In a sense this is the core of one's being and is the end result of all of one's experiences.

The concept of self first begins to emerge from the child's conception of his body image. As he experiences feelings and sensations from his body, he begins to mark off his *self* boundaries. His concept of "I" or "me" is learned first from his own actions and reactions and, later, from the actions and reactions of others toward him.

The identifications the child makes with others, the standards, attitudes, and values that he incorporates as a result of this process, and others' attitudes toward and appraisals of him are all assimilated as part of the self-concept. All of this learning helps the child evaluate himself. Therefore, the esteem the child holds for himself is determined by the degree to which he meets internalized expectations and the ever changing external requirements of his environment. If the child is unsuccessful in meeting the goals his parents set for him, or if the goals are beyond his capacity to reach, he will not develop self-esteem or an adequate self-concept.

With the many expectations the child encounters, the varied social roles he must learn to play, and the con-

tinuous changes he experiences in his growing body, it is little wonder that he has so much difficulty formulating his self-concept. However, if the child experiences consistency in the demands and appraisals of others, he can crystallize a concept of himself. That is, his behavior and his characteristic way of thinking about himself gradually begin to approximate the views others have of him. He learns to behave according to certain role prescriptions that are associated with his being Johnny Jones who lives in a yellow house on Palm Drive. These anchoring points, as well as the relatively standard role prescriptions given to him by his parents and the social class in which he lives, help him crystallize his view of himself.

Although it is generally recognized that the child's concept of himself is a result of interactions with those in his immediate family, the role of his peer group is often not given the emphasis it deserves. With children of his own age he has an equal standing and thus finds his peers' judgments about himself most fair and just. The more he interacts with his peers to evaluate himself, the more he uses them as measuring rods to determine the adequacy of his accomplishments. Particularly in adolescence the standards of his peers may become the primary mirror that he uses to catch reflections of his developing self. Unfortunate indeed is the adolescent who does not measure up in this comparison.

The importance of an adequate self-concept and self-esteem cannot be overemphasized. Above all else, these are a child's greatest developmental achievements. Once the self-concept has been substantially defined (and it probably is defined sooner than we care to think), all of the individual's experiences are carefully screened and evaluated by this concept. As a matter of fact, the degree to which a person finds life pleasant, happy, and successful is largely determined by the adequacy of his self-concept.

Combs (2) has discussed with sensitivity the attributes and behavior of the person who has a positive view of self. He has suggested that the person who feels adequate behaves in a manner that enables him to be successful. He trusts himself and his impulses, and he is able to identify with and accept others. The adequate person, being at home with himself, is freer to respond to events outside himself. Since he is open to experience and is not preoccupied with inner conflicts, he is less defensive, can be more objective, and can see issues more clearly. The person who has a positive view of self can make the utmost use of his experiences, since there is little or no need to distort, deny, or repress them. With more data available, the individual is able to deal more accurately and realistically with his environment. And, being relatively free from threat (internally and externally), the adequate self is able to grow and develop unique talents without excessive concern for conformity.

Conversely, the individual with an inadequate self-concept approaches life cautiously. He carefully screens his experiences in order to avoid personal threat, and he anticipates failure as he moves further out into life. Because he questions his capacities and often feels guilty about his impulses, he struggles continually with feelings of low self-esteem. Feeling unworthy, he is ready prey for anxiety and depression. In extreme instances such an individual may feel despicable and lonely and may entertain notions of suicide.

The first five or six years of a child's life are crucial in the development of his self-concept and, therefore, the important developmental processes that occur during these early years should be considered in detail. Presented here will be the psychoanalytic view of infantile sexuality—modified, however, by Erikson's (4) sensitive insight.

STAGES OF PSYCHOSEXUAL DEVELOPMENT

The psychoanalytic theory of infantile sexuality postulates three important zones or orifices in the psychosexual development of the person. We learned in the first chapter that each of these three zones—the mouth, anus, and genitals—is associated with the satisfaction of an important need and performs life-preserving functions. In addition, these zones are especially sensitive to stimulation. Because stimulation of these areas produces sensual pleasure, they are referred to as erogenous zones. The pleasure arising from stimulation or manipulation of any of these erogenous zones is considered sexual in nature. This conception of sexuality is quite different from adult sexuality, although many of Freud's critics have often interpreted him to mean they are synonymous (7).

Blum (1) has indicated three distinct differences between infantile and adult sexuality: (a) the area in which sensitivity is the greatest in infantile sexuality need not be the genitals; (b) the goal of infantile sexuality is not intercourse, although activities associated with it play a part in the forepleasure of adult sexuality; (c) infantile sexuality is not directed toward objects but is autoerotic. These zones are the first important sources of excitation and pleasure. Being such, activities involving the erogenous zones (particularly the anus and genitals) are the focus of much interest by both child and parent. It is natural, therefore, for these zones to create conflict, frustration, and concern.

The Oral Stage

The first erogenous zone of interest and focus in the pleasure seeking of the infant is the mouth or oral cavity. His early sucking needs are obvious, and observation of the infant of one to two years of age reveals his practice of placing practically everything he can maneuver into his mouth. It is assumed, therefore, that the first major aims during this stage are nourishment and pleasure derived from oral stimulation.

The infant also receives stimulation through his eyes and tactile sensations which help him become aware of the person who feeds and attends to him. The sensations received through tactile stimulation must be of proper intensity. That is, the tactile contact must be affectionate and tender, rather than rough and threatening, for the child to associate pleasant and pleasurable feelings with feeding. If there is mutuality between the infant and mother, the infant learns to receive love and, later, develops the capacity to give of himself. Such mutuality of relationship seems to be a prerequisite for identification with the mother (4).

Inasmuch as the mouth is the focus for the child's first significant learning and social interaction, his manner of responding at this time tends to be prognostic of the future. To get what he wants, the infant learns five main methods or modes of functioning: (a) incorporating or taking in, (b) retaining or holding on, (c) biting, (d) getting rid of or spitting out, and (e) closing. These modes may serve as models for the child's personality traits in the future. For instance, incorporation may be the forerunner of acquisitiveness, retaining of determination, spitting out of rejection, and closing of negativism (10).

The extent to which these modes of functioning become fixed as part of the infant's personality is probably related to the relative frustration or satisfaction he gets at certain critical points during the oral stage. Fenichel (6) has advanced several explanatory hypotheses for fixation at oral modes. According to his view, fixation may occur when there is (a) excessive satisfaction, (b) excessive frustration, (c) marked vacillation between satisfaction and frustration, and (d) simultaneous satisfaction of biologically based drives and security needs.

Fixation at this or any other stage is crucial in a child's development. Fixation at a level or stage of development means that the person will tend to retain to an excessive degree the psychological characteristics of that stage. If a person is fixated at the oral stage, in later periods of stress he will tend to adapt by regression to the point of fixation. Thus, orally fixated people tend to meet problems in later life by regression to passivity or dependency (11). Also, because oral satisfactions are associated with love during this period, it is understandable why loss of love in later life may lead one to revert to oral satisfactions as a means of compensating for the loss.

Fixation at any level, such as the oral stage, tends to retard the individual's growth at succeeding levels. For example, if an individual is fixated at the oral stage, some of his resources for growth are arrested and cannot participate in the development that should take place at later periods or stages.

Although the child may experience many problems during the oral stage, one of the earliest and most severe arises when teeth appear. Teething involves pain for the child, and he attempts to relieve the pain by biting. It is natural, therefore, that during the course of nursing he may bite down on his mother's breast. If this process is repeated often and the child is denied gratification, he may clamp down harder and more often to ensure gratification. This causes the mother to withdraw more often, and regardless of the reason for her withdrawal of the breast, the act establishes ambivalence in the child. He is angry at the withdrawal; he is angry at his mother. Thus, he develops ambivalence toward his first love object, whom he now both loves and hates. The child's ambivalent feelings may later be expressed by his rejection of food or milk.

The oral period of development also marks the child's beginning sense of trust or mistrust (if things go badly). The development of a sense of trust arises, according to Erikson (5), from a mutually qualitative relationship between mother and child. It is not based on the quantity of food or love given by the mother but upon her capacity to meet consistently and predictably the child's needs as they are expressed. Problems arise for the child who has not had a wholesome relationship with his mother. He may grow up distrustful

of life, seeing it as undependable or unpredictable. In later years he may return to the fixations established here, solving his problems in infantile and incorporative ways. However, if the child feels assurance that his mother will predictably meet his needs, he is not overly anxious when she is gone. Thus, he attains his first "social achievement"—letting mother out of sight.

This is a magnificent achievement. The child is no longer completely dependent and, consequently, need not fear his separateness. With his developing sense of trust, the foundations for establishing his own identity have been laid. He is then ready for the next level of development, which must also be successful if he is to realize his potential.

The Anal Stage

When the child is between ten and sixteen months of age, his oral concern is superseded by preoccupation with the anal region. This change of erogenous focus accompanies the maturation of the anal muscular system and continues to about the third year. During the anal phase the child develops (or further elaborates) two modes of dealing with the world—retaining or holding on, and expulsion or letting go (4). As these modes are contradictory, conflicts experienced during this period are likely to cause the child to expel or retain at inappropriate times.

The anal stage is a highly significant one for several reasons. It represents the parents' first intensive and systematic efforts to socialize the child, and as part of the child's socialization, he is trained to control bowel and bladder in culturally determined ways. Also, with the beginning mastery of his muscular system, he seizes every opportunity to exercise his awakening motor capacities by exploring his environment. His explorations may lead him into difficulty, depending on his mother's attitudes.

The effects of the anal stage on the child's personality development are determined primarily by parental training methods and attitudes regarding defecation, control, cleanliness, and responsibility. Strict, unyielding, and punitive methods may make the child rebel against the whole procedure. As he grows, his rebellion may result in messiness, wastefulness, irresponsibility and disorderliness. Or he may adapt to the frustration by developing a reaction formation expressed by excessive orderliness, cleanliness, and thriftiness. These ways of dealing with the world may extend to many areas of one's life. For instance, the adult may hoard his money or become very wasteful, since at the unconscious level, feces tend to be equated symbolically with money. The punctuality that is demanded in going to the toilet may generalize to other events involving appointments or the use of time (10). The individual may be excessively punctual or always late.

It is difficult to know exactly what interpretation the child places on his new source of pleasure and the developing power arising from the maturation of his muscular system. It is probably safe to say that it is a time of considerable awakening for the child. He is no longer completely helpless or dependent, and as he experiences some mastery of his activities, he begins to set even more definitely the boundaries of the self. As he perceives this "I-ness" and separateness from others, he feels a greater need to assert himself. That is, he needs the freedom to try himself out, to make choices, to gain confidence in his capacity to manipulate the environment.

It is understandable why Erikson (4) has stated that the crisis at the anal stage is autonomy versus shame. A severe, strict, prohibiting regime of toilet training and control may communicate to the young child that selfhood, curiosity, and independence are unsafe and are to be avoided at all costs. It is here that he may begin to develop a series of compromises with life. Instead of developing confidence in his beginning independence, he may withdraw shamefully, desiring not to expose himself, feeling it is safer to be unnoticed.

If the child has not had the good fortune to experience relationships that develop a sense of trust or autonomy, he may turn the urge to manipulate against himself. He will, according to Erikson (5), develop a "precocious conscience" and "overmanipulate himself." Instead of testing things out by repetitive play, he becomes preoccupied and obsessed "by his own repetitiveness." He will become a slave to orderliness and addicted to ritual. His conscience becomes oppressive; impulses are excessively restricted, and he is subjected to shame and guilt.

It is apparent, then, that if a child experiences too much frustration during the anal stage, he will leave part of the forces of growth fixated at this level of development. With such fixations, he cannot face confidently or move readily into the next level of development which is the phallic stage.

The Phallic Stage

The third period of psychosexual development makes its appearance at approximately three years of age and continues until about the age of five. Dominant during this stage is an erotic interest in the genitals, which produce intense feelings of sensual pleasure upon stimulation. This erotic interest in genitalia is a gradual development. It is well known that even very young children gain satisfaction from manipulation of the genitals; however, interest in the genitals is magnified during the phallic stage. This conception, as a part of the child's psychosexual development, has been widely refuted. In fact, some people vehemently dispute the idea because they do not recall the experience from their own childhood. Such refutation is invalid, since many things about our childhood cannot be recalled because of repression or simple forgetfulness. With the inhibitions governing sexuality in our culture, it is no wonder that such memories are relegated to the unconscious. Erikson (4) has pointed out that in cultures where erotic stimulation and sexual experimentation are freely accepted, children readily engage in sexual exploration, and relegation to the unconscious is unnecessary.

According to the psychoanalytic view, the phallic stage is significant for two major reasons. First, it is the time when the Oedipus complex develops. Second, upon the resolution of the Oedipus complex, the superego is formally established.

By the time the male child has entered the phallic stage, he has usually developed strong emotional attachments and dependency ties to his mother and desires to have her all to himself. Consequently he recognizes his father as an intruder into this relationship. He does not wish to share his mother and resents the position his father is accorded in her affections.

However, if he has previously had positive relationships with his father, he also has affectionate feelings toward him. Thus, the boy is faced with the dilemma of feeling both love and resentment toward his father.

The degree of the child's ambivalent feelings depends upon his past relationship with his father. If the father has been punitive and unloving, the child's resentment and hostility are likely to be greater and more apparent. Also, if the boy has been overprotected by or excessively attached to his mother, he is likely to feel more resentment toward his father for intruding into the triangular relationship.

The child is aware, of course, that his erotic attachment to his mother may incur the father's displeasure. For isn't it true that the father may not wish to share his love object with his son? Isn't it also possible that the father resents the time and attention the mother gives to her son?

With all of these complications, it is understandable that the boy may fantasy something happening to his father or to himself. The son may expect his father to retaliate in some way, and during this period when the boy's interest and erotic pleasure are focused on the genitals, it is natural for him to fear castration. At least this is presumed to be the decisive fear that leads to the boy's reappraisal of the situation.

Because of castration fears, the boy gradually renounces his sexual strivings for his mother and solidifies his identification with his father. Ultimately his attitude changes from wanting to be his father to wanting to be like his father. The Oedipus complex is resolved when the boy identifies with his father, incorporates his standards, and accepts his own male role. When this happens, the boy is presumed to have established his superego.

At this point one may ask, "Can all of these strivings, fantasies and ambivalent feelings really be attributed to a child during the phallic stage?" Perhaps an actual case taken from my experience will illustrate that such formulations are quite credible.

A boy who was doing poorly in school and who had a number of conflicts and fears was referred to me for study. He was seven years old at the time and was making a very poor social adjustment. Upon reviewing his developmental history with the mother, I learned that he had always been very dependent upon her and over a period of two years had been excessively fearful of his father. The relationship between the father and the son had never been particularly strong, but there was no evidence to suggest that the father had been rejecting or punitive toward the boy. The boy had been permitted to sleep with the mother for several years, and the mother had been quite overprotective.

Besides the boy's difficulties at school and his marked fear of his father, one other symptom seemed particularly noteworthy. Whenever the father was out of town, and in one instance when he was hospitalized, the boy steadfastly refused to eat. On one occasion the boy could not be persuaded to eat until his father returned home from a business trip.

Projective tests revealed many hostile fantasies directed toward the father, a fear of being hurt, and an excessive amount of guilt. The boy's TAT stories (a personality test which reveals motivations of the child through the stories he composes) indicated marked preoccupation with marriage and very possessive strivings toward the mother. Whereas a healthy seven-year-old would be well into the phallic stage with the typical concerns characteristic of this developmental level, the data in this case pointed to a classical, unresolved oedipal conflict. The boy's refusal to eat appeared to be a means of atoning or punishing himself for his hostile, destructive wishes toward his father and his yearnings for his mother. Each time his father returned home, the boy was reassured that his hostile fantasies against his father had not come true, and he could eat once again. However, his fear in the presence of his father continued unabated. He constantly acted as if the father might hurt or injure him. Perhaps it was castration that he feared. Certainly there is little doubt that this boy's reactions are characteristic of oedipal conflicts.

The oedipal situation for a girl is more complex. In general her oedipal problems are similar to those of the boy, complicated by her physical differences in body structure and the fact that her first love object is also her mother, a person of the same sex. Similar to the boy, the area of sexual primacy for the girl is the genitals or the clitoris. There is, according to theory, a similar focus of interest and erogenous pleasure in this area. Early in this stage of development the girl wants to be her mother but experiences the same destructive wishes against her that the boy feels against the father. She wants the father all to herself. The decisive reasons for the girl's original renouncement of her mother and turning toward the father seem somewhat speculative. It is assumed that discovery of the absence of external genitals leads her to the feeling that she has been castrated, for which she blames her mother. Envy of her father and disappointment in her relationship with her mother lead to further strivings for the father (8). As the girl progresses through this phase, she recognizes that she risks her mother's displeasure because of her desire to possess her father. Imagined fear of punishment and loss of mother love leads to a second renouncement—the wish for her father. Then she wants to be *like* her mother, thus re-identifying with her mother and her female role.

Hopefully a child can progress through the phallic stage successfully because an unresolved oedipal situation will create problems in further personality development. Perhaps the most obvious problems are those involving proper sex-role identification and, later, successful consummation of heterosexual and marital relationships.

Along with the oedipal struggles, the child experiences other maturation processes during this period. It was noted that during the anal stage the rudiments of the child's identity were established in broad outline. During the phallic period his identity is further elaborated. He is intent upon finding out about himself—what type of individual he is, and his ego becomes firmly established. He is still very much imbued with the sense of power that comes from greater refinement of locomotion and growth of mental capacities (4).

His drive to find out about himself, to use his developing capacities, launches him into various manipulations of his environment. These manipulations are both physical and mental and are expressed in an infinite variety of play activities. Indeed, this is an active "play age" in which he attempts to experience the wholeness of himself. His developing imagination leads him into numerous experiments with his environment as well as fantasy explorations that transcend space and time. But he is also concentrating on tasks that help him differentiate proper sex roles. For instance, parents often complain that their developing little girls have inconveniently appropriated lipstick, high-heeled shoes, and other objects of feminine attire for their play. These explorations during play are crucial because the child is learning about his own capabilities, limits, and boundaries.

During this stage the basic structure of the superego is established and, depending upon that structure, the child is either more or less free to develop a sense of initiative. If the superego is rigid and strict and must maintain vigilance in respect to impulses, the child gives up this sense of initiative. He becomes incapacitated by a sense of guilt (5). His play and all of his explorations are characterized by inhibitions. However, if his superego has not been so encumbered, he is free to focus his energies without excessive fear or guilt.

The child with a healthy superego, then, is ready to learn some of the formal tasks of life. When he reaches school age, he is ready to engage in curricular undertakings set by the school. These academic enterprises are crucial for a number of reasons, but perhaps the most important is that the child now senses "I am what I learn." He is ready to give up some of his imaginary explorations for learning how to do and accomplish new things. He is ready, therefore, to take the next step in active mastery of his real world. He needs and wants to be useful. At this time he reaches the next psychosexual level of development—industry versus inferiority (5).

The child's progression through and successful resolution of this phase depend upon a number of things. Most important is the degree of success he experienced through the earlier stages of development. However, he must also learn that he can make adequate progress in the formal academic setting. It is obvious, therefore, that the school has much to contribute to a child's sense of industry or its opposite, a feeling of inferiority. For instance, if a child already feels inadequate, his school experiences may greatly influence his confidence in facing the world of work.

Latency Period

The phallic stage formally closes with the coming of the *latency* period —so named because it is assumed that the sexual curiosity and strivings of the phallic period are repressed and remain dormant until the genital phase. Sexual interests, it is said, are sublimated into intellectual activities and educational enterprises. The superego begins to exercise more rigid direction of the sexual drives. And, with this increased direction by the superego, the child's behavior becomes more moral and his conformity to rules more absolute (7).

There is some reason to doubt this conception of the latency period. Anthropological evidence suggests that a child's conformity may be more culturally than biologically determined. The sexual activity and interest of children in primitive cultures tend to diminish little during this time. In American society, children do continue to masturbate and make sexual explorations during the latency period. However, these activities are more covert than at younger ages. Then too,

the world of the child in the latency period is expanding rapidly; his orientation is more sociocentric. His interests move away from himself and other things absorb his energies.

The Genital Stage

Sexuality is reawakened and begins to assume its adult form at puberty. This is the beginning of the *genital* phase of development, ushered in by the capacity of an individual to procreate. It is a time of striking changes, both physiological and psychological. There is an increase in sexual drives, in sensitivity of the genital organs, and in secretion of sex hormones. With these changes, secondary sexual characteristics develop (7).

During the early part of the genital stage, at least in our culture, there is considerable psychological disequilibrium. The individual may be faced with old, unresolved conflicts that now demand solution. And, with increased sexual drives, anxieties and guilt may rise to new levels. Indeed, if the superego structure is rigid and the ego functions falter, the individual may face intense stress. Heterosexual relationships may be so threatening that the individual may feel more secure by withdrawing from them. Such concerns may lead him to homosexual experiences.

Although the adolescent struggles to free himself of parental reins, perhaps his chief problem at this time is his effort to establish his own true identity. From his earlier years he has made some relatively firm identifications, but the adolescent does not feel entirely secure with these. The revolution that he is experiencing within himself and his new relationships with the world that are so rapidly developing give a tentativeness to his earlier identifications. He must now synthesize all of his previous identifications with the demands and expectations of his new social roles.

As Erikson (5) has said, the chief crisis at this time is that of identity versus identity diffusion. The adolescent is struggling not only with who he is but with what he should be. It is natural, then, that his inability to settle on an "occupational identity" is very distressing. His identity struggles may lead him to over-identify with the heroes of his clique. Furthermore, in order to defend himself against identity diffusion, the adolescent erects most exclusive membership rules to govern participation in his tight little group. He may be intolerant of outsiders and their differences in dress and background. Inherent in such behavior is the security he feels in not having to make choices. His behavior is so stereotyped that discrimination among ideals and roles is temporarily avoided.

If the adolescent achieves an adequate sense of identity, he is ready to enter the first of three adult stages leading to maturity. The crisis of the first adult stage is intimacy versus self-absorption. The person who has developed a sense of intimacy is able to enjoy emotionally close relationships with others and to involve himself in the intimacies that are prerequisite to mature sexuality. He can, therefore, experience satisfactory sexual relations with the opposite sex (5).

When mature genitality has been established, the healthy person finds satisfaction in having and caring for children. Generativity versus stagnation is the second adult crisis he must resolve. Successful accomplishment of generativity is more than desiring children; it is the genuine fulfillment that accompanies the nurture and guidance of a child.

People who have made inadequate identifications with parents, or individuals who are bound to themselves by self-love, do not successfully resolve this crisis. Rather, they remain slaves to themselves, unable to move away from their own self-centeredness. Their interest and emotion are largely confined to themselves.

The crowning achievement of the healthy, mature personality is integrity —the result of the successful resolution of all previous psychosocial crises. It is acceptance of what one is and the life cycle of which one is a part. Integrity, as Erikson (5) defines it, is the mature assumption of responsibility for one's life and acceptance of what one has experienced in the past. The person who has achieved integrity accepts death without regret or despair. Integrity is the summit of maturity, a state or point in time when one has found substance and satisfaction in life.

MASLOW'S THEORY OF HUMAN MOTIVATION

The discussion of psychosocial development has directed our interest to some of the crucial processes and stages in the socialization of the child. We have seen that psychosocial development proceeds through a sequence of stages, and that one's readiness to embrace successfully each of the more advanced stages is determined by his adequate resolution of the prior stage. It was seen also that the child faces psychological hazards particular to each stage he experiences.

The task of considering a more systematic theory of human motivation remains. Maslow's (14) theory of motivation has been selected because it is consistent with the general conceptual framework already considered. That is, achievement of certain tasks, resolution of certain crises, and gratification of specified basic needs are necessary to establish one's maturity or to actualize one's potential.

Maslow postulates five levels (or sets) of needs: physiological needs, safety needs, belonging and love needs, esteem needs, and the need for self-actualization. These needs are organized into a "hierarchy of relative prepotency." That is, the most basic needs must be satisfied before higher needs have the power to motivate behavior.

Physiological Needs

As is typical of most theories of motivation, Maslow's theory rests on the biological or physiological drives. If a person is deprived of everything, his behavior will be motivated primarily by a desire for food, water, oxygen, and proper temperature regulation. That is, he will attempt to gratify first those needs that are most basic to survival, and other needs will become relatively unimportant or even nonexistent.

When a person is dominated by physiological needs, all of his capacities are placed in their service. The individual uses all of his ego resources to satisfy his hunger, and his concept of the world about him is colored by his search for physiological gratification. A very hungry man wants food and, until he has it, concern for others or the desire to learn are relatively unimportant.

Once the individual's physiological needs have been sated, he is released

from their domination and new, higher levels of needs motivate his behavior. Physiological needs, when they are relatively satisfied, fade into the background as active organizers of behavior. If, however, at a later time these needs are ungratified, they will arise again and dominate the individual's behavior.

Safety Needs

The emergence of safety needs as motivators of behavior rests on the prior satisfaction of physiological needs. Once given this satisfaction, the individual searches for a predictable, orderly environment. He needs surroundings that are consistent and organized so he need not fear the unexpected.

As Maslow has indicated, the child's need for safety is seen in his desire for predictable routines. He wants structured relationships he can count on, people who are the same from day to day. People who vacillate in their moods or in their relationships with children cause him much apprehension and anxiety. Understanding the importance of these needs clearly indicates that total permissiveness with young children can be harmful to their development.

When (as was true of the physiological needs) an individual is dominated by his need for safety, his security, relationship to others, and philosophy of the future are defined in terms of safety gratification. More than anything else, he will need a predictable, orderly environment. A person who feels unsafe may reveal his safety strivings in a number of ways. He may be generally apprehensive and act as if something unexpected will happen. Or he may rigidly overorganize everything to ensure predictability. The tendency of some people to over-insure themselves (take out an excessive number of insurance policies) may reveal pronounced safety strivings. Some children may express their safety needs by clinging unreasonably to a familiar adult.

Belonging and Love Needs

With the satisfaction of physiological and safety needs, belonging and love needs become active motivators of behavior. Once again the behavior of the individual assumes a new focus, with affectional needs serving as the core of motivational strivings.

The importance of love needs in our society hardly needs emphasis. Maslow has indicated that inadequate satisfaction of these needs is one of the most frequent causes of maladjustment. Indeed, individuals who have been deprived of adequate affection in childhood will value it most highly and seek it continually. Other goals will have a secondary position until the craving for love has been gratified. When these needs are the predominant motivators, the individual may be described accurately as an affection-seeking animal.

Esteem Needs

Observations of people in everyday life readily confirm the importance of self-esteem and the respect of others. However, the appearance of these needs, according to Maslow, rests on the adequate and prior satisfaction of the needs at the lower end of the hierarchy.

Maslow has classified esteem needs into two sets (a) the desire for competence in dealing with the world, and (b) the desire for recognition, status, and importance in the eyes of others.

Adequate self-esteem promotes a sense of personal worth, self-respect, and confidence. Lack of self-esteem induces a feeling of helplessness and inferiority that, in turn, can create an excessive need to compensate for these inadequacies.

The person who lacks adequate esteem can be identified by his defensiveness in respect to his performance. He is frightened by competition or by activities involving challenge. He would rather *not* perform than risk revealing his inadequacies. Some school children who feel little self-esteem and are unsure of others' evaluations of them prefer to do little school work in order to avoid exhibiting their inadequacies to others.

Self-Actualization Needs

The peak of the hierarchy of basic needs is the desire to be what one is able to become. When one arrives at this level of motivation, he has a restless urge to actualize his capabilities and to use all of the resources of his being. To be content, he must do what he can do.

The self-actualizing person is relatively free to use his abilities. He is not hamstrung by inner battles, anxiety distractions, or fixations at lower levels of need, all of which suppress expression of abilities. Indeed, his abilities function like a flawless machine and as they do, the world opens up as a thing of beauty, complexity, and awe-inspiring mystery. The self-actualizing person, having had sufficient gratification of physiological, safety, love and esteem needs, finds a oneness with himself and the world. He has found a relatedness to things and people that epitomizes integrity.

References

1. Blum, G. *Psychoanalytic theories of personality.* New York: McGraw-Hill, 1953.

2. Combs, A. A perceptual view of the adequate personality. In *Perceiving, behaving and becoming.* Washington, D.C.: Association for Supervision and Curriculum Development, 1962, pp. 50–64.

3. Diamond, S. *Personality and temperament.* New York: Harper & Brothers, 1957.

4. Erikson, E. *Childhood and society.* New York: W. W. Norton, 1950.

5. Erikson, E. Identity and the life cycle. *Psychol. Issues,* I, No. 1, 1959.

6. Fenichel, O. *The psychoanalytic theory of neurosis.* New York: W. W. Norton, 1945.

7. Freud, S. *The basic writings of Sigmund Freud.* Translated by A. A. Brill. New York: Random House, 1938.

8. Freud, S. *Collected papers.* Vol. V (1925). London: The Hogarth Press, 1956.

9. Goldfarb, W. Psychological deprivation in infancy and subsequent adjustment. *Amer. J. Orthopsychiat.,* 1945, XV, 247–255.

10. Hall, C. *A primer of Freudian psychology.* New York: Mentor Books, 1954.

11. Hutt, M., and Gibby, R. *Patterns of abnormal behavior.* Boston: Allyn and Bacon, 1957.

12. Lorenz, K. Morphology and behavior patterns in closely allied species. In B. Schaffner (ed.), *Group Processes.* Josiah Macy Jr. Foundation, 1955, pp. 168–220.

13. Martin, W., and Stendler, Celia. *Child behavior and development.* New York: Harcourt, Brace, and Co., 1959.

14. Maslow, A. *Motivation and personality.* New York: Harper & Brothers, 1954.

15. McCandless, B. *Children and adolescents: Behavior and development.* New York: Holt, Rinehart and Winston, 1961.

16. Mussen, P., Conger, J., and Kagan, J. *Child development and personality,* 2nd ed. New York: Harper & Row, 1963.

17. Stokes, S. An inquiry into the concept of identification. In W. E. Martin and Celia Stendler (eds.), *Readings in child development.* New York: Harcourt, Brace, 1954, pp. 227–239.

18. Watson, R. *Psychology of the child.* New York: John Wiley and Sons, 1959.

19. Young, K. *Sociology: A study of society and culture.* New York: American Book Company, 1942.

CHAPTER THREE

Parental Impact on Child Behavior

The family provides the child with his first sustained experiences in relating to others and his first and most significant learning environment. In miniature, the family is the chief cultural representative of the larger society and the major agent for the child's socialization. Furthermore, families seem to settle on certain crystallized ways of living together and coping with problems, and these life styles tend to remain consistent from year to year. And since the child spends the major portion of his preschool years almost exclusively with his family, it is there that the foundation is laid for later development of personality structures, coping mechanisms, self attitudes, and life styles.

While one may question whether this early environment forges a personality structure that cannot be changed, he must recognize that after the first five or six years it is strenuously resistant to change. Certainly, human beings can change. However, they rarely change significantly after the first six years. When changes do take place, they are usually related to marked shifts in one's life circumstances or changes in the quality of his interpersonal relationships.

With this brief introduction, let us analyze some of the problems children develop as a result of their early relationships with their parents. In assessing these relationships and resulting problems, attention will be focused on the origin of parental attitudes, dimensions of parent-child relationships, problems of mothers and fathers, and difficulties that arise from certain child-rearing orientations. These analyses should help to clarify the connection that exists between children's maladaptive patterns and their parental relationships.

ETIOLOGY OF
PARENT ATTITUDES

The attitudes parents have toward their children are determined by many things. Ausubel (1) has grouped these determinants into four general areas: (a) the general culture, (b) situational variables, (c) the family and childhood experiences of the parents, and (d) the personality structure of the parents.

The norms that exist in a culture, as we have previously noted, determine in a general way the interaction that takes place between parent and child. That is, cultural norms do orient parents toward certain child-rearing goals and methods, although parents vary considerably in the methods they use. In general, conformity to contemporary child-rearing methods is closely related to the extent of the parents' formal education and their social class membership (1); however, conformity is also related to the amount of guilt the parents experience for nonconformity. Furthermore, regardless of the cultural norm, formal education, and social class membership, extenuating circumstances that cannot be predicted or controlled may significantly influence the way parents relate to and rear their children. For instance, reversals in the parents' economic circumstances or an inherited mental or physical abnormality may greatly affect the way parents feel about and rear a particular child. Similarly, health problems, of a parent or the child, can greatly modify the child-rearing process.

It is obvious, too, that parents' child-rearing practices are influenced by the childhood experiences they had with their own parents. Parents tend to rear their own children in much the same way they were reared. Any significant changes occur usually as a result of the parents' strong reactions to their own parents' attitudes and methods, and such changes are usually in direct contrast. That is, if one's parents were unusually strict or authoritarian, he may rear his own children more permissively.

Furthermore, a parent's child-rearing methods are influenced by his own personality structure. If his past experiences have left him with feelings of inadequacy, unmet emotional needs, and inner conflicts, he may have great difficulty rearing his child in a psychologically healthy way because his own needs, anxieties, and conflicts will interfere in ways that are detrimental. For example, a mother who is aggressive and domineering may experience great difficulty accepting a child who expresses the same behavior. Yet, the same mother may be able to accept a submissive child with comparative ease. In this instance, the decisive determinant is the mother's conflict with her own hostile impulses. An aggressive child may tempt expressions of aggression in the mother and seriously threaten her capacity to maintain control, which may be a necessary condition for her own security.

Block (3), in summarizing some of the literature on parental attitudes and child rearing, has indicated that mothers who rear prejudiced children display child-rearing attitudes that are authoritarian, and they experience difficulty tolerating children's annoying and disruptive behavior. Similarly, restrictive child-rearing attitudes are associated with conservative political opinions. The Sears, Maccoby, and Levin study (8) of the child-rearing techniques of 379 mothers also concluded that the personality traits of the mothers were expressed in the ways they related to, controlled, and trained their children.

DIMENSIONS OF PARENT-CHILD RELATIONSHIPS

Parent-child relationships may be conceptualized in terms of four major dimensions (1): (a) degree of emotional responsiveness and acceptance, (b) type of control and training, (c) degree of valuation of the child, and (d) level of aspiration or expectation for the child. Let us consider in detail each of these major dimensions.

Emotional Responsiveness and Acceptance

The degree to which a parent is sensitive to the needs of his child and is able to accept and approve of him may range from complete acceptance to absolute or total rejection. It is, of course, a rare parent whose behavior can be correctly described by either of the two extremes. Also, with the exception of the emotionally disturbed parent, it is rare to find one who intentionally rejects a child. It is not unusual, however, to find a parent who expresses rejecting attitudes of which he is unaware. The ways in which a parent may exhibit rejection toward his child are infinitely varied. However, the following patterns appear most typical.

1. Failure to assume adequate responsibility for the care, growth, and protection of the child. The child is permitted to care for himself and his needs from an early time. Thus, he may not be properly clothed or fed and is given freedom to roam about the neighborhood with little or no direction.

2. Absence of the expression of affectional warmth, often revealed in a minimum of physical contact with the child.

3. Long periods of separation from the child with little or no concern about his welfare. A mother escapes into an unnecessary full-time job, leaving the child in the care of others.

4. Marked mistreatment, punishment, or abuse expressed verbally or physically.

5. Excessive deprivation of material things and experiences that are considered common or natural for all children.

6. Excessive criticism, frequent reprimand, and humiliation of the child.

7. Mental, physical, and behavioral expectations beyond the child's capacity to perform.

8. Excessive indulgence or protection, as a reaction formation to compensate for unconscious hostility or guilt toward the child.

9. Transfer or projection of hostility. A parent may express toward his child the hostility he feels for the other parent, thus making the child the recipient of an emotion felt for someone else.

The reasons for rejection are also infinitely varied and uniquely determined by the characteristics and life circumstances of parent and child. For example, a parent may have been deprived of love as a child and simply not have the capacity to love another. A child may be an economic burden, or he may interfere with the ambitions of the parents to achieve status or success. Also, the child himself may fail to achieve the social or intellectual standards that are considered important by his status-conscious parents. Or a child may be an intruder in a relationship between the parents that is symbiotic and leaves no room for a third person.

Type of Control and Training

A second major dimension of the parent-child relationship is the type of control and training methods used by the parents to socialize the child. The disciplinary techniques of parents tend to vary along two major dimensions that are not mutually exclusive. On the one hand they may range from permissiveness to strictness, and on the other, from overprotectiveness to domination.

When we speak of control and training methods, we refer to the means or strategy the parents use to limit, inhibit, or stop a child's immediate behavior and to influence his future behavior in certain prescribed ways and directions. That is, the object of control and training is to influence certain functions, traits, and behavior to comply with the goals a society has set for its children. The major areas upon which parents focus rigorous training and control practices are feeding, weaning, elimination, sex, dependency, and aggression. In these areas parent and child often experience marked conflict because societal goals demand that these functions be properly socialized. Therefore, if children develop problems, they often stem from the skirmishes between parents and child in the process of socializing these behaviors.

There is not, of course, a one-to-one relationship between child-rearing practices and child behavior. McCandless (7) has suggested that style of feeding and time of weaning have less influence on the child than the mother's attitudes of affection and acceptance. Similarly, early toilet training, when associated with harshness and restrictiveness, retards motor development, and the child requires more time to develop control.

The child-rearing methods that parents employ influence the structure of the relationships between parents and children, and, as these relationships are structured, the child's learning and feelings about himself and others are significantly patterned. It is interesting to note that, even though we are a future-oriented society, the control and training techniques used by many parents are oriented toward control of a child's immediate behavior. The concerns of the moment—what the child is doing right now—seem to be more important than the type of superego or the ego strengths the child is developing. Of course, one must deal with a child's immediate actions when they are harmful or destructive, but the manner in which a child is handled in the present may have significant consequences for his future development. One often sees, in clinical practice, clear demonstrations of the effects of training methods on the child's behavior, both present and future.

A case in point is that of a seven-year-old girl who was referred to me because of her excessive fear, inability to concentrate, and poor performance in school. She was enuretic (a bed-wetter), had difficulty sleeping at night, and had frequent night terrors. Her manner of relating was compliant and ingratiating.

Examination of the child and an interview with her guardian revealed many examples of disturbed relationships. However, of significance for our present discussion were the control and training techniques used by the guardian in "disciplining" the child. Control methods were excessively strict, authoritarian, and punitive, ranging from physical punishment to constant criticism and reprimand. Inasmuch as the child was enuretic, the guardian had determinedly launched upon a strategy to stop this problem. She had purchased a mechanical device with a loud bell that was activated when the child began to wet the bed each night. At the sound of the bell, the child was reminded to go to the toilet. In order to ensure that the complete operation was duly performed, the child was told that if she did not go to the toilet when the bell sounded, her legs would be severed from her body!

One's reaction to this illustration may be that the guardian obviously did not love the child, and the training techniques were a reflection of the negative emotional relationship. This may have been partially true, but the guardian seemed most sincere in her wish to help the child develop in ways that were considered desirable. Of course, the most glaring mistake was the guardian's failure to consider the effects the control and training measures would have on the total personality of the child, both then and in the future. Obviously, a symptom, such as enuresis, cannot be dealt with in isolation. The part it plays in the over-all personality of the child must be thoroughly understood.

In this case illustration, it is understandable that the child was unable to concentrate, had excessive fear, and was unable to sleep at night. Each of these symptoms was intimately related to the training and control methods and the disturbed child-guardian relationships. Interestingly enough, the child had developed the symptoms at the time she entered the home of the guardian.

The impact on the child of various types of control and training techniques will be more dramatically demonstrated when parent types are discussed later in this chapter. However, the present discussion should alert one to the importance of control and training techniques as one dimension of parent-child relationships.

Parental Valuation of the Child

The term valuation refers quite literally to the degree or amount of value a parent holds for a child. The child may be overvalued, as a pearl of great price, or undervalued, as a thing of insignificant worth. He may be valued intrinsically for what he is, or he may be valued extrinsically for what he does and for the credit he reflects on the parents. The type and amount of value attached to the child significantly affects the nature and quality of parent-child relationships (1).

The child who is overvalued by his parents may become an object of adoration to be handled with delicate care and protected from the "bad" influences of life. He may be regarded as a fragile thing made of glass. If so, he is likely to be indulged and given the freedom to "write his own ticket." He grows up, therefore, in the center of the stage, reacting to the world in a narcissistic way. In later years, he will expect adoration and love but will lack the capacity to give and to love in return.

The child who is undervalued by his parents receives a very different reaction from them. He does not enjoy their emotional concentration. He is a standard fixture around the house and may even be considered an emotional and economic burden. Because he does not enjoy parental closeness and affectional warmth, he will have an inadequate self-concept and limited capacity to establish positive emotional relationships with others, and will feel an affectional void. If his parents have given him minimum but inadequate affection, he may value it highly and seek it vigorously from others.

The child who is intrinsically valued is accepted for what he is, with his capabilities and limitations. His parents do not make pre-judgments about what he should be. Because they need not project their own needs upon the child, they are better able to rear him in ways that are consistent with his own needs and maturity.

The circumstances of the extrinsically valued child are in real contrast to the intrinsically valued one. These circumstances are discussed in the following section.

Parental Level of Expectation and Aspiration

The fourth and last dimension of parent-child relationships to be considered is the level of expectation or aspiration the parents have for the child. Expectation implies an obligation on the part of the child to perform, while aspiration is a parental desire for the child to achieve a wished-for future goal. The things parents *expect* children to do differ from what they *wish* them to achieve primarily in relation to the parents' emotional involvement. Parents *expect* children to act and behave in certain ways, and little latitude is given in regard to expectations. That is, parents demand that a child not lie, steal, cheat, or behave in ways that are considered unacceptable. On the other hand, they hope or desire that their child will be a teacher, engineer, lawyer, or businessman. An expectation is immediate and

pursued with intensity and vigor. An aspiration is not; if it is, it becomes an expectation, not an aspiration.

Parental expectations and aspirations for their children vary according to their own childhood experiences, the social class with which they identify, and the unmet needs and unfulfilled aspirations that are basic to their motivational system. It is in this dimension of parent-child relationships that the unconscious purposes and needs of the parents have a fine opportunity to flourish.

A child can easily become the vehicle for actualization of his parents' status needs. Parents who are dissatisfied with their social status often pressure their child to behave in ways that are socially esteemed. They may expect the child to conform excessively to highly valued social norms, or they may set unreasonably high academic expectations. The danger is that expectations may not coincide with reality. The child may be too immature or his capabilities and temperament may be such that he cannot meet the expectations.

When faced with such demands, the child has two alternatives. One, he may struggle gallantly to meet all demands, fearing that, if he does not, he will lose precious parental acceptance. In this case, he will be generally anxious about all expectations, always fearing he will fail. He will, because he is unable to meet all demands, begin to internalize prominent feelings of inferiority. Two, he may strenuously resist or rebel against all parental demands, recognizing his inability to meet many of them. In this instance, his resistance is a result of the frustration produced by the expectations.

The success parents have in setting reasonable expectations and aspirations for their children appears to be intimately related to their insight into themselves, their own feelings of adequacy, their sensitivity to the child's developing needs and capacities, and the amount of their ego involvement with the child. Parents usually do not seek to enhance themselves through their children when they are satisfied with what and who they are. In fact, the degree to which parents project their own unrealized aspirations and needs on the child often indicates whether the child is intrinsically or extrinsically valued. Also, the child who is extrinsically valued seems to receive parental affection in direct ratio to the degree to which he behaves and performs according to parental expectations.

The parent who must rigidly maintain unreasonable expectations and aspirations for a child reveals, by his attitudes, an unconscious need involvement with his child. Such involvement is interesting, if pathetic, to observe. The unreasonableness of the demands is readily revealed by numerous conflicts and symptoms in the child. Yet, when the relationship between the demands and the child's conflicting behavior is identified for the parent, he constructs a great variety of defenses to block recognition of reality.

Almost any unsatisfied need, conflict, feeling of inadequacy, or unfulfilled aspirations of a parent may be translated into goals, expectations, and aspirations for a child. The teacher, administrator, or counselor who seeks to understand and help children should, therefore, carefully investigate the four dimensions of parent-child relationships to achieve a reasonable understanding of the parents' impact on the child.

In the following sections, we will delve more deeply into disturbed parent-child relationships.

DISTURBANCES IN PARENT-CHILD RELATIONSHIPS

Disturbances in parent-child relationships will be considered in three ways: a) a discussion of some of the characteristic problems of the mother and the father and their effects on the child, b) an identification of fairly common parent types and their impact on the child, and c) a summary of certain detrimental home conditions and ineffective parent-child relationships.

Problems of Mothers

The problems of mothers that negatively influence the personality development of a child have been carefully outlined by Slavson (9). Six of the seven problem areas he identified will be considered. These are problems of mothers who are (a) not adapted to the feminine role and have masculine drives, (b) unable to resolve their oedipal involvements, (c) self-centered, infantile, and unable to give of themselves, (d) unable to establish the ego boundaries between themselves and the child, (e) weak, vacillating, and ambivalent personalities, and (f) affectionally deprived and overdependent.

A mother who has not successfully adapted herself to the feminine role may become very disturbed over becoming a mother. Having a child not only confirms her femininity, but forces her into a female role. The relationship that develops between such a mother and her child depends upon the extent to which she must deny her femininity by rejecting the child. For example, a mother may develop a reaction formation and disguise the rejection of her child by pampering and overindulging him. Another mother may become competitive with a male child and seek to emasculate him, as she does her husband. Consequently, the son develops anxiety and may become effeminate in his behavior. A daughter may, under these circumstances, unconsciously identify with the mother's masculine drives and later develop homosexual fantasies. Because the mother is unable to express tenderness and love, both son and daughter may grow up feeling emotionally deprived and lonely.

The primary difficulty of the mother who is unable to resolve oedipal involvement with her father is her inability to perform, on a mature level, her psychosexual role as a wife and to function adequately as a mother. She seeks from her husband and children the love, protection, and service that are more befitting a child than an adult. In a sense, the mother's role is reversed; the care, affection, and service that are usually given *to* a child are demanded *from* him. These distortions in the mother-child relationship produce a child who feels deprived and guilty, and such feelings often lead to strict superego development. The father, feeling ungratified in his relationship to his wife, may seek satisfactions from the child. Thus, further disturbances are created in the child.

The self-centered, infantile woman also has difficulty performing adequately the mother role. She indulges herself and attempts to organize the world to meet her needs. Such a mother can usually be identified by the time and money she spends on herself and the effort she devotes to holding the center of the stage. Also, she may unconsciously use the child to satisfy her own emotional needs. That is, she may attempt to mold him in ways that will bring her admiration and praise from others, even though her expectations are contrary to his needs. The child's achievements are personal triumphs for the mother, and she uses them to solicit praise from others.

The disturbances produced in a child with a self-centered, infantile mother are obvious. Since the mother has difficulty being other-centered, she does not meet the affectional and growth needs of her child; consequently, he does not feel secure, nor does he feel that his needs will be met. The child grows up feeling neglected and deprived of many of the qualities necessary for successful socialization; as a result, he may act out impulsively against his environment, demanding that of which he has been deprived. Or, he may become exploitative, using others for his own ends in the same way that he has been used.

Many mothers in our culture fit into the next category—the mother who is unable to establish properly the ego boundaries between herself and her child. This is the mother who does not clearly delineate herself (or her individuality) from the child. The child becomes an appendage of the self, an outward extension of the "I." This type of mother is domineering and overbearing. The child's autonomy is seriously restricted, and practically everything he does is dictated by the mother.

Primarily, this type of mother-child relationship produces a child who is excessively dependent, compliant, and submissive. He surrenders his independence, cannot assert himself, does not accept responsibility, and is fearful of success. Because the child has had no opportunity to develop self-dependence, in later years he has difficulty in separating himself from the parents in order to marry (9).

Another type of problem mother is the one who is vacillating and ambivalent in her treatment of the child. As we have observed, a basic condition for developing trust and safety is an environment that is predictable. A child has great difficulty adapting when his relationships with people are always changing. Personality development is healthier in the child who is even treated cruelly than it is in the one constantly exposed to parents who are unpredictable. A child can build defenses for himself against cruelty, or any other treatment that is consistent, but he is traumatized by vacillating relationships. Unpredictability makes it impossible for him to learn the ground rules, the expectations, or the code by which he is to live.

Consequently, this ambivalent treatment of the child produces intense anxiety and weak ego organization. The child is in a constant state of threat, and, since he has not been able to erect stable defenses or well-reinforced adaptive modes, he can be readily victimized by his impulses. Furthermore, the excessive anxiety reduces his intellectual efficiency to the extent that he may be unable to use his potential. He is the child often characterized by teachers as "tight as a G string."

The final type of problem mother—the one who is affectionally deprived and overdependent—is, in some outward appearances and behavior, similar to the one with unresolved oedipal problems. Both types make excessive demands on their children for service, and both are dependent. Perhaps the major difference is the excessive demand of the affectionally hungry mother to have the child assume adult responsibilities. Along with the executive responsibilities, he is expected to meet his mother's affectional need. Such burdens are beyond the child's capacity to perform; therefore, he grows up with anxiety and a damaged self-concept.

Problems of Fathers

The father's contribution to the development of the child is not as direct, and certainly not as clear, as the mother's. Being the chief breadwinner, the father is frequently absent from home; consequently, his interaction with the child is less frequent, and his impact on the child is more diluted than is the mother's. This pattern is changing somewhat (particularly in the middle class); however, the father's problems and his influence on the development of the child are still vague and poorly defined.

Research studies to determine the father's influence on the development of the child have been primarily of the father-absent type. That is, children whose fathers have been away from home for frequent intervals have been compared with children whose fathers have been consistently present in the home. It is generally assumed that any personality differences between the two groups of children (when they have been carefully matched) can be indirectly attributed to the presence or absence of the fathers. Such studies (7) show generally that the boys whose fathers have been away from home are the most intimately affected of all the children studied. They tend to be less masculine and more immature, experience some difficulties in social relationships, and feel less secure in their identification with their fathers than the boys whose fathers are consistently present.

According to these studies, then, the father is somewhat influential in the son's development and in the total psychic economy of the family group. Nevertheless, his adequacy in performing his father role and his own problems are bound to exert additional influence on the entire family group.

Problem fathers, like problem mothers, often create difficulties in the family situation because of their inability to perform the paternal role due to personality inadequacy or weakness. As Slavson (9) has indicated, the child has a basic need for a strong father. The father has the primary responsibility for the survival of the family, and his successful performance not only complements the mother role but helps to establish basic security in a child. Indeed, weakness in the role performance of the father often invites the son to substitute himself in the paternal role. In such instances, the boy may become provocative and aggressive as a means of forcing the father to perform a more controlling, authoritative role.

The inadequate, weak father attempts to resolve his difficulties in one of two ways. First, recognizing his weakness, he may seek to develop a dependent or parasitic relationship to his wife and children. Second, he may attempt to come to grips with his weakness by being very dominating. Since he must over-react to his inadequacy by overdomination, he may terrorize the household with his authoritarian manner (9).

The family with an inadequate father of this type experiences considerable instability. Because the father performs his role poorly, the mother must carry a double responsibility. This places the mother in an impossible dilemma, and she is unable to meet the children's emotional needs. Consequently, the children may develop anxiety and insecurity because they are required to exercise their independence too early.

The father also exerts influence on the children when they are experiencing the oedipal conflict. The father must be sensitive and adequate enough to deal with the hostility his son directs toward him as a result of the son's desire to possess the mother exclusively. Similarly, he must sensitively understand and handle his daughter's excessive attachment to him during the oedipal stage. If the father is sufficiently masculine and can constructively exert his rights in the oedipal triangle, the son is able to contain impulse strivings toward his mother and will later identify positively with the father. However, if the father is punitive and hostile, the son submits, gives up a large share of his autonomy, and seeks to ingratiate himself. In such cases, the boy may grow up assuming a somewhat passive, effeminate role (9).

There are, of course, numerous other problems of fathers that can adversely affect healthy development in children; however, the two mentioned above are perhaps the most common and the most difficult. It seems logical, next, to focus our discussion on certain pervasive child-rearing patterns and parental types in which both parent personalities may be intimately involved.

The Compulsive-Perfectionistic Parent

Generally, the ways parents relate to, control, and rear their children can be explained by several descriptive terms. That is, a particular parent's (or parents') approach may be described as primarily democratic, authoritarian, perfectionistic, overanxious, or some other approach that is more prominent than others. This is not to imply that parents rigidly adhere to one specific pattern or that they are pure types, but some consistency does exist in their over-all approach, and that approach can be identified meaningfully by labeling its general structure.

The compulsive-perfectionistic parent is one who is driven to perform the child-rearing role in a very precise, exacting way. To such a parent, compulsive perfectionism is not only a pervasive approach to child rearing; it is an overall approach to life. The child, then, becomes intimately woven into the parent's need to structure rigidly the order of his world as a means of making it more predictable. Consequently, to such a parent the task of rearing his child is a job that must be conscientiously and meticulously done.

The child who has been reared in a compulsive-perfectionistic atmosphere often develops adjustment problems, for a number of reasons. First, because the parent is so intent upon molding him into a predetermined, flawless product, little allowance is made for his individuality, ability, and maturity. For example, he is often urged to be something that his maturity and capability will not permit him to be. Second, his behavior is frequently scrutinized as if it were placed under a high-powered magnifying glass. He is given little opportunity to deviate or to grow in ways that are appropriate for a child. Typically, the parent constantly suggests, orders, and advises. And, when the child does not readily conform, he is excessively scolded, nagged, and criticized. The high standards of the parent are carried to practically all routines; he is carefully watched and supervised in his eating habits, his bedtime routine, his studying habits, and his play time (3). Indeed, the child finds himself in a straitjacket; his autonomy is seriously restricted. Third, because of a rigid personality, the parent does not seem to profit or learn from the mistakes he makes in rearing the child and continues to force or pressure the child even more tenaciously.

Under such a regime, the child may seek to accommodate himself in a number of ways. If he discovers that his security and survival are seriously threatened when he rebels, he may submit, ingratiate himself, and give up his active, autonomous strivings. If he adapts in this way, he may feel a strong sense of inadequacy for failing to live up to parental expectations and may rigidly conform to demands made by those in authority. He may grow up having a very rigid superego, carefully restricting all impulse expression.

Depending upon the ego strength of the child, he may take a contrary route as a means of adapting to parental demands. Instead of complying, the child may exhibit more reactive, overt resistance. His protests may be loud and vehement. He may become a rebel against most, if not all, authority. He may resist all limits, as another form of tyranny, and take secret joy in resisting responsibility and the demands made on him at school. As he grows older, he may be truant from school, become involved in delinquent activities, and seek out age mates that embody, in their behavior, his own resistance to authority.

Of course, if the parent has enough affectional warmth and the child is able to identify with him, he may accept his orientation and standards. However, because the parent's requirements are extreme, it is more likely that the child will adjust by passive submission or overt rebellion.

The Authoritarian Parent

The authoritarian parent is one who places an excessively high premium on the child's unquestioned compliance to demands and commands. It is an orientation characterized by firm control, unreasonably high standards, and limited tolerance for behavior deviations in children.

As is characteristic of the compulsive-perfectionistic parent, this parental orientation is deeply rooted in the personality of the parent. It is not a chosen response; it is a parent's unconscious way of adapting to the world. An authoritarian parent often has strong feelings of inferiority and is, therefore, greatly upset when his authority is questioned. Open challenges to his authority tend to increase feelings of inadequacy; consequently, the parent attempts to avoid challenge by issuing authoritative edicts.

McCandless (7) has advanced several hypotheses to explain parental authoritarianism and the resulting behavior in the child. He suggests that an authoritarian parent tends to be (a) intolerant of ambiguity, (b) highly conforming and responsive to approved standards of adults, and (c) more oriented toward power and status than love and affection. Each of these authoritarian personality trends has significant impact on the child.

Because the authoritarian parent has difficulty in tolerating ambiguity and the indefinite, he is prone to use the either-or approach to child rearing. He tends to be all-loving or all-punishing. Consequently, the child acquires certain attitudes and behavior that are difficult to change because they are inconsistently reinforced. The child tends to see the world as black or white, good or bad, right or wrong; he does not see it in shades of gray.

Inasmuch as the authoritarian parent excessively conforms to approved adult standards, he places strong pressure on the child to behave in an orderly, quiet, conforming way. Since the authoritarian parent cannot tolerate

nonconformity in himself, he is provoked to anger and is anxious when it appears in his child. Consequently, the child usually responds in stereotyped ways to familiar situations but experiences doubts and confusion regarding expected behavior in unfamiliar situations. He anticipates punishment. His behavior will tend to lack flexibility, to be unduly rigid.

The authoritarian parent's orientation toward power and status also significantly influences the child's development. The child is usually perceived by the parent as an ego extension—a way to enhance his own power and status. The child, therefore, is often exploited rather than valued for his own individuality and uniqueness. The child gains love by achieving power and status. He learns to value the material, external signs of success. Moreover, he is prone to more than a normal amount of prejudice (7).

Symonds (10) has indicated that the child of authoritarian parents tends to be submissive, conforming, and lacking spontaneity—relying on repression to deal with hostile impulses. He develops a somewhat rigid, strict superego and, as a consequence, is not likely to find real pleasure in life. Because the child has rarely had the opportunity to make his own decisions, he tends to be dependent and to lack the ability to think for himself.

Bakwin and Bakwin (2) have suggested that children of authoritarian parents are likely to be accident-prone and susceptible to illnesses that are psychologically based. Obviously, when a child must rigidly inhibit his impulses and feelings and must suffer extreme guilt for even slight behavior deviations, his own body may become an object of self-punishment.

The authoritarian parent, then, may

teach his child to conform to authority without overt protest, but the child's capacity to use independence wisely and to think creatively may be dealt a severe blow. Apparently, obedience of this type is much too expensive.

The Overprotective Parent

The final parental type to be considered here is the overprotective one. Parental overprotection manifests itself in emotional overconcentration or overattachment to the extent that the child becomes the primary focus of the parent's life. Levy (6) has identified four symptoms of maternal overprotection: (a) excessive contact or constant attention to the child, (b) infantilization or doing things for the child beyond the usual time, (c) prevention of independent behavior, and (d) lack of or excessive maternal control. All of these symptoms may not appear in a particular instance; however, one can usually observe a parental pattern of overdevotion, constant attention, and excessive care of the child in cases of overprotection.

Etiologically, there are two basic types of overprotection: (a) pure, and (b) guilty or compensatory (10). The pure type of overprotection arises as a result of biological or hormonal factors in the mother that produce in her a strong need to care for a child. Other factors that may be instrumental in creating excessive maternal needs (the pure type) are certain situational or external factors. That is, the mother may have had difficulty conceiving a child, or she may have had to wait a long time before she had a child. Also, the death of a previous child may cause the parents to overvalue the present one. Another reason for overprotection of the pure type relates to the mother's

emotional deprivation during her childhood. In this instance, the mother establishes a relationship to the child in which she attempts to satisfy her own emotional need.

Overprotection of the guilty or compensatory type arises as a result of the parent's rejecting or hostile feelings toward the child. The parent, in order to deny the real feelings of rejection, develops a reaction formation. That is, the rejection of the child produces guilt in the parent, and the parent, in an effort to compensate for the guilt, displays excessive feelings of love and concern for the child. The manifestations of this defense mechanism are often a parent's extreme, unrealistic concern that the child may be injured, or his tendency to shower the child with an unreasonable number of material gifts.

Extreme overprotection has a detrimental effect on a child's development, and when overprotection is a manifestation of a parent's unconscious needs, it is likely to be more damaging to the child. For instance, if a parent attempts to gain from a child satisfactions that he did not receive in his own childhood, or if he turns to the child because of an unsatisfying relationship with his marital partner, the child is quite likely to be emotionally exploited and impeded.

Typically, overprotection manifests itself in either one of two basic patterns, indulgence or domination. Depending on which pattern is emphasized, the child's personality and behavior develop quite differently. In essence, the overprotective and *indulgent* parent does almost anything the child wishes him to do, while the overprotective and *dominating* parent feels it is necessary that the child do what the parent wishes (6).

The overprotected-indulged child

exhibits fairly standard traits and problems. He tends to be selfish and demanding; he expects constant affection, attention, and service. He has little frustration tolerance, is impatient, and is prone to have temper tantrums. He may have a good deal of charm, be a good conversationalist, and be skilled at manipulating others; but, when he is thwarted, he may forcefully take what he desires. He may be bossy, self-centered, and aggressive at school. If he excels at school, it is likely to be in the language arts; arithmetic is often the area of poorest academic performance (6, 10).

Although overprotected and indulged children may often give the appearance of reckless abandon and be relatively immune to the comments of others, they do suffer from anxiety, guilt, and feelings of unworthiness. Because they have weak egos, they have great difficulty controlling their impulses; consequently, they are always evoking disapproval from others. Furthermore, as they encounter situations away from home where control is required, their anxiety may increase considerably. The child, recognizing his inability to control his impulses properly, may become very provocative in an attempt to get the environment to set limits for him.

The overprotected-dominated child exhibits behavior that is in striking contrast to that of the indulged child. In the first place, the overprotected and dominated child is not as likely to be considered a problem. His behavior often conforms to standards that are considered "proper." Generally, he is neat, docile, obedient, polite, inhibited, and apologetic. Like the child of authoritarian parents, he must submit to the parents' will to feel safe. So, in order to accommodate himself to his environment, he becomes submissive,

anxious, and fearful. He is rarely a problem in school. Rather, because his behavior is so well controlled, he is a "model" citizen.

Levy (6) found that the overprotected-dominated child is not subjected to the same type of infantilization and emotional overattachment that is so typical of the indulged child. The mother lacks maternal warmth and exercises her protectiveness chiefly in the form of domination. In essence, she carefully controls and supervises the child. The child is rarely allowed to participate in activities characteristic of his age group (particularly those involving risk or danger) and is almost completely stripped of opportunities to make decisions or assume responsibilities.

Although parents rarely intend to hurt, warp, or impede the healthy growth of their children, their own needs and unconscious motivations subtly filter into the parent-child relationship. In order to underline some of the significant factors of parental impact on child behavior, ten key points are summarized below (4). In each instance, the undesirable condition or ineffective child-rearing practice is first stated, and the resulting effect on the child is expressed in summary form.

Unreasonable or punitive discipline. The child tends to be excessively conforming or reacts with extreme hostility. Cruelty is often expressed secretly, and the child may feel low self-esteem or personal condemnation, which causes him to be self-punishing.

Emotional deprivation and rejection. The child experiences difficulty in relating to and forming emotionally satisfying relationships with others. He feels emotionally insecure and displays an inability to give and receive love.

He may be constantly seeking affection, demanding, and negativistic in his behavior. He may also have difficulty in forming proper identifications.

Marital conflict. The child feels tense and anxious and has marked feelings of insecurity. He tends to regard the world as a frightening, dangerous place.

Parent sex-role confusion. Difficulties in the assumption of proper sex role, effeminacy, and latent homosexuality may be characteristic of the child's reactions. He may experience rejection by peers, difficulty in learning social skills, and, in later life, be unable to form satisfying marital relationships.

Parent authoritarianism. The child tends to be stereotyped, rigid, submissive, and obedient. He may be intolerant of ambiguity and may experience marked anxiety in unstructured situations. He may be overly prejudiced and accident-prone. He tends to think in either-or terms.

Parental ambivalence and inconsistent discipline. The child often suffers from extreme anxiety and insecurity. He may experience difficulty in controlling impulses and developing consistent values. He vacillates when he deals with problems.

Parent perfectionism and unrealistic expectations. The child incorporates unrealistic standards which leads to perpetual frustration, guilt, and self-depreciation. He may experience much anxiety about achievement and have a chronic sense of failure.

Parental overprotection (indulgence). The child is often demanding and selfish and has low frustration tolerance. He may be hyperactive, bossy, manipulating, and resistant to authority. Frequent bids for attention and difficulty with self-control are also characteristic.

Parental overprotection (domination). The child lacks initiative and has marked feelings of inadequacy. He tends to be submissive, conforming, passive, and dependent. A lack of originality and creativity is often characteristic.

Excessively high moral standards. The child grows up with a strict, rigid superego and experiences much conflict between impulse expressions and superego restraints. As a consequence, he feels marked guilt, low self-esteem, and self-condemnation.

References

1. Ausubel, D. *Theory and problems of child development.* New York: Grune & Stratton, 1958.

2. Bakwin, H., and Bakwin, Ruth. *Clinical management of behavior disorders in children.* Philadelphia: W. B. Saunders, 1953.

3. Block, J. Personality characteristics associated with father's attitudes toward child rearing. *Child Develpm.,* XXVI, 41–48.

4. Coleman, J. *Abnormal psychology and modern life,* 2nd ed. Chicago: Scott, Foresman, 1956.

5. Kaplan, L. *Mental health and human relations in education.* New York: Harper & Brothers, 1959.

6. Levy, D. *Maternal overprotection.* New York: Columbia University Press, 1943.

7. McCandless, B. *Children and adolescents: Behavior and development.* New York: Holt, Rinehart and Winston, 1961.

8. Sears, R., Maccoby, Eleanor, and Levin, H. *Patterns of child rearing.* Evanston: Row, Peterson, 1957.

9. Slavson, S. R. *Child psychotherapy.* New York: Columbia University Press, 1952.

10. Symonds, P. *The dynamics of parent-child relationships.* New York: Bureau of Publications, Teachers College, Columbia University, 1949.

CHAPTER FOUR

Approaches to Understanding
the Child

The prime prerequisite for helping a child with a problem is an understanding of the problem in relation to that particular child, and real understanding is not easily acquired. Regardless of the problem the child presents, the first and most basic step is to attempt some analysis of the cause, the developmental source, and the severity of the problem. Without some basic understanding of these factors, one can make serious mistakes in attempting to help a child.

Bush (3) found in his study of teacher-pupil relationships that those teachers who knew most about their pupils and were sensitive to their needs and interests had more influential and effective relationships with a greater number than did teachers whose paramount concern was knowledge of subject matter. His study also confirmed that teachers differ greatly in the amount of information they have about their pupils and in the effectiveness with which they use the information they have.

Ojemann and Wilkinson (6) obtained similar results. They wished to determine whether understanding of children's behavior enhances teaching effectiveness. In their study they used a control and experimental group, each composed of 33 ninth-grade children. The children were matched in relation to chronological age, intelligence, achievement, and home background. The teachers of the children in the experimental group were given assistance in the accumulation of comprehensive information on each child, while the control group was not given such aid. The compiled information was used to discuss modifications in classroom procedures. An analysis of the experimental and control groups at the conclusion of the study revealed that the experimental group made significantly greater progress academically, exhibited fewer psychological conflicts and disturbances, and had a more positive attitude toward school.

Certain teachers sometimes assume that their relatively vague descriptions of a child's behavior constitute understanding. For example, they may label a particular child's reactions as insecurity; and then, having so labeled the reaction, they erroneously presume it has been explained. They fail to consider that a general feeling of insecurity can arise from a great number of conditions, and it can be expressed in a variety of symptoms. A boisterous, seemingly self-sufficient child may actually feel very insecure. Yet, cursory observations of his behavior might lead one to the mistaken notion that he is conceited or snobbish. A teacher should avoid this mistake and pose two crucial questions. What does the child's behavior really mean? What experiences and relationships in his background have caused such behavior?

Many people greatly overwork certain key phrases or terms in the name of understanding. One such term is the word "immaturity," which is often used in the school setting to explain the poor academic performance of young children. But, like the word "insecurity," "immaturity" may have a great many meanings. A child may be immature in at least four different ways —intellectually, physically, emotionally, and socially. Depending upon the type of immaturity, the nature and solution of the child's problems will vary considerably.

Descriptive terms such as insecurity and immaturity are much too vague to be helpful in understanding the deviant behavior of a child. Human behavior is much too complex to be explained

so simply. If one is to acquire real understanding of a child and his problems, he must delve beneath the surface behavior of that child.

Furthermore, human behavior can be very deceiving, particularly if one focuses on the manifest behavior or an overt symptom. Unfortunately, symptoms have no standard meanings. They may sometimes be helpful in formulating useful speculations about deviant behavior; however, the same symptom has a different meaning in different people. For instance, individual children can exert excessive amounts of aggression for quite diverse reasons. One child may be reacting to a punitive father. The aggression in another child may be a response to affectional deprivation or parental indifference. Still another child's aggression may be a convenient disguise for a basic fear. A symptom always has a unique meaning based upon the particular dynamics of the individual who presents the symptom.

AREAS BASIC TO UNDERSTANDING

What, then, does understanding the child really mean? What areas are of most basic concern in arriving at this understanding?

Practically speaking, it is always wise for one to consider the most obvious things first. For example, it is important to determine whether the child has any intellectual, physical, or sensory deficiencies, because he cannot be expected to perform or behave normally if he has impairment in any of these areas. Such deficiencies or impairments may be apparent or obscure. They may be present at birth—through inheritance, fetal anomaly, or birth trauma—

or they may be the result of illness or injury. The deficiency may be permanent or temporary, depending upon its cause, severity, and chronicity. All of these possibilities should be considered when a child is not performing adequately; and, at the very minimum, the teacher should have an accurate idea of the child's ability to perform, with a normal amount of energy, the academic tasks expected of him.

Depending upon the nature and severity of the deficiency, the child will have either more or less difficulty adjusting to his situation. For example, it is not unusual for children who are retarded mentally to have excessive fears and to experience difficulty in adjusting to their environment. Similarly, blind children often have difficulty growing up to be independent, socially adaptable people because of the limitations imposed by blindness. Obviously, the individual's capabilities are adjustive tools which may help or hinder his adaption to the environment (5).

Perhaps of primary importance is one's determination and understanding of a child's own conception of his capacities and limitations, his experiences, and himself as a person. Does the child see himself as an adequate, happy, lovable person, or does he regard himself as an inferior person, unworthy of love? In a general way, any person's behavior is understandable and predictable on the basis of his self system (4). Moreover, people tend to respond differently to the handicapped child, thereby increasing his own feeling of being different from other children.

A person's conception of himself develops from his relationships with others and, to a lesser extent, from his experiences in meeting cultural demands. In the process of relating to others, the child's needs are met in varying degrees of satisfaction, and his self-concept is an outgrowth of these experiences. The nature of these relationships is crucial in understanding dynamic personality trends in the developing child. Thus, it is essential to examine the child's feelings toward his parents, siblings, peers, and teachers. These are the people with whom he lives and becomes most involved emotionally. If the child experiences difficulties, they are bound to arise in those relationships that are most intense and highly charged emotionally. When his feelings in these relationships are understood, the motivation for his behavior can be more readily explained. The key is to understand his *feelings*. Generally, if a child feels angry, he reacts with anger; if he feels sad, he acts sad (1). If a child always reacted as he felt, one would have the key to understanding. However, this is not the case, for most children learn relatively early to hide or deny the less acceptable feelings (those involving anger, dependency, or sex); yet, these feelings are the ones that cause the most difficulty and therefore must be understood if we are to get a clear picture of the child and his problems.

However, feelings which cause the most difficulty are frequently not available to the child for conscious inspection. They are often disguised behind an intricate network of psychological defenses. The child, like any adult, soon learns to adapt, to deal with excessive anxiety and threats to his survival in particular defensive ways. His overt behavior may give an impression that is the opposite of his true feelings and problems. For instance, a child may act and consciously feel excessively loving toward a brother or sister, when in reality he may have considerable hostility toward the sibling. His behavior is a reaction formation against the undesirable impulse.

In order to gain real understanding and insight into a child's behavior, to discover "where he really lives," one must have reasonable understanding of his psychological defense system. With such knowledge, one is in a much better position to predict the child's future behavior. This capacity to predict behavior is invaluable to a teacher in estimating a child's response to learning and various phases of school life. Moreover, the teacher with this knowledge may be able to help a child avoid situations that are unnecessarily upsetting or frustrating to him.

METHODS OF OBTAINING INFORMATION

Theoretically, any expression of behavior, ranging from a pupil's performance on an intelligence test to the kinds of humorous stories he tells, can be useful analytically. All behavior has interesting and significant meaning. Most behavior is multi-determined. There is rarely, if ever, a single cause behind a particular behavior deviation.

Nevertheless the classroom and playground behavior of a shy child gives the sensitive teacher numerous opportunities to observe and speculate about the meaning of the child's behavior. By watching and listening, he can get significant clues to aid his understanding of the troubled child. The teacher can readily capitalize on situations and activities that occur spontaneously. For instance, a few subtle questions introjected during "share and tell time" can quickly lead to some of the private concerns of the child.

Some techniques for acquiring information about a child have more practical value and utility than others. For busy school personnel, practicality is often the most important consideration. What are some of the techniques that meet these criteria?

Talks with School Personnel

Perhaps one of the most efficient ways to gain some understanding of the problem child is to talk with others who have had intimate contact with him. In the school situation, this usually means former teachers, the supervisor, and the principal. If the child has had difficulties in the past, these people will know something about them. Also, the fact that inquiries are made alerts them to the problem and subtly invites their cooperation in the course of its solution.

There are several important aspects of information that a teacher will want to acquire from school staff members. First, he will want to know how longstanding and severe the child's problem is. If the problem is an old one of considerable severity, the teacher should realize the fact that "the old tricks of the trade" have been tried and found wanting. Furthermore, if the problem is severe, the usual corrective measure will be of little value; the teacher will have to modify his goal from "changing the child" to "softening" his symptoms.

The teacher will want to know the areas in which the child has experienced most of his difficulties in the past. For instance, has he had difficulty in one subject area or several? Which school rules has he consistently violated? What in his personality structure makes him so resistant to these particular rules? With what type of teacher does he seem to experience most difficulty? At what times during the day do most of his infractions occur?

Answers to these questions can provide important clues that the teacher may use in modifying the program to help the child. Such modifications may not do much to change the child, but they may be serviceable in facilitating greater harmony in the classroom while allowing the teacher to meet the needs of other children.

The sooner the teacher acquires such basic information about a deviant child, the sooner he is able to develop an appropriate relationship with him. After all, the first prerequisite for helping a child is a positive relationship with him. Only then will he be willing to modify his behavior or accept correction.

In talking with others about a child with a behavior problem, the teacher will also want to inquire about his skills or talents that can be used to enhance his self-concept. It is always more beneficial to build on existing strengths than to focus on "casting out" existing difficulties. If one encourages a child's skills, talents, and interests, the child is much more willing to deal with and assume responsibility for his difficulties. With greater self-esteem and renewed confidence in his selfhood, problems do not seem so insurmountable to a child.

Parent Interviews

The teacher will not be able to acquire enough information from school personnel for complete understanding of a child's problem. An interview with the parents can provide rich information and can assist the teacher in understanding its nature and depth. When the time for study is limited, an interview with the parents is most economical and rewarding. The parents have, of course, been in constant interaction with the child over the years and generally are aware of his problem, although they may not recognize its source or the extent of their own involvement. Moreover, any substantial modifications of the child's difficulty must inevitably involve the parents.

Parents of a child who has a problem generally express some resistance to exploring it. The more serious the problem, the more resistant the parents are likely to be. It is usually at this point that school personnel become anxious and fearful. As a result, the parent interview may be delayed too long or even forgotten, and the teacher continues to struggle with the problem rather than face the defensiveness of the parent.

Parents are people, too. Deep down, most parents want to help their child, if they can feel assured that they are not blamed for their mistakes, and if they are given the same type of understanding that we ask them to give the child. It is relatively rare to find parents who will not come in for an interview if the stage has been properly set. How the teacher approaches the parents is particularly significant.

In the beginning, when the teacher is making his first contact with the parents, he can reduce their defensiveness considerably if he indicates that he wishes to become better acquainted with them and the child. The teacher can indicate further that the better he understands a child, the more he is able to provide a beneficial school experience for him. If the teacher's attitude conveys sincerity, helpfulness, and acceptance, the parents will usually respond. The teacher's attitude is probably the most significant factor that influences the parents' response to his request.

When a child is known to have behavioral difficulties, it is crucial to have the first parent interview early in the school year. If a child has had problems in other grades, it is very probable that his new teacher will soon be involved emotionally in them—unless this teacher initially has considerable understanding and objectivity. If the child's behavior has become too distressing to the teacher before he engages the parents, the teacher's feelings are likely to alienate them when he does see them.

There are several reasons why it is useful to have the parents describe the child and his difficulties. In stating their perception of the child's problem, the parents reveal their acceptance of him, their involvement with him and his problem, and their level of insight or the understanding they have reached. This knowledge about the parents provides direction for the teacher and helps him avoid parental defensiveness by not asking direct questions about highly sensitive areas.

If the parents seem hesitant or reluctant to state the problem as they see it, the teacher can make a good beginning by asking the parents to relate the child's specific reactions to school. The teacher can also encourage them to talk about the school activities the child most enjoys. If the parents are receptive, the teacher can encourage them to talk about things the child dislikes about school. This approach communicates to parents that the teacher is accepting and objective, is willing to consider his own involvement, and sincerely wants to understand the child. It is important for the teacher to remember that a non-judgmental attitude is essential if he is to obtain the information he needs.

From the initial request for the parents to describe the child's feelings or reactions toward school, one can easily lead into his past school history: his reactions to past teachers of both sexes, his favorite teacher's personality characteristics and ways of relating to the child, and the subject areas of his greatest strengths and greatest weaknesses. If a teacher has had a child in his room for awhile, he will probably be fairly well acquainted with his weaknesses; however, he may not have discovered the child's strengths. These strengths provide areas of positive contact and a point from which to build.

Obtaining information about the child's reactions to school, the teachers he liked best in the past, and the general approaches that have been used with him helps the teacher plan a more effective program. Such information communicates to a teacher the pitfalls to be avoided if past methods have proved ineffective. Moreover, the teacher's objective comparison of the characteristics of the child's best-liked teacher with his own may often reveal some personality conflict between teacher and child.

Another area which is important for the teacher to know, and which favorably involves the parents in the conference, is the child's favorite activities at home. What specific intellectual or academic interests does he have? What type of play does he engage in? Which roles does he assume in group play? Is he accepted and integrated into the play groups or his peer groups in the neighborhood? These questions will elicit information that can help the teacher evaluate the child's interests and the things in which he emotionally invests himself. The information can be helpful to the teacher also in motivating the child in school—interests do have motivational value.

An area of inquiry closely related to the one just mentioned is concerned with *the things the child enjoys doing with his parents*. This question can be broadened to an inquiry about *the activities the child enjoys with his family, including brothers and sisters*. Exploration of this kind subtly moves the teacher into the areas of family relations, solidarity, and integration. He can determine with which parent the child seems to interact most frequently, which parent provides acceptance and support, and what roles various family members take. Inquiries of this nature can also provide information about day-to-day routines, the kinds of responsibilities the child is asked to assume, and the persistent expectations placed upon the child; the teacher can use this information in planning work and activities for the child in the classroom.

The parents' perceptions and acceptance of the child can be further determined if one asks them to state *what they enjoy most about the child*. By listening to what they enjoy or like about the child, one can infer what they probably do not like about him. The parents may state, for example, that they like the way he gets a job done and the way he conforms to or obeys all commands. From these responses, one might speculate that the parents are rather exacting and controlling. This type of questioning can reveal a great deal about the parents' philosophy in rearing children.

The parents' general child-rearing philosophy is important to know because parent-child interactions tend to evolve from it. If one learns and understands their philosophy, the behavior the parents sanction, reward, punish, or control is easier to predict. Thus, the areas of conflicted parent-child relationships can be more readily analyzed.

In clinical practice, one often finds that parents do not have a well-thought-out or crystallized child-rearing philosophy and cannot, therefore, directly state it. The teacher can, however, acquire some understanding of their implicit attitudes about child rearing by asking the parents to describe *what they consider desirable or undesirable behavior on the part of a child*. The parents' attitudes about correction or discipline can be elicited by a question like: "Do you believe in the old cliché 'spare the rod and spoil the child'?" One can get further insight into child-rearing attitudes by inquiring about *the aspirations the parents have for the child this year, next year, or ten years from now*. Children react to pressures disguised as parents' aspirations; these pressures affect a child's performance in the classroom.

Since one often finds organic and health factors playing a significant role in a child's behavior, it is essential to inquire about the child's general health, the nature and severity of any illnesses and injuries, and any sensory problems—especially eye or ear problems. Even when the teacher can do nothing directly to alter such problems, knowledge of their existence is important in planning a school program that does not intensify the difficulties.

Finally, the teacher should gain information concerning *the things that are upsetting to the child, the things that frustrate him the most*. A child may, because of his low anxiety tolerance, be unable to work at a task as long as his age mates are able to. Thus, the teacher will have to arrange instruction for him in shorter time and instructional units. Another child may experience great frustration in competitive situations, so that the teacher will have to reduce to a minimum most competitive hurdles. Knowledge of problems such as these assists the teacher in actively planning a program for the child before the full impact of his problem is felt.

If the teacher has been successful in acquiring and understanding the information that has been suggested as essential, he will have a fairly good picture of the conflicts to which the child may be reacting. Moreover, conferences with parents can serve not only as an information-getting device for the teacher, but can assist the parents in gaining a better understanding of their child. At the end of an effectively directed conference, parents often say that they have a clearer understanding of the reasons for a child's difficulties. This does not happen magically or as a matter of course. It happens when and because the conference has been skillfully directed and certain pitfalls have been avoided.

From beginning to end, the teacher attempts to focus the conference on the needs of the child, not on his faults or failures. The conference or interview is directed so that it is need and problem centered, rather than personality centered. Throughout the interview one should encourage the parents to think together and relate information to each other. This can often be done by asking a question such as "Is Johnny's fear of competition related to his failure in competing with his twin brother?" Continuing in this vein, one might ask, "Do you suppose there is any connection between his fear of competing and the expectations placed upon him?" With this approach, the teacher helps the parents to gain insight by offering a leading question for their considera-

tion rather than making a direct interpretation for them.

The teacher should be careful to avoid blaming past school or teacher mistakes (2). If such mistakes have been made, it is better to ignore personalities and focus on the meanings such experiences have for the child's present difficulties. It is, of course, extremely rare for a particular teacher or a particular school year to be the cause of all a child's problems. Healthy children seem to survive quite well in spite of inept teaching.

The teacher should also be extremely cautious about giving advice. Advice works only when it is based upon deep understanding of personality and group dynamics and rarely as a single successful solution. If the teacher has helped the parents to formulate a statement of the child's needs and their own involvement in them, there is less need for the parents to ask for specific advice. It is wise to encourage parents to formulate their own plans for helping the child. If parents are to develop insight into the problem and transform this insight into appropriate action and behavior, it is much more effectively done when they are encouraged to go through the process of thinking it out themselves. Parents need help in "working through" the problem emotionally if any solution is to be effective. The wisest man cannot force parents to accept something for which they are intellectually and emotionally unprepared.

Classroom Activities as Diagnostic Tools

The classroom offers many opportunities for obtaining information about the behavior of children. As was suggested earlier, every expression of behavior on the part of a child has some diagnostic value. However, some classroom activities and curriculum content provide more opportunities than others. The following activities have good potential for yielding useful information about children.

Fiction and general readers. From the first grade on, children are subjected to several kinds of general readers. Most readers describe people or animals in various situations or relationships. Therefore, reading activities provide excellent opportunities for one to discover how a child feels about certain types of relationships and events. A teacher can use almost any story about an animal or a person to learn (a) the child's interpretation of the motivation of the characters in the story and why each person probably did what he did; (b) the traits or actions of the characters in the story that a child likes or dislikes most; (c) the child's ideas about how the central character or characters in conflict situations might have behaved differently for a more favorable result; (d) the person or animal in the story the child would like to be and why; (e) how, according to the child, each character in the story probably felt and why he felt that way. If the teacher is careful to question the child on these major points, he is able to get some understanding of the child's motivation, the kinds of people he likes and dislikes, his feelings about authority figures, and his self-concept.

Biographies. Most school libraries have selected biographies of people whose lives portray various experiences, interpersonal relationships, problems, and events. A child's reaction to the struggles and problems described can often reveal his own problems and conflicts. The teacher should pay

particular attention to the child's discussion of the motivation of the central character, his relationship to others, how and why he reacted as he did to certain situations, and what might have made him the type of person he was. At times it may be revealing to the teacher and helpful to a particular child to direct him to a biography that is related to his particular situation and have the child report to the class on it. The child will tend to express some of his own feelings through this medium and may provide some insight for other class members who are having difficulty accepting this specific child.

Themes. Theme writing is a wonderful way for a child to express his attitudes and feelings about a great variety of things. If the teacher has good relationships with all of the children in the classroom, they will grasp at the opportunity to share their hopes, joys, aspirations, and even conflicts through the avenue of writing.

There is, of course, an infinite variety of topics about which teachers can ask children to write. When this type of activity is initiated, however, it is wise to select "safe" topics that do not arouse the defensiveness of the troubled child. For example, the teacher can have the children write about various phases of classroom or school life, their interests or hobbies, or things they like to do with their friends or at home.

If the teacher is assured of his rapport with the class, he can suggest more intimate or confidential topics. For instance, after a particularly disturbing classroom incident, he might have the children write a theme about it. He can ask the children to describe what seemed to have gone wrong, what might be the causes of the incident, and how each felt about it. Similarly, the teacher can have the children write about topics such as Things that Happen at School that Bother Me, Things I Like about School, The Ideal Teacher, My Favorite Classroom Friends, and My Most Embarrassing Moment at School.

Topics for themes can be selected for practically any situation, event, or person about which the teacher wishes information. If the teacher is interested in discovering more about a child's intimate concerns and conflicts, a well selected theme topic can often reveal what he wishes to know. If he is interested in learning more about the child's family situation, he might suggest theme topics such as Things My Family and I Do Together, My Most Boring Times at Home, Things My Parents Do I Dislike, or Some Things I Wish Were Different in Our Family. A more intimate look at the child's concerns can be gleaned from themes about Things I Am Afraid of, The Person I Would Like to Be, People I Like the Most, Things I Hate, Things I Wish I Could Do, or My Dreams.

Themes can be used not only to gain insight into the behavior of children, but also to serve a cathartic value. The value that can be derived in this sense depends upon the teacher's skill in using the children's productions. The teacher may wish to use the themes for a class discussion to permit the children to air some of their feelings. In order not to reveal the intimate concerns of a particular child, the teacher might read certain illustrative themes without revealing the child's name. The teacher may also indicate that he will be available to individual children to discuss any of the themes in greater detail. This procedure gives the child the opportunity to keep confidential anything he may wish to, and it still provides the opportunity for him to express some conflicted feelings with someone who will accept him.

Drawing. Young elementary school children may not be able to use themes as a means of expressing themselves because of their limited ability to write; their drawings, however, can often be as useful as themes. The basic procedure is to have the child draw a picture about a person, situation, or event that will express his feelings in an area about which the teacher desires information. After the picture is drawn, the teacher asks the child to tell a story about it, describing how each person feels. The teacher may make this a project for class discussion or have each child tell his story in private.

The subject of the picture or the type of picture the teacher asks the child to draw will depend upon the purpose he wishes the activity to serve. If the teacher wishes to learn more about the family circumstances of the child, he might ask him to draw a picture of the family home and then describe the people who live in the house, what they like to do, what makes them happy or sad, and how they get along together.

A young child readily identifies with and often uses animals in symbolic ways to express his feelings. The teacher can use this symbolism by having the child draw animals he would like to be and asking his reasons for choosing the animals he draws. Some children will select aggressive animals, while others will select passive or docile ones. By his selection a child often reveals his conception of himself and some of his conflicts and needs.

The teacher can also have the child draw pictures about his wishes, people or situations that upset him the most, or things that frighten him. Practically any situation, event, or feeling can be pictorially described by a child if he is given sufficient opportunity to do so.

Other classroom activities. Another classroom activity that the teacher can use effectively for gaining insight into a child early in the school year is an activity that might be called "This Is My Life." The teacher can initiate this activity by asking each child to tell something about himself in a manner similar to the television program "This Is Your Life." In this instance, the child serves as his own informant. Each child gives a brief sketch of himself based upon a general outline provided by the teacher.

This activity can be made to approximate more closely the "This Is Your Life" program by having the children serve as informants for each other. This approach helps the children get better acquainted with each other, provides the teacher with clues for better understanding of the children, and may develop for each child an understanding of the others.

Some activities, in addition to being diagnostic, may serve as a useful channel for a child's expression of his feelings, aspirations, and desires. One such activity might be referred to as *The Wishing Well.* It is, of course, most applicable to the younger child.

For this activity the teacher constructs a cardboard box that is appropriately decorated to serve as a wishing well. He can explain the activity by suggesting that people are always wishing for something, and that it is sometimes fun to share our wishes or talk about them with each other. The teacher then directs each child to write out three of his most important wishes and drop them into

the wishing well. The child may make his own decision as to whether he wishes to write his name on the wishes. When this activity has been completed, the teacher takes time on different days to read the wishes and discuss them with the children. A carefully directed discussion can often reveal the motivations behind a child's wishes and can provide useful information for the teacher in understanding the child.

Another activity that can aid a teacher might be called a *Pet-Peeve Box.* This device provides each child with a channel for expressing some of his dissatisfactions in respect to the classroom. It gives him an opportunity to be heard and, as a consequence, conveys to him the feeling that what he has to say is important. This activity is carried out simply by having the child submit peeves or gripes to the box without signing his name. Periodically, the peeves or complaints are read by the teacher and discussed with the class. The teacher should carefully indicate that the procedure will be used only so long as the children express sincerely their concerns or complaints and it serves to make their life in the classroom more productive and happy. The teacher should actively involve the children in working out solutions to their peeves or complaints.

The diagnostic activities listed here are just a few of the many that are available to the teacher. The creative teacher will think of many more. He must keep in mind one basic fact: the child is constantly expressing his needs, strivings, and conflicts in one form or another. To make sense of this behavior, one must learn to watch, listen, and analyze. Behavior must be understood before effective, positive action can be initiated.

References

1. Baruch, Dorothy. *New ways in discipline.* New York: McGraw-Hill, 1949.

2. Bühler, Charlette, Smitter, Faith, and Richardson, Sybil. *Childhood problems and the teacher.* New York: Henry Holt, 1952.

3. Bush, R. N. *The teacher-pupil relationship.* Englewood Cliffs, New Jersey: Prentice-Hall, 1954.

4. Lecky, P. *Self consistency: A theory of personality.* New York: Island Press, 1945.

5. Maslow, A. *Motivation and personality.* New York: Harper & Brothers, 1954.

6. Ojemann, R. H., and Wilkinson, F. R. The effect on pupil growth of an increase in teacher's understanding of pupil behavior. *J. exp. Educ.,* 1939, VIII, 143–147.

CHAPTER FIVE

Maladaptive Behavior

Frequent reference has been made to various types of behavior deviations and maladaptive patterns. In this chapter, we will consider specifically the nature of deviation and maladaptive behavior, criteria by which they may be identified, and the relative seriousness of various types of maladaptive behavior.

The incidence of maladjustment in school children is much greater than is commonly recognized. The public is generally aware of the incidence of mental illness in the adult population, yet maladjustment in children has received relatively little national publicity. Therefore, much less study has been devoted to it. Perhaps a major reason for this difference in interest and emphasis is that maladjustment in adults is more easily recognized, while deviant behavior in children is often regarded as a phase they will outgrow. Consequently, the beginnings of maladjustment in children are not often regarded with alarm.

Kaplan (15), however, has made an excellent summary of thirteen studies dealing with the incidence of maladjustment in children from preschool through college years. Each of these studies reveals that the incidence of moderate or serious maladjustment varied from 16 to 50 percent. The median percent for all thirteen studies was 25.

If we use the median of 25 percent as the incidence-of-maladjustment indicator, in a typical public school of 700 children 175 will be in need of special or professional assistance. Then, if one adds to this figure the number of children who have mental retardation, orthopedic handicaps, brain injury, and visual and auditory handicaps, the magnitude of this problem becomes impressive.

IDENTIFICATION OF
MALADAPTIVE BEHAVIOR

Identification of maladjustment in children is not a simple task. It is generally recognized that maladaptive behavior may be expressed by poor academic performance, negativistic or aggressive behavior, stealing, truancy, and delinquency; however, even when overt behavior clues reveal behavior deviation, they do not necessarily reveal the cause and severity of the deviation. Furthermore, many children who are emotionally upset do not exhibit these symptoms. For example, some children accept the demands made of them, exhibiting no behavior that calls attention to themselves; yet, they do have internalized conflicts which silently take their toll. These are the children who live out their lives in "quiet desperation."

Others disguise maladjustments by overconforming to the goals parents and middle-class society hold as important. They are often "hooked" by an anxious drive to succeed or to give up certain normal needs—even during childhood. These are the children who strive for flawless academic performance in order to maintain or gain self-esteem and parental acceptance. Such relentless strivings burden the children with anxiety and warp their personalities in other ways.

As a first step, let up consider what is meant by maladjustment.* For our purposes, a child may be considered maladjusted when he is so thwarted in satisfaction of his needs for safety, affection, acceptance, and self-esteem

* Throughout the book, the terms *behavior deviation*, *maladjustment*, and *disturbance* are used synonymously to connote the behavior described in this definition.

that he is unable intellectually to function efficiently, cannot adapt to reasonable requirements of social regulation and convention, or is so plagued with inner conflict, anxiety, and guilt that he is unable to perceive reality clearly or meet the ordinary demands of the environment in which he lives. With this definition as a focus, we can extend and elaborate the analysis.

There is no point at which maladjustment suddenly begins or ends. Behavior reactions arrange themselves along a continuum from adaptive to maladaptive, from adjustive to nonadjustive. Maladaptive behavior differs from adaptive behavior more in degree than in kind. And, we should note, abnormal behavior evolves from normal behavior. All of us have physiological and psychological stress limits; when these limits are reached, our behavior begins to deviate in certain prescribed ways, depending upon what our experiences have been.

Therefore, in considering criteria, signs, or symptoms for evaluating the existence of maladjustment, several points should be noted. First, each criterion or sign is not mutually exclusive but is interrelated. This simply means that maladjustment generally expresses itself in broad areas of experience, not in isolated pockets. Each of the criteria is singled out simply for convenience and clarity of presentation. Second, the criteria identified as indicators of maladjustment are *not* equally diagnostic and helpful in determining the severity of disturbance. Furthermore, some behavior deviations are more ominous than others. As a rough rule-of-thumb, we may use Cleugh's (5) intensity, frequency, and duration as indicators of the severity of a reaction.

The intensity of a reaction refers

to its sending power—its force, or the quantity of energy by which it is expressed. For example, if a teacher, upon viewing a hostile act, determines that it is one of the most extreme reactions he has seen in a fourth grader, he can usually infer that such hostility is indicative of serious maladjustment.

Frequency refers to an often-repeated act which, by itself, is indicative of disturbance. For instance, a child who exhibits a disturbed reaction once a day has a problem of greater magnitude than a child who expresses a similar reaction once every month or every year. Therefore, a repetitive series of disturbed reactions occurring in short intervals of time is a good indicator of maladjustment.

Duration refers to the length of time a reaction or a series of reactions has been exhibited. The longer a child expresses deviant behavior, the more thoroughly entrenched, better crystallized, and more resistant to change his behavior becomes.

With these qualifications and diagnostic statements in mind, we are ready to discuss the criteria. As each is analyzed, those signs that are especially indicative of serious maladjustment will be identified.

Degree of Tension or Anxiety

In Chapter one we said that whenever a person's basic psychological needs are insufficiently gratified, or he experiences a serious threat to his self system or survival, the inevitable result is anxiety. Anxiety acts as a warning signal to the ego that vigilance must be exercised to defend against or to ward off approaching danger. Therefore, it logically follows that the existence of excessive anxiety (or its derivative states) is a reliable sign of conflict or disequilibrium.

Anxiety appears in many forms and is expressed overtly in a number of ways. The most common manifestations are inability to concentrate, restless or hyperactive behavior, tremors, twitching, finger-tapping, and nail-biting. In its more severe forms, anxiety may be expressed by chronic apprehension or extreme sensitivity and reaction to slight changes in the environment. The more tension or anxiety indicators the child presents, the more evidence we have of his maladjustment.

Efficiency of Intellectual Functioning

A second important sign of maladjustment is one's apparent inability to use his intellect efficiently. Efficiency of intellectual functioning refers to the degree of correspondence between one's academic performance and his *capacity* to perform. In other words, does the child make the progress in school that one might reasonably expect, based on both quantitative and qualitative estimates of his capacity? Is he a consistent and productive worker in all subject areas? Or is his performance spasmodic and variable? Is he academically retarded in some or all academic areas?

In addition to these considerations, other aspects of intellectual functioning should be evaluated. For instance, are the child's thought processes (as indicated by oral and written expression) logically organized, clear and coherent? Or does he express a series of disconnected ideas? Does he exercise judgment appropriate to his age? These evaluations of thought organization are crucial in determining the severity of a child's disturbance. Pathology of thought processes rarely appears in a child whose adjustment is within normal limits. Therefore, the appearance of pathology, if it persists, suggests the need for immediate professional assistance.

Appropriateness of Emotional Response and Affect

Just as the amount and kind of anxiety are an over-all indicator of maladjustment, so are the child's characteristic emotional responses and feeling tone useful clues to his general stability and psychological health.

The stable child generally enjoys life and is able to invest himself emotionally in others. He accepts affection easily and is able to give it. On the other hand, he is sad when sadness is appropriate; he cries when he gets hurt. Moreover, the emotionally healthy child may experience disintegrating emotional reactions at times when things are upsetting or go wrong, but he has emotional "bounce" (21).

The maladjusted child presents quite a different picture. He may be impulsive and over-react emotionally to failure, mild slights, and trivial mistakes. Sometimes he reacts to praise as if he had just been given a large dose of castor oil. The upset or disturbed child frequently does not relate appropriately to others. He may unreasonably attach himself to one or two people rather than relate to a broad circle of friends. Often he is a "fringer" or isolate, rarely moving into the mainstream of peer activity.

In addition to these signs of emotional maladjustment, other symptoms are more serious in nature. In the serious category are children who exhibit marked vacillation in feeling tone (varying from elation to depression) or excessive emotional constriction (showing little expression of any kind). The latter are not emotionally flexible and react to situations that have emotional impact with the deadpan expression of the poker player.

In the serious category also are children who have rigid or tyrannical superegos, whose reactions are permeated with guilt feelings. These are the children that "walk the tight rope"; they are fearful of expressing almost any impulse. When their behavior does not conform to the exact requirements of acceptability, they are guilt-ridden and excessively apologetic. The inner lives of such children are often filled with despair and they face the world with a distorted sense of duty.

The Nature of Self-Concept

We have already noted in Chapter two that the way an individual regards himself affects the way he perceives and reacts to the world. His self-concept is a distillation—a product of all his experiences. Consequently, his psychic economy is mirrored in it, and one important aspect of his stability can be determined by an assessment of his self-concept.

White (22) has convincingly argued that we all need to feel competence in our environment. Consequently, individuals riddled with self-doubt feel worthless and inadequate, are plagued with chronically low self-esteem, and make brittle adjustments to the world around them.

An inadequate or low self-concept is relatively easy to identify. Perhaps the most usual sign is one's excessive need to be continuously reassured that his productions are of acceptable quality or that he is valued and worthwhile. Sometimes the person with low self-esteem expresses unreasonable concern about his appearance, even though he is physically attractive; he may frequently verbalize that he feels ugly or repulsive. Or, this person may magnify, out of realistic proportions, a minor defect or flaw.

Others express a low self-concept by their inability to accept genuine and deserved praise graciously; instead, they become upset or readily convince themselves that the praise is insincerely offered. However, some children who are deprived of acceptance will react to a genuine offering of praise as if they have been given the world's most powerful energizer. They devour it like a starved man and immediately crave more. These reactions may be equally indicative of a battered self-concept.

A low self-concept may be expressed in other ways. A child may be so uncertain of himself that he steadfastly refuses to participate in anything competitive, or he may qualify excessively his every act, statement, or opinion. Occasionally, a child may also refuse to do any school work. This refusal may be interpreted as laziness or negativism when, in fact, the child would rather not perform than face another sign of his inadequacy.

Finally, there are behavior reactions of people with disturbed self-evaluations that are extremely deviant and maladaptive (people who exhibit extreme self-contempt). They regard themselves as totally worthless; they are greatly depressed and often unconsciously launch upon a course of self-punishment and self-destruction. In such a person suicide ideation, the entertainment of suicidal thoughts, is not uncommon. Obviously, these reactions are indicative of extreme maladjustment and require prolonged psychiatric treatment.

Appropriateness of Behavior

To some extent, the healthiness of a child's adaption can be determined by the degree to which his behavior corresponds to that of other children his age. This determination is relatively simple for most teachers since children are age graded in most schools, and an individual child's behavior can be compared readily with the typical behavior of the other children in his class or grade.

This criterion, however, has some inherent problems. Careful observation of children's behavior quickly reveals that retardation in physical and mental maturation impedes development of behavior appropriate to one's age. Mentally retarded youngsters, particularly, tend to behave more in accordance with their mental age than with their chronological age. As a matter of fact, behavior appropriate to one's mental age appears more typical than exceptional; therefore, the teacher will be wise to consider a child's mental age as the better predictor of appropriate or inappropriate behavior.

When age-appropriate behavior is used as a criterion for evaluating maladjustment, there are several personality patterns that should be considered. For example, is the child's behavior appropriate to his age regarding self-direction, caring for himself, and assuming responsibility? Or, is he unusually dependent, requiring excessive assistance from others? On the other hand, does his behavior express a pseudo-maturity so that it is apparent that he cannot let himself enjoy the pleasures of his years and peers? All of these are signs that the child may be troubled.

In summary, age-appropriate behavior is reflected in a child's ability to handle and perform the tasks that are characteristic of most children living in his culture. He accepts reasonable social controls and makes substantial progress in the internalization of standards, morals, and values; to the degree that he does not, he is on the maladjusted end of the continuum.

In its most severe form, this latter problem is expressed in the behavior of the *sociopath*. Such a person has marked defects in his superego structure, has few internalized values, and constantly commits anti-social acts without experiencing appropriate guilt reactions (4). The sociopath is, as is any individual who has limited capacity for empathy or guilt, seriously maladjusted, and psychological or psychiatric assistance is indicated; however, the prognosis for change is poor.

Adequacy of Reality Contact. Most people distort reality at times and in various degrees, but usually such distortions occur when one experiences a traumatic event, when his security is jeopardized, or when his self-esteem is threatened. Such behavior is not unnatural and certainly not atypical. However, when a person persistently makes perceptual distortions of many things in the world of objects and facts, he has a serious problem.

The inadequate child may distort reality by reacting to minor achievements as great victories. The anxious child may misperceive reality by interpreting an extraneous sound in the night as the footsteps of a burglar. The economically deprived child may distort the real value of a dollar. The child who is constantly in trouble at school often changes reality by denying responsibility for his unacceptable behavior. All of these examples represent difficulties in dealing with and maintaining contact with reality. To the degree that they persist and endure, they are indicative of maladaptive behavior.

Adequacy of reality contact differs not only in kind, but in degree. It approaches pathological proportions when an individual experiences marked difficulty in properly differentiating between reality and fantasy. For instance, when one has persistent difficulty in orienting himself to time, place, or person, his condition is probably pathologic. This individual may be unable to determine who or where he is or to relate the proper date (day, month, or year). These symptoms are exceedingly rare in children and need not be considered at any greater length here. It is sufficient to say that such distortions or confusions of reality (especially when accompanied by delusions or hallucinations) are probably the most serious of all signs of maladjustment.

Defense Instability. Defenses, discussed in an earlier section, operate to ward off unacceptable impulses, protect us from dangerous temptations, and reduce excessive tension. It is apparent, then, that the effectiveness of one's defense-mechanism system is a significant clue to his stability. Therefore, the extent to which a person acts impulsively, has chronic anxiety, or distorts reality indicates the degree of his defense system's instability.

At another level, the more defensive a person is regarding his actions, opinions, and feelings, the more certain we can be that his adjustment is rigid. Teachers can readily call to mind a child whose behavior illustrates extreme defensiveness. Typically, such a child goes to great lengths to deny his failures, to attribute responsibility for an unacceptable act to someone else, or to elaborately defend his own opinions.

It should be kept in mind that defensiveness is not necessarily maladaptive. Indeed, it is human, and very often healthy, to use defense mechanisms. Defensiveness becomes maladaptive, however, when a person must defend every action. Such behavior reflects deep feelings of inadequacy which the person is struggling desperately to avoid. Obviously, these defensive reactions, if used in the extreme, block out continually greater parts of one's reality or distort reality to unmanageable proportions. In addition, the more one's reality is distorted, the more difficulty he has in successfully resolving his conflicts or problems.

Under constant and excessive stress (threats to survival or self, demands one cannot meet, impulses one cannot control), defenses begin to falter or break down. This failure of the defenses to perform their functions effectively is referred to as *decompensation*. When decompensation occurs, various degrees of personality disorganization can be observed and identified. Typically, the symptoms are characteristic alarm and immobilization reactions. The individual may try strenuously to exert self-control; become extremely sensitive, alert, and hyperactive; vacillate in mood from fearfulness to depression; and exhibit various physical abnormalities. Signs of increased tension and lowered efficiency are also characteristic of defensive decompensation (6). Obviously, anyone with symptoms of psychological decompensation is disturbed or maladjusted, and disturbances of severe proportions require expert psychological or psychiatric care.

Now that the major criteria for determining maladjustment have been identified, let us consider their use. It is not expected that teachers will or should make diagnostic judgments that are better made by psychologists and psychiatrists. But, if teachers are to do the job their roles require, they must be able to identify disturbed or maladjusted children and to know when expert assistance is needed. If expert help is not available, it is important that the teacher understand the type of problem with which he is dealing and work intelligently with the parents in interpreting the child's problems to them.

In applying the seven major criteria for maladjustment, one may find it helpful to think of them quantitatively as well as qualitatively. The more signs or symptoms a child presents, the more realistically one can evaluate the extent of his maladjustment. Differential weights should be given to those symptoms that indicate serious maladjustment; however, quantification does not supersede the value of a sensitive qualitative analysis of each sign. The seriousness of particular behavior deviations will become clearer when a diagnostic classification of maladjustment is considered.

A CLASSIFICATION OF MALADAPTIVE BEHAVIOR

Although we have made some progress in identifying criteria by which maladaptive behavior in children may be detected, the task of delineating a sensible classification system remains. It is important to classify behavior deviations for three main reasons. Classification helps to (a) identify and structure certain meaningful relationships among a great range of behavior deviations, (b) elucidate the dynamics common to related behavior deviations, and (c) differentiate the etiology and severity of disorders. With minor exceptions, the classification system is essentially the same as that published by the American Psychiatric Association in 1952.

Behavior disorders (or maladjustments) may be grouped into two broad categories—organic and functional. Organic disorders include behavior deviations in which the etiology is primarily associated with hereditary conditions, physical disease or defect, and convulsive states. Impairment in body function and structure frequently occurs. Functional disorders are so labeled because their origin is considered to be primarily psychogenic or psychological in nature; they have no demonstrable organic basis (1, 6). We are primarily concerned with the functional disorders.

Functional deviations may be further grouped into primary behavior disorders, psychoneurotic disorders, character or personality disorders, psychosomatic disorders, and psychotic disorders. From this group we will focus particularly on the primary behavior disorders and specific aspects of psychoneurotic deviations. We shall discuss some of the other disorders in very general terms. The delineations are made because these problem areas are the ones which the classroom teacher most frequently encounters.

Primary Behavior Disorders

Primary behavior disorders are divided into habit disorders, conduct disorders, and neurotic traits. Psychodynamically, the primary behavior disorders arise as a result of disturbances in parent-child relationships. The child expresses the conflicts he experiences in these relationships by acting out or externalizing them. The symptom picture varies according to the adaptive patterns that have been most strongly reinforced. The child does not usually manifest excessive anxiety since he has felt a certain amount of security during infancy. His difficulties typically begin, and negative treatment usually occurs, when the child becomes assertive and independent (1, 19).

Developmentally, habit disorders appear earlier than conduct disorders. The child with habit disorders cannot satisfy and has difficulty projecting his affective needs. He expresses his inadequate gratification by various forms of tension-reducing behavior. The emotional deprivation he experiences produces painful inner tensions that are manifested in particular forms of autoerotic activity. Feeding disorders, sucking, biting, vomiting, scratching, masturbation, enuresis, rocking, and head-banging are often symptomatic of this disorder (1).

When the child has acquired the psychomotor maturity to fight back or attack his family because of his emotional deprivation, he exhibits a conduct disorder. When conduct disorder occurs, the child is revealing his parents' inability to love and appropriately meet his needs. His revolt is open and expresses his desire to force his parents to be more indulgent. Since the child does not receive the emotional acceptance which fosters healthy identification and permits the internalization of standards, he exhibits deficiencies in self-control and superego functioning. Indeed, his needs for nurture and autonomy plague him, and he lets the world know about it. He expresses his need by such behavior as tantrums, defiance, destructiveness, cruelty, lying, stealing, and deviant sex behavior (1).

The needs of a child in this type of conflict are unrelenting; his problems become progressively more severe. The development of neurotic traits reflects this transition. Neurotic traits represent that phase of personality development in which identification with and internalization of parental standards are incomplete. Impulses are not fully controlled, and fear of parental hostility because of them is displaced to an object or symbol. Thus, the greater fear is not of inner guilt, but of punishment originating from an external source. The conflicts are partly internalized and partly externalized. Characteristic expressions of these difficulties are inhibition of play and aggression, sleep disorders, night terrors, sleepwalking, enuresis, and fear of animals, darkness, and thunder (1).

Psychoneurotic Disorders

Neurotic traits, as we have noted, are transitional between primary behavior problems and psychoneurotic reactions. A person cannot develop a psychoneurosis (or neurosis) until the personality structure has established the superego. Central to the development of a psychoneurosis is conflict between two opposing strivings or forces. Id drives, which the individual evaluates as dangerous, strive for discharge while superego promptings move to block expression of the drives. As conflict develops between these two opposing sets of strivings, anxiety is created, the ego is warned, and defensive operations rush into action. However, the ego defenses do not completely contain the conflict,

and symptoms of various types appear. Generally, symptoms are symbolic disguises or substitutes for impulses that cannot be directly expressed (1, 3, 13).

The id strivings that lead to the psychoneurotic conflict are unconscious and repressed. The individual is usually not aware of the exact nature of the impulses involved. However, he does experience anxiety, apprehension, and guilt and strives hard to rid himself of these uncomfortable feelings.

The essential difference between primary behavior problems and psychoneurosis should now be apparent. In psychoneurosis, the conflict is largely internalized and unconscious. The child is more or less in conflict with himself, although the source of the conflict is a result of his earlier experiences and interpersonal relationships. He suffers greatly, but he usually does not react against the environment. However, in primary behavior disorders, the child rebels against the treatment he receives, and he reacts against his environment in a retaliatory way. In other words, he acts out his distress and conflict.

Berkowitz and Rothman (2) have captured the essence of this difference in the following example. A child who suffers guilt because of an unconscious death wish against the father is considered to have a behavior maladjustment (primary behavior disorder) when his aggression is expressed in bullying, stealing, and other forms of antisocial behavior. The psychoneurotic child may handle the anxiety associated with the death wish by developing a phobia. In this instance, the phobia is symptomatic of the unconscious wish.

Although in previous sections considerable attention has been devoted to the types of experiences and relationships that lead to behavior deviations, it may be helpful to note how psychoneurotic reactions develop. These reactions almost invariably occur as a result of inadequate, depriving, and harsh parent-child relationships. Parents who inadequately accept, constantly threaten, and harshly punish their child create hostile impulses in him that he cannot express for fear of retaliation or loss of love. In his effort to maintain some sense of security, he represses (and defends in other ways) his hostility. Nevertheless, the unconscious hostility continually strives for discharge, with each hostile impulse leading to anxiety and guilt; thus, the cycle repeats itself. Finally, when the child's personality structure can no longer defend against the conflict, symptoms develop, and the child exhibits psychoneurotic reactions. He may regress to stages or points of fixation, and he may become greatly preoccupied with old, unresolved problems.

Symptoms and types of psychoneurotic reactions vary with the personal history of the individual. While it is beyond the scope of our discussion to consider in detail specific psychoneurotic reactions, the general syndrome is worth noting. That is, psychoneurotic disorders may be characterized by considerable anxiety, marked difficulty in functioning at capacity level, rigid and repetitive behavior, hypersensitivity, egocentricity (self-centeredness), immaturity, varied physical complaints and fatigue, dissatisfaction and unhappiness, and limited insight into one's own behavior (6, 7).

Psychoneurotic reactions are more severe and represent more serious disturbances than primary behavior disorders. Unless the psychoneurotic person receives appropriate professional help, his symptoms usually persist; he does not outgrow his conflicts, and the advice freely offered by friends and relatives is of little value. While some personality disintegration usually occurs, a psychoneurosis does not seriously impair one's capacity to test reality; however, one's efficiency is impaired in a number of ways. In summary, if the person with psychoneurotic reactions is to be helped, he will require expert psychological or psychiatric treatment.

Psychosomatic Disorders

Psychosomatic disorders result from severe or chronic psychological stress in which there is direct physiological malfunctioning. Disruption of the internal homeostatic balance of the body occurs, and almost any organ system may be involved. Psychosomatic symptoms in children usually appear at a young age, when children are poorly equipped to adapt to situational dangers and other stresses. Such children, when faced with threatening situations, handle the resulting excessive anxiety by turning it inward on the body, where it is expressed by psychosomatic malfunctioning. Typical of such psychosomatic symptoms are colic, vomiting, constipation, diarrhea, breathholding, asthma, and other disturbances (1, 7).

Psychosomatic disorders—different from the psychoneuroses—are not generally symbolic expressions of a conflict. Instead, the emotion associated with the conflict (which cannot be expressed by acceptable verbal or physical activity) is discharged through the visceral organs. Usually, the anxiety, fear, and hostility which an individual cannot express openly are basic to the psychosomatic malfunctioning. These feelings, which are associated with the original stress, are to a large extent unconscious. Therefore, the person has minimal understanding or awareness of the reactions taking place. By the use of repression, the threatening events and feelings remain unconscious and the whole process is perpetuated (6).

Why a particular organ system is selected to discharge the tension associated with the stress is not completely understood. Any of the organ systems (gastrointestinal, cardiovascular, respiratory, skin, musculoskeletal, and others) may be selected. Some authorities have suggested that six major factors may be involved: (a) constitutional susceptibility of a particular organ system, (b) the previous accident and illness history of the individual, (c) the type of emotional stress, (d) predisposition because relatives have had illness of the organ system involved, (e) the symbolic meaning given to the organ by the individual, and (f) the nature of the secondary gains accruing from the selected symptom. Individuals who adapt by developing psychosomatic problems generally are immature and unable to handle responsibility adequately; they rely excessively on repression and have had the reaction reinforced during childhood (7).

Psychosomatic disorders, like other maladjustments, have their adaptive aspects. First, physical illness replaces a current situation which would otherwise be emotionally intolerable. By unconsciously dealing with a situation in this way, a person substitutes a more acceptable form of illness for a less acceptable one. That is, physical illness is socially accepted in our culture more than is emotional illness. Second (as a by-product), the psychosomatic illness may be used unconsciously to gain interest, care, and affection which cannot be achieved in other ways. Third, and even more important, a psychoso-

matic illness may protect the person from developing a more severe disorder. For example, some patients with ulcerative colitis have developed a paranoid psychosis when the psychosomatic disorder has been alleviated; others, with the same physical illness, may develop a psychotic regression (4).

Psychosomatic illness varies in intensity and severity; therefore, it is not possible on the basis of the symptomatology to evaluate the depth or seriousness of the psychological problems. One should recognize, however, that psychosomatic problems require very early and expert diagnosis and treatment. Otherwise, the affected organ may become permanently damaged; physical treatment may occur too late, even if the psychic problem has been resolved.

Psychotic Disorders

The final type of deviant behavior to be considered is psychosis.* Psychotic disorders are popularly referred to as insanity and are among the most severe disturbances known to man. They are characterized by extreme personality disorganization, defense decompensation, and loss of contact with reality. Because the illness is so debilitating, the psychotic person finds it difficult or impossible to relate appropriately to others and to perform his ordinary responsibilities on the job and at home.

The chief features distinguishing psychotic from non-psychotic reactions

* Maladjusted reactions referred to as personality or character disorders will not be discussed because they consist of heterogeneous deviations, varying in seriousness and underlying dynamics. These deviations occur so rarely in children that it is not necessary to discuss them here.

are the integrative qualities of various functions; marked disturbances in memory, attention, and imagination; bizarre thought processes; and extreme inappropriateness of affect. The psychotic person typically manifests delusions (false beliefs) and various types of hallucinations. He is often disoriented to his environment (evidenced by lack of awareness regarding time, place, and person) and usually exhibits behavior that is markedly regressive (6, 13).

The conscious mental activity of a psychotic is similar to the unconscious mental activity in dreams of a non-psychotic person. In dreams, ego controls exert minimum influence (although much material is censored or symbolized), and the dream activity may transcend the bounds of time and space. Ideational representations of impulses which would shock his conscious awareness are experienced in the dreams of the non-psychotic person. Because the psychotic's ego defenses are greatly decompensated, he experiences the conscious unmodified expressions of id drives and the torturous promptings of the superego; yet, he cannot (as the non-psychotic can) cast these impulses aside as simply dreams. They compose his reality.

The etiology of functional psychoses is still not entirely clear. Some investigators (17) have pointed to constitutional predispositions that later lead to abnormal brain-functioning as causal factors. Similarly, Escalona's study (10) of seventeen psychotic children makes a good case for postulating constitutional etiology. Undoubtedly, both psychological and constitutional factors play a part in creating this most debilitating illness.

There is some general agreement among investigators that the childhood of an individual who later becomes psychotic is not particularly happy or stable. Parent-child relationships are frequently characterized by rejection, overly strict or inconsistent discipline, excessive superego development, rigidity in sexual morality, and chronic insecurity. These relationships and developmental problems tend to impede the satisfactory development of the child's ego strength and his capacity to adapt to the various stresses which are so much a part of our world today (6).

Fortunately, psychotic reactions in children are somewhat rare; consequently, we need not elaborate our discussion on the complexities of the psychotic process. The information that has been discussed should, however, sufficiently alert one to the general characteristics and magnitude of this very serious illness.

CHANGING MALADAPTIVE-BEHAVIOR PATTERNS

Now that we have identified various types of maladjustment and have classified various types of behavior deviations, we face the problem of changing maladaptive-behavior patterns. This is an awesome task. No "pat" solutions exist because no two people are exactly alike. Nevertheless, some attention must be given, in a general way, to the often repeated question of teachers "What do we do next when we know the child is disturbed?" Before a theoretical discussion of this question, a number of general questions should be considered. They are significant questions that all people who work with maladjusted children must ponder before attempting to implement a strategy that may be helpful. These questions are (a) How much and in what direction should a child's maladaptive behavior be changed? (b) Is one's aim to change the symptom or to bring about basic personality changes? (c) To what extent is the helping person's personality impeding more healthy growth? (d) Considering the seriousness of the maladjustment, what realistic limitations should be set regarding goals for changing deviant behavior? Let us consider each of these questions.

The first question is a crucial one for several reasons. As we have noted previously, disturbed behavior often represents the best compromise a child can reach because of his life circumstances. However, if one attempts to change the behavior, the attempt should be in the direction of more healthy adaption rather than inhibition or repression of the behavior that is annoying or provocative. Furthermore, if one decides that change of the maladaptive behavior is desirable, intelligent planning and work are required. Many people are motivated to help a child until they recognize that appropriate change will require much effort and dedication. Maladjusted children do not change by the magical implementation of a trick, technique, or an ingenious form of punishment. A great deal of giving is required if one wishes to help a child.

The second question is related to the first. The helping person should carefully consider whether the plan for change should be oriented toward symptom removal or toward the basic cause of the maladjustment. While it is sometimes beneficial to give symptomatic relief, a major focus on symptom removal rarely helps the child resolve the basic problem. For example, in clinical practice one usually finds that a symptom removed by this method is only replaced by another and sometimes more devastating one. Therefore, any plan aimed at symptom removal tends to be temporary at best and should be carefully considered.

The third basic consideration refers to the emotional involvement of the helping person. The disturbed behavior of some children tends to set up negative, dissonant reactions in all of us. Sometimes our reactions are conscious and at other times unconscious. Consequently, in spite of our best efforts, we often develop relationships and set up expectations that intensify rather than alleviate a child's maladjustment. Therefore, when our diligent efforts fail to produce change, we should carefully consider and evaluate our relationship with the child.

The final consideration is a realistic judgment of the degree to which we can expect to change the behavior of a maladjusted child. A reasonable assumption is that the more seriously disturbed a child's behavior is, the more likely it is that unconscious motivational forces are at work. Unconsciously determined behavior—or maladaptive behavior that is firmly entrenched and has persisted over a period of time—is very resistant to change. In addition to the severity of a child's disturbance, one must carefully consider and evaluate his personality resources and his life circumstances. If his personality resources are inadequate or if his environment should be but cannot be changed, limited goals must be set because even the most skillfully executed therapeutic plans may not be productive under these circumstances. In some cases, then, simply helping the child to maintain a certain amount of stability is a worthwhile aim and accomplishment.

With the above general questions in

mind, we can now focus on the teacher's question "What do we do next?" This discussion will be a general one since later sections deal specifically with principles and procedures for working with the maladjusted child.

When we consider conditions conducive to influencing or changing maladaptive behavior, we are considering therapeutic procedures. To the degree that therapy involves learning, we are also considering the creation of an effective learning environment. If we conceive therapy and learning to be substantially the same, our quest becomes that of establishing conditions under which the disturbed child can unlearn defeating patterns, thus freeing him to learn emotionally adaptive or satisfying ones.

Drawing upon certain therapeutic and learning principles, we can formulate some conditions that are believed helpful with the maladjusted child. *A child can be assisted in modifying his behavior by experiencing an accepting, predictable, and safe relationship with a helping person* (11, 18, 20). Practically all of the well-established systems of psychotherapy make this assumption. For example, Fiedler (11) found that successful therapists, regardless of orientation, were successful primarily because they were sensitive to the patient's meanings and feelings and displayed warm interest in him without becoming over-involved emotionally. Psychoanalysis, a form of psychotherapy, also relies heavily on certain standard procedures that lend consistency and predictability to the therapeutic relationship.

When one person completely accepts another, there is an absence of threat. When there is an absence of threat, one can be himself. Energy that is normally used in dealing with personal threat can be productively employed in other pursuits. Indeed, with such conditions prevailing, defensiveness and anxiety are at a minimum, conditions for effective learning are enhanced, and one can efficiently utilize potential resources. Complete acceptance also allows the person to get better acquainted with aspects of himself that have previously moved him in self-defeating directions.

A helping relationship that is consistent and predictable is the basis for the development of trust (9, 18). We cannot develop satisfactory (or satisfying) relationships with others until we learn to trust. As we experience a feeling of trust in another person, we are able to relax our defenses and relate to others more freely and warmly. Therefore, if a teacher or any other helping person relates in a predictable and accepting way to a child, the child is better able to identify with the goals of the teacher and is freer to allow his potentialities to develop.

An attitude of helpfulness is also an essential ingredient of this first condition. For instance, Frank (12) has pointed out that simply the perception that one will be given help often leads to symptom relief.

A child tends to move in the direction of more healthy adjustment when he is permitted the opportunity to express his feelings and concerns without censure or disapproval. This statement follows logically from the previous discussion and has considerable empirical support (3, 18, 20). Symonds (20) has indicated that therapeutic gain depends little on what the therapist does but rather on what he encourages the client to express, to think, or to do. Freedom to express oneself in an accepting setting or relationship (in the absence of emotional over-involvement by the helping person) tends to desensitize a person to his conflicted feelings. Stated in learning-theory terms, the constant working through of feelings associated with conflict without negative reinforcement leads to extinction of the conflicted feelings.

Miller and Dollard (8) have suggested that any condition that reduces excessive anxiety and fear (approval, reassurance, interest) acts as a potent reinforcement. As a matter of fact, they have pointed out that simply remaining silent when a patient is verbalizing reduces fear and stimulates emotional catharsis.

The simple procedure of listening intently to what one is saying has startling results with people who are *not* experiencing emotional difficulties. As a class assignment (following a rather complete discussion of these ideas), I asked that each member select another person to relate to in the following manner. For a period of fifteen minutes he would focus his complete and concentrated acceptance on that person. He would encourage the person to speak freely and, by listening intently, would attempt to conceptualize the inner world of the person as if he were going to draw a portrait of the selected person.

A teacher who was a student in my class used the procedure with *her* class. She reported that a number of the children remarked that they had not previously recognized what a fine, wise teacher she was. Others of my students were amazed at the rapidity with which some people revealed deep, personal concerns. Still others reported the remarkable change in attitude of their wives or husbands when this procedure was used for a more extended period of time.

It is not to be expected that deep or serious maladjustments will be cured or substantially modified simply by encouraging freedom of expression. However, it is well known clinically that catharsis in a therapeutic environment is a useful technique that enables one to gain insight into his problem. The maladjusted person needs not only to verbalize his conflicted feelings but also to connect them to the unconscious strivings or experiences that were instrumental originally in creating his conflict.

A *child tends to change to more acceptable behavior when his relationship to a helping person fosters healthy identification.* While there appear to be several reasons why one person identifies with another (see Chapter two), healthy identification and incorporation of values and attitudes seem to proceed best when acceptance and approval are part of the relationship.

Therefore, when the person with whom one identifies is a healthy model, his healthy attitudes, standards, and coping methods tend to become a part of the personality of the identifier. For example, a teacher who is reasonable, calm, and unemotional in dealing with a child, provides that child with an opportunity to assimilate and incorporate the attitudes and behavior of the teacher (8, 19). Such opportunities become very important to children with certain types of maladaptive reactions whose set of values is distorted or deficient. The teacher's attitude may enhance a child's desire to identify with him and, consequently, to accept his set of values.

A *child's adjustment is facilitated when inappropriate or distorted superego attitudes are corrected.* In some types of maladjustment the superego is excessively rigid and severe. Consequently, the person feels an unreasonable amount of guilt, worthlessness, depression, and lowered self-esteem; a reduction in the harshness of the superego, however, leads to a decrease in the intensity of these painful feelings (14, 19).

Opportunity to verbalize guilt associated with ideas, impulses, fantasies, and actions—in the absence of censure or disapproval—often reduces the tyranny of the superego. As the superego becomes less tyrannical, impulses that have been excessively thwarted can be more freely expressed and can participate in the psychic economy of the person. Moreover, if the teacher or helping person takes a matter-of-fact, everybody-makes-mistakes attitude, the guilt-ridden person may gain a more realistic perspective.

For example, with a decrease in feelings of guilt and worthlessness, there is a corresponding increase in self-esteem. It is as if one's lost parental love has suddenly been restored, and this is a powerful tonic. With increased self-acceptance the person is able to relate more effectively with others and feels more confident to engage in activities in which he is now more likely to be successful. As this cycle occurs, the success feeds back to further enhance his self-esteem.

Psychological growth is promoted and adjustment is enhanced when a child finds that he is able to deal more adequately with his environment. White (22) has convincingly suggested that one of the basic motives of all human beings is to feel competence in dealing and interacting with the environment. The maladjusted child perceives the environment as unsupporting and feels inadequate to deal with it; thus, he is blocked in his efforts to satisfy his needs and victimized by his self-concept.

The environment in which a child can feel adequate varies with his particular circumstances; however, there are always certain general demands and expectations with which he must cope to feel competent. He must, for example, feel reasonable success in mastering the formal intellectual tasks prescribed by his school. He must master the social skills that permit him to find a place in his peer group. Similarly, he must develop reasonable competence in learning those physical skills that prove his boyishness (or girlishness) and help him to perform the roles appropriate to his age. Failure in any one of these areas can produce in him feelings of incompetence. Consequently, assistance to a child who is having difficulty in any of these areas will enhance his self-concept, which will in turn enhance his ability to deal with his environment.

Veteran teachers are well aware of the changes in behavior that take place in a child when he is brought to the point of mastering a skill at which he has previously failed. As a matter of fact, many remedial reading experts are convinced that therapy is unnecessary to change the maladaptive behavior of the disabled reader; his behavior will change as he learns to read.

Since most maladjusted children have associated academic problems, it is highly beneficial to them for the teacher to set up an instructional situation that will lead these children to a feeling of mastery. In the beginning it is particularly crucial to grade the tasks carefully to ensure that the child cannot fail. Success must be immediate and lead step by step to daily mastery.

A teacher once asked how he might encourage a pupil to participate in art when the pupil was convinced that he had absolutely no aptitude. My immediate response was to ask in which type of art form he wished to encourage the pupil's participation. This comment immediately alerted the teacher to the numerous art forms in which the child might be encouraged and the knowledge that the child could most certainly have success with one of them. I suggested further that, if the pupil were capable of dropping ink on a sheet of paper, cutting a bar of soap with a knife, or immersing his hands in finger paint, he was capable of producing some type of art form. The very practical moral here is that, as long as one is not rigidly bound to a lock step procedure, almost any activity can lend itself to pupil mastery.

In a somewhat old but significant study, Keister and Updegraff (16) found that instructing a group of children in problem-solving tasks graduated in difficulty led to significant changes in their post-test behavior. One of two groups of children (trained group) who were generally inadequate in solving problems was given instruction in this skill. A second (non-trained) group was not given the benefit of this training. At the conclusion of the training period the trained group was significantly better in problem solving and reflected a decrease in immature and dependent behavior. In addition, the trained group exhibited more desirable behavior at the end of the training even though the non-trained group was superior in most of these traits in the beginning. Apparently, carefully graded tasks structured to lead to success not only increase skills related to training but lead to significant changes in social and emotional behavior.

A *child's behavior may be appropriately modified when his environment is made more rewarding and his basic needs are satisfied.* The maladjusted child, as we have discussed, experiences great difficulty in satisfying his basic needs. Because of unsatisfactory interpersonal relationships in the past, he expects others to reject him. Consequently, he may be suspicious and keep others at a distance to avoid more psychological hurt. Or, as we have also mentioned, his superego may be so rigid that he cannot permit himself the satisfactions necessary to his emotional well-being (14).

Besides developing a one-to-one relationship that is emotionally satisfying with the child, the helping person can assist in manipulating other aspects of his environment. Since most of the child's needs are intimately tied up in his relationship with his parents, assisting them to better understand his needs is extremely important. Most parents want to help their child if they feel respected and understand their involvement in his problems.

It is also important for the helping person to encourage other people at school who have contact with the child to help him. For instance, an art teacher can help him express his conflicts through the medium of drawing or finger painting. An accepting physical education teacher can develop a relationship with a boy that provides the masculine identification he needs. In a similar manner, classmates can provide helping relationships if a teacher encourages them to make the problem child their friend.

As we conclude our discussion of the nature of maladjustment, it is appropriate that a statement or two be made regarding the assistance process. Although one may have concluded from the discussion that the teacher is expected to be a psychotherapist to the maladjusted child, this meaning is not intended. What is suggested, instead, is that in order to help the child we must seek to implement those conditions that are therapeutic. Our knowledge of those conditions that are believed to be conducive to behavior change or therapeutic gain is crucial.

It should be apparent from the conditions we have identified and discussed that there is no magic, no secret formula, for solving the problems of the maladjusted child. If there is a central focus, it is the establishment of a satisfying and safe relationship with the child so that he can feel better about himself.

References

1. Ackerman, N. W. *The psychodynamics of family life.* New York: Basic Books, 1958.

2. Berkowitz, Pearl H., and Rothmann, Esther P. *The disturbed child.* New York: New York University Press, 1960.

3. Cameron, D. E. *General psychotherapy.* New York: Grune & Stratton, 1950.

4. Cameron, N. *Personality development and psychopathology.* Boston: Houghton Mifflin, 1963.

5. Cleugh, M. F. *Psychology in the service of the school.* New York: Philosophical Library, 1951.

6. Coleman, J. C. *Abnormal psychology and modern life,* 2nd ed. Chicago: Scott, Foresman, 1956.

7. Coville, W. J., Costello, T. W., and Rouke, F. L. *Abnormal psychology.* New York: Barnes & Noble, 1960.

8. Dollard, J., and Miller, N. *Personality and psychotherapy.* New York: McGraw-Hill, 1950.

9. Erikson, E. *Childhood and society.* New York: Norton, 1950.

10. Escalona, Sibylle. Some considerations regarding psychotherapy with psychotic children. *Bull. of the Menninger Clinic,* 1948, XII, 127–134.

11. Fiedler, F. E. Quantitative studies on the role of therapists' feelings toward their patients. In O. H. Mowrer (ed.), *Psychotherapy: Theory and research.* New York: Ronald Press, 1953.

12. Frank, J. D. *Persuasion and healing.* Baltimore: Johns Hopkins University Press, 1961.

13. Hutt, M. L., and Gibby, R. G. *Patterns of abnormal behavior.* Boston: Allyn and Bacon, 1957.

14. Jourard, S. M. *Personal adjustment.* New York: The Macmillan Company, 1958.

15. Kaplan, L. *Mental health and human relations in education.* New York: Harper & Brothers, 1959.

16. Keister, Mary E., and Updegraff, Ruth. A study of children's reactions to failure and an experimental attempt to modify them. *Child Develpm.,* 1937, VIII, 241–248.

17. Radzinski, J. M. Constitutional vs. accidental factors in mental disease. *Ill. Med. J.,* 1943, LXXXIV, 1925–1931.

18. Rogers, C. R The characteristics of a helping relationship. *Personnel & Guid. J.,* Sept. 1958, pp. 6–15.

19. Slavson, S. R. *Child psychotherapy.* New York: Columbia University Press, 1952.

20. Symonds, P. M. *Dynamics of psychotherapy,* Vol. 1. New York: Grune & Stratton, 1956.

21. Wattenberg, W. W. Your child's mental health. *NEA Journal,* LIII, 1964, 35–50.

22. White, R. W. Motivation reconsidered: The concept of competence. *Psychol. Rev.,* 1959, LXVI, 297–333.

CHAPTER SIX

The Mental Health and Therapeutic Potential of a School

The time a child spends in school and the relationships he has there are secondary in importance only to the first five years of his life, which he spends almost entirely with his family. Consequently, the increasing emphasis on helping the child with behavior problems in the school setting is natural and significant.

While one may question whether the school's helping the child with problems is philosophically justified, experience indicates that such responsibility is quite inescapable. The child brings his problems to school with him. The aggressive child, the shy child, the child who struggles with limited ability—all have to be coped with; for if their problems are not considered, they can, and will, disrupt the learning process. Unless the school finds acceptable methods and curriculum arrangements to meet the problem of individual differences, one of its major therapeutic impacts is lost. Schools must, first and foremost, maximize their resources to do the job that has traditionally been theirs—to help each child learn in a manner consistent with his nature. Learning, after all, affects the way in which a child regards himself, and this in turn affects his adjustment.

Every school has plus or minus influences that significantly determine its mental-health potential. These influences are primarily in three general areas: (a) the administrative philosophy, organization, and curriculum; (b) the teaching staff; and (c) the sociocultural setting.

ADMINISTRATIVE PHILOSOPHY AND ORGANIZATION

The educational and administrative philosophy of a school determines the way individual differences in children will be handled. If the school ignores the existence of these differences and does not structure a program for them, children will have less opportunity to grow educationally and emotionally. When this situation prevails in a school, classes are likely to be large, the curricula out of harmony with children's needs, and the existing programs inflexible and unimaginative. As a result, children in the same grade will receive the same academic diet. Furthermore, a teacher's strengths and latent resources cannot be utilized unless he is supported and helped in his efforts to individualize instruction.

A similar stalemate frequently arises if the prevailing school philosophy places almost exclusive emphasis on the tool subjects. When the three R's are overemphasized, the social and emotional needs of the child are usually underemphasized. The child with a behavior problem then has a very difficult time. Even the teacher who tries to understand and help such a child will probably find little support from the administration. There is also a characteristic tendency in such schools to treat all children with relatively standard disciplinary techniques. In this climate, the child with problems not only fails to learn what is expected, but his emotional and social growth is impeded.

A significant result of this philosophy is an increase in disciplinary cases in or around the principal's office. Management of the child's behavior is often only that which is temporarily expedient—a behavior stopper—rather than management that is therapeutic. Depending upon his personality, the principal may become overwhelmed or displeased with the disproportionate amount of time he spends on disciplinary cases. Furthermore, if he has

hostility problems, the disciplinary cases may provide a channel for expression of his own unresolved conflicts.

In addition, an educational philosophy that places excessive emphasis on the academics often fails to consider appropriately the influences of feelings in the educative process. Because the human organism is essentially unitary, it reacts to every experience on several levels. Reaction to an experience at only one level (for example, intellectual) is never possible. How a child feels about learning is as important as what he learns. A learning situation that fails to take account of a child's feelings will be rather sterile in helping him acquire appropriate attitudes, values, and appreciations. The fact is that the acquisition of myriad facts alone rarely leads one to rational behavior or makes him a productive, happy citizen.

The philosophy of the school administration also determines how many teachers and administrative and specialized personnel are hired and the size of the class that each teacher must teach. Furthermore, if the developmental and emotional needs of children are not carefully considered, the school will have few programs for children whose needs differ significantly from those of the group. Any specialized services that do provide assistance for the deviant child will have considerable difficulty surviving; even if they do survive, such programs will probably be too inflexible for much therapeutic help to the child with problems.

The Administrator's Personality

The educational philosophy in operation in a particular school is a reflection of the person or persons who embody or propagate it. We might even say that the person who directs the school program largely determines the school's philosophy. Within this framework, great variability is possible. For illustrative purposes, let us consider some of these possibilities.

The administrator who has a rigid personality structure is concerned with his own adequacy and is likely to control the school program autocratically. Such control may be a protective device against threats to his feelings of adequacy—if one's authority is never challenged, his adequacy is not threatened. This type of administrative control stifles initiative and the germination of new ideas and requires excessive conformity from subordinates. When ideas are not allowed to germinate, the latent resources of a school remain latent, and rigid administrators generally have narrow, rigid programs.

Furthermore, an autocratic control places limitations on appropriate two-way communication. The needs of the subordinates and the problems they experience are not sufficiently identified or discussed. Consequently, needed modifications in programs may not be instigated. Also, any conflicts between subordinates and their superiors have a fine opportunity to flourish.

Quite a different kind of organization evolves from an administrator who is at home with himself, feels confidence in his abilities, and is willing to engage his subordinates in the problem-solving and decision-making process. Such an administrator obviously respects the contributions of others. Under this administrator the resources of the school are better utilized and problems are more easily identified and effectively solved than under the autocratic administrator. More important, the people in this organization become closely identified with the school program and are willing to make it work.

To summarize, the prevailing philosophy of the administration filters down to all levels of a school and affects the relationships in its social system. Also, the dominant model of the administration is usually sanctioned at all levels. For example, if the administration is autocratic, there is strong sanction for this same model in the principal-teacher relationship and in the teacher-pupil relationship.

To elaborate the importance of the model, Bush (2), in his study of teacher-pupil relationships, points out the important effect administrator-teacher relationships have on teacher-pupil relationships. He indicates that just as the administrator-teacher relationship varies, so does the teacher-pupil relationship. Furthermore, he suggests that a teacher's morale is significantly determined by the administrator-teacher relationship and that a disturbance in this relationship causes the quality of teaching to deteriorate.

Administrative Philosophy and Teacher Selection

The philosophy of the administration usually determines teacher selection, and teachers are rarely picked when their philosophy is alien to the predominant one in the school or district. For example, the administrator who stresses the three R's will probably select teachers who are subject-matter oriented. On the other hand, if the administrator's philosophy is to develop the many facets of the child, teachers will be selected for their understanding and competence in this educational area.

THERAPEUTIC IMPACT OF THE TEACHER

Of all the people on the school staff, the teacher has the greatest and most direct effect on the child. He is primarily responsible for the child during school hours, and the child interacts more frequently with him than with any other adult at school. Furthermore, the teacher determines how learning is organized, the type of social and emotional relationships that develop in the classroom, and the kind of living that takes place. The whole teacher, like the whole child, comes to school. He brings his loves, dislikes, prejudices, fears, and enthusiasms with him. Some of his feelings and attitudes are in his conscious awareness and others are not, yet they all significantly influence the teaching-learning process.

Teaching, then, involves more than the dissemination of knowledge; it involves the teacher's use of himself in the process of creating new learning experiences for the pupil. In this process, regardless of how much the teacher guards against it, he will be himself, and everything he teaches will be influenced by his past experiences.

Teacher Personality and
Pupil Relationships

Teachers and children may develop either helpful or damaging relationships with each other, depending upon their individual personalities. For instance, one teacher may contribute immeasurably to the emotional growth of a child, while another teacher may be completely at odds with the same child. To elaborate further, some teachers have difficulty with a particular type of child but may be successful with another type. In any case, both the teacher and the child give something to each other or contribute to each other's problems.

It is unrealistic to expect that all teachers will be able emotionally to accept all children. Teachers are not, and cannot be, fathomless sources of love. Such a belief denies that teachers are human beings. Teachers have emotional problems too, and sometimes they use a child in an attempt at partial resolution of their own conflicts. The important fact is that a teacher will affect children differently depending upon his personality structure, his psychological defense mechanisms, and the way he deals with his conflicts.

Some examples will illustrate how these factors operate. Consider a teacher who is dealing unsuccessfully with an excessive amount of hostility. Such a teacher often attempts unconsciously to weave the children into expression of his hostility. Thus, his classroom control is autocratic, and most breaches of behavior are punitively handled. In this situation the children are controlled through fear, and the shy child's security is jeopardized. He may become even more withdrawn and conforming, relying on further suppression or repression to keep his impulses in check. As a result, his anxieties will increase, with a comparable decrease in intellectual functioning.

However, another teacher who has difficulty dealing with hostility may have a different psychological defense system and thus have a quite different relationship with his pupils. If this teacher uses a reaction formation as a defense against hostile impulses, he may place a premium on love and use guilt-producing techniques to deal with any overt expression of anger in the classroom. Thus, a child may feel guilty for weeks after an aggressive episode, sensing the subtle withdrawal of the teacher's approval. As a result, the child's self-esteem will probably be lowered. Yet, such a teacher may be commended by the principal for using such "positive" disciplinary techniques.

Rigid group control on the part of a teacher, regardless of the disguises under which it poses, stifles normal group interaction. Bovard (1) found that children in group-centered climates like the group and each other better than do children in leader-centered climates. From this, one might assume that strict or rigid teacher control limits interaction among pupils, because the children do not have the opportunity to relate to, get to know, or enjoy each other.

Generally speaking, a teacher's personality seeps through and subtly determines his relationships to children. Consider, for example, the overly moral teacher who is often upset by the "bad" or "sexy" language of a child, and the rigidly compulsive teacher who is annoyed by a dirty child or the child who does his work sloppily. Consider, also, an unmarried female teacher who may quite unconsciously play a mother role and develop excessive attachment to a child, making him excessively dependent. Furthermore, a particular child may epitomize the living expression of some old, painful conflict in the teacher, and he may, as a consequence, become a scapegoat. Whatever the dynamic trend, which may be unrealistic and infinitely varied, its impact will be felt in the teacher's relationship to the children in the classroom.

In summary, it is important to recognize that any time a teacher is excessively and inappropriately upset by a pupil's mannerisms or behavior, that teacher may have conflicts around the behavior in question. Similarly, if the teacher's relationship to a child is disproportionate to the situation—intense or over-attentive—some unconscious determinants may be operating on the teacher's part that could be damaging to the child. Under such circumstances, it is usually unrealistic to let the teacher and child try to work out the problem. It is more advisable to separate teacher and child by placing the child in another classroom.

Effective placement of a child is one of the more important therapeutic avenues available to a school. For example, it is common to find that a child may have an inordinate amount of difficulty relating to one teacher, but much less difficulty with another. Although the significance of appropriate pairing of teacher and child is generally recognized by school personnel, such pairing is rarely done in a systematic manner. One reason may be that administrators usually do not have sufficient insight into a teacher's personality. Too often the pairing is done superficially. For example, the child who is considered a "discipline problem" is placed with a teacher who maintains good discipline. If the teacher's motivation produces suppressive classroom control, yet the child needs to express himself, such a placement will probably submerge more deeply the child's real problems. To really know what effect this teacher will have on the child who is a "discipline problem" requires that one know the teacher's motivational forces which produce "good discipline." Superficial pairing of teacher and child, then, is not often therapeutic for the child with problems.

In educational circles, one often hears that it is highly desirable to have well-adjusted teachers. The assumption is, of course, that well-adjusted teachers have few problems that interfere in the teaching situation, and they are free, therefore, to develop helpful relationships with children. Of course, a high correlation probably exists between personal stability in teachers and positive growth in pupils; however, the mythical well-adjusted teacher is more an educational ideal than an existing actuality. Teachers, like people in general, are more or less well-adjusted. Furthermore, one could even say that a teacher need not be well-adjusted in all areas of living to have a healthy, beneficial effect on children; however, in order to have such an effect, he should have stability.

A distinction is drawn here between well-adjusted and stable. A well-adjusted person is probably stable, although a stable person may not be entirely well-adjusted. For instance, a teacher with stability may have areas of conflict and unmet needs, but his defense system protects him from expressing these needs or conflicts in the teaching situation. Furthermore, if the teacher with unmet needs and conflicts has outlets outside the classroom to serve as important need-satisfiers or conflict-resolvers, he probably will develop a favorable growth-producing climate in the classroom.

On the other hand, a teacher might generally be quite healthy emotionally but use children to resolve a relatively isolated, single area of conflict. The crucial point is not the teacher's emotional difficulties but the manner in which he attempts their resolution.

One may wonder, at this point, what type of teacher personality is most likely to have a beneficial effect on children. Although much research has been conducted to assess the personality traits of "good" teachers, it has produced few definitive answers. The following studies are typical of those that have addressed themselves to the question.

LaBue (7) attempted to differentiate between students who exhibited a "persistent" as opposed to a "non-persistent" interest in teaching by using the Minnesota Multiphasic Personality Inventory (MMPI) to analyze personality differences. As subjects he used fifty "persistent" women and forty-nine "non-persistent" women. A number of differences appeared between the two groups. "Persistent" women scored significantly lower on the scales for Schizophrenia, Hypochondria, Psychopathic Deviate, Psychasthenia, and Hypomania. That is, the "persistent" women showed less disturbance on these scales than did the "non-persistent" women. Of forty-seven "persistent" men and twenty-eight "non-persistent" men similarly studied, the two groups differed only on the Psychopathic Deviate scale; the lower scores of the "persistent" men indicated their better adjustment in regard to this personality trait.

Hedlund (5) did a study to determine whether the MMPI could be useful in differentiating between students who would become effective teachers and those who would not. The study was done in eighteen New York State colleges and involved 840 students in one- and two-year training programs for secondary teachers. The scores on the MMPI were compared with teacher effectiveness, and only two scales appeared to differentiate between good and poor teachers. The good teachers received lower scores on the Paranoia and Lie scales.

Perhaps the most extensive study has been reported by Ryans (9). His research included approximately 6,000 teachers in 1,700 schools and involved numerous individual studies as a part of the larger project. A substantial portion of the research was directed toward classroom observation by trained observers to identify patterns of teacher behavior and related pupil behavior.

Because of the numerous individual projects and findings, only relevant and highly selected parts can be presented here. Of particular importance for our purposes are the findings that pertain to differences in characteristics regarding sex of teacher and grade level taught. Some apparent trends are the following:

1. At both elementary and secondary levels, male teachers were more stable than female teachers.

2. Secondary teachers were more traditional in respect to educational viewpoints than were elementary school teachers. Generally, elementary teachers were more permissive.

3. At the elementary school level (on the four dimensions of classroom behavior studied), men tended to be less businesslike and assume less responsibility, to have a greater affinity for democratic classroom practices, to be more child-centered and permissive in educational viewpoint, and to be more stable emotionally than women.

4. At the secondary school level, women teachers obtained significantly higher scores on scales measuring favorable pupil attitudes; democratic classroom practices; friendly, stimulating and responsible classroom behavior; permissive educational views; and verbal understandings than did men teachers on the secondary level.

5. Marital status seemed to affect certain classroom behaviors and attitudes, although other factors, such as grade and subject taught, also affected these behaviors and attitudes. Married elementary school teachers scored better on child-centered viewpoints and businesslike classroom behavior. However, at the secondary level, unmarried teachers attained better scores on the same variables.

6. Those teachers who reported activities in childhood and adolescence such as "playing school" and "reading to children" obtained higher scores on scales that reflected favorable pupil attitudes; friendly, stimulating, and responsible classroom behavior; and democratic classroom procedures than did teachers who did not report such activities during their youth.

It is apparent from these studies and from the opinion of those who have made exhaustive reviews of existing research on teacher personality and effectiveness (4) that little that is definitive has yet appeared. Consequently, I have attempted to set down, in the material that follows, some personality characteristics and dynamic trends that appear to be prerequisites for teachers if they are to facilitate wholesome psychological development in pupils. These characteristics are based on my observation of hundreds of teachers over a decade.

Perhaps the first prerequisite that a teacher should possess is *a reasonable degree of basic need satisfactions in addition to or beyond those derived from teaching.* That is, if a person derives satisfactions of basic needs that are sufficiently sustaining from sources external to the teaching situation, a child is not likely to become a prominent need-satisfying tool. Thus, the teacher is free to be more objective and sensitive to the needs of children.

A second basic quality that a teacher should possess is *the ability to establish and maintain wholesome human relationships.* This ability indicates that a person has the capacity to relate to people and is able to give and to receive. This capacity is important not only in relating to children but also in relating in positive ways to others with whom the teacher works. The capacity for meaningful relationships significantly influences a teacher's success. For example, the ability to make and maintain wholesome human relationships helps the teacher to maintain personal stability through continuous basic need satisfaction. Therefore, his emotional tone and his manner of approaching the teaching situation are not as likely to be colored by his projected or displaced needs.

Conversely, if a teacher is not capable of forming warm, sustaining interpersonal relationships, he probably will not be sensitive to the needs and feelings of children. Moreover, the children are unlikely to identify with him. Only when a child feels important to and accepted by the teacher will he desire to subscribe to the teacher's goals. And, obviously, it is through the process of identification that a child develops standards, values, and attitudes important to his personality development. Furthermore, a certain amount of identification with his teacher seems necessary if a child is to grow educationally and emotionally.

In summary, the importance of the teacher's ability to relate warmly to children is suggested in a study by Christensen (3). Using fourth and fifth grade school children, he studied the relationship between pupil achievement and teacher warmth and permissiveness. He found that arithmetic and vocabulary achievement, as measured by the Iowa Test of Basic Skills, was significantly greater for pupils having teachers who were high in (affective) warmth.

A third basic requirement that a teacher should have for the favorable influence of pupil growth is *a psychological defense system which operates* *sufficiently well to control excessive amounts of guilt, anxiety, hostility, and unusual impulsivity.* Thus, the teacher can maintain predictable relationships to children. If his psychological defense system functions efficiently, the teacher is able to look for meaning in a child's behavior without being personally involved in it. Therefore, he is not prone to act impulsively or discipline severely in helping the deviant child.

On the other hand, the teacher who is overtly anxious or impulsive has difficulty appropriately organizing learning and establishing acceptable routines. His behavior prevents children from developing safe, secure relationships with him because few things are more upsetting to children than inconsistency and fluctuation. Also, his expectations are likely to be highly variable, producing an anxious emotional climate for the children. Those children who already have insecure relationships with their parents will have difficulty in the identification process and will not readily subscribe to the teacher's goals.

Moreover, unless a teacher has a defense system that functions reasonably well, he will be unable to use his own intellectual resources efficiently. He will exert a great deal of energy dealing with, or being preoccupied with, his own conflicts, and his frustration tolerance will not meet the excessive demands of the deviant child.

The fourth quality that a stable, effective teacher should possess is *sufficient knowledge and competence.* Part of this knowledge should relate to his subject matter and part to an understanding of the individuals he teaches. This understanding should go beyond the usual child growth and development and should include the emerging personality and the dynamics of its deviation.

Even more important, a teacher should understand and enjoy the changing, living, growing world around him. He must not only know about it, but have the capacity to appreciate and share it. The effective teacher is able to embark on each new learning experience with a spirit of adventure; he can make learning live. He is able to enter into the world of the child, sharing his confusion and nourishing his enjoyment of things and people.

The previous discussion is a sketch intended not to be all inclusive, but to illustrate, in dynamic personality trends, a basis for assessing a teacher's influence on the growth of children.

INFLUENCE OF SOCIO-CULTURAL FACTORS

Depending upon the predominant cultural and social class influences in operation in a school setting, the child's attitudes, values, aspirations, and patterns of sanctioned behavior will differ. As these influences vary, so will the task of educating children. While it can be stated generally that the ultimate educational objectives for children are the same, the manner of approach and the successes involved will vary as a result of the socio-cultural factors of a particular setting. Cultural and social class differences also pose problems for the child and school and restrict the range of possible solutions.

Of particular concern are the manner in which these influences affect the behavior and personality adjustment of the child and the limitations imposed upon the school in helping the child. Before discussing these relationships, we will summarize some of the more significant effects of social-class membership upon behavior.

Social-Class Membership

Shaffer and Shoben (10) have summarized especially well the attitudinal and behavioral differences resulting from different social-class membership.* According to their study, members of the lower class generally place a high premium on immediate gratification and appear to have little capacity to plan for the attainment of long-range goals. They seem to "seize upon the pleasures of the moment" and, in contrast to the other classes, exercise less control or restriction upon emotional expression. Consequently, lower-class children are much less inhibited in the expression of sexual impulses and anger. Fights within the family, between children and parents or mother and father, are not unusual. As a matter of fact, these parents urge their children to learn how to defend themselves. This ability is a means of acquiring status and is a highly valued skill. Furthermore, in this group, the tendency to band together into gangs as a protection from threats is a rather frequent phenomenon. Also, because parents tend toward physical discipline (whipping and slapping), the lower-class child experiences more overt aggression directed toward him. Thus, the aggressive model of the parents is a prominent one.

* It should be noted that studies are not completely consistent regarding social-class differences in behavior and child-rearing practices. The author has selected Shaffer and Shoben's work as a major reference because it is consistent with his own experience. The reader who wishes to pursue this further should read the article reported by Maccoby and Gibbs listed at the end of this chapter.

The middle-class child views the world quite differently since his major formative influences are directed toward his future—in the home, the school, the church, and certain kinds of informal relationships. For example, the child is asked to postpone immediate gratifications, to delay rewards, and to value more highly long-range goals. He is asked to develop foresight, self-control, and independence, in the hope that he will achieve well and improve his future position. Since a premium is placed on restraint and control, the middle-class child is strongly urged to control physical aggression and to restrict carefully improper expression of sexual impulses. The learning of proper protocol and social manners is strongly ingrained in middle-class culture.

The upper-class child has already "arrived," so it is logical to expect that the formative influences in his life will be somewhat different from those of the other two classes. The pressures upon him are those of good taste, good manners, and preservation of his family's reputation. Since he is taught to regard himself as superior, some of the pressure for upward mobility is absent. He dares not be too individualistic, however, and must reflect credit upon the family name.

The impact of formative influences on children in the lower and middle classes is marked and fairly well-crystallized. The urging and molding in the life of the middle-class child frequently focus around a strong desire to achieve, to be something. Thus, he is urged to do well in school and to look toward a college education. If he does not perform adequately, he may have an excessive amount of anxiety about achievement. In seeking to achieve goals, the middle-class child is likely to have heavy burdens placed

upon his control or defense system. Thus, he may rely upon compulsion, repression, and rationalization as defensive operations (10).

Because of the unusual amount of deprivation in the life of the lower-class child, his needs are immediate. Sustained dedication to long-range goals has little meaning in his system of values. The emphasis on conformity, so prevalent in the middle class (and the teacher's code), is a marked contrast to the leniency he has experienced in earlier childhood in respect to organically based drives.

The importance of these differences in socialization to the education of children is not always sufficiently considered in the school setting. The manner in which they determine children's problems and the means available in the school for assisting the child are even more frequently overlooked. The school psychologist has the unique opportunity to observe some of these influences in operation.

The cultural conditioning that takes place in the three social classes has significant implications for the child and the school. As one might suspect, the lower-class child, in contrast to the middle-class child, does not readily subscribe to the middle-class goals of the school. He is often in school only because the law requires him to be there. His background has frequently not prepared him to launch upon the learning enterprise with enthusiasm. Although he may see the need to conform to the teacher's standards, he has a tendency to react against them. When he rebels, he is likely to be openly aggressive, as his social class membership has taught him to be, and his aggressive manner may shock the teacher. Therefore, he may act out rather than disguise his conflicts neurotically, because, as a general rule, the lower-class child does not have great anxiety or guilt about his aggression or poor performance in school.

Since academic performance is not so highly valued in the lower class as it is in the culture of the middle class, the lower-class child tends to perform less well than does the middle-class child. Also, his school attendance is not so continuous; it is often disrupted by his responsibilities at home or because his family is transient. Consequently, the lower-class child is often deficient or retarded academically, and his retardation usually increases with each succeeding year or grade level.

The impact of these problems on the lower-class child can be substantially reduced if the school has a curriculum structured to his needs and appropriate remedial programs to give him assistance at crucial times. However, if such programs do not exist, he is likely to feel even greater alienation. His problems will elaborate, and he will begin to express his confusion and conflict openly. He may, depending upon what the school allows, disguise his frustration by spasmodic school attendance, truancy, tardiness, or general indifference.

The middle-class child generally is anxious to begin school and to do well. He is frequently sent to nursery school or kindergarten, so there is a tendency for him to be "ready" for school. His parents usually have introduced him to books almost from the time he was able to sit up and listen. He has often had "field trips" in his early years that were educational. Since he has had repeated exposure to such experiences, the importance of education and learning have been strongly reinforced. When he enters school, he may learn that his parents' love is sometimes con-

ditional, depending upon what he does there.

The middle-class child is not likely to feel a tremendous clash between his values and those of the school. The school embraces the same middle-class values and is likely to make him more of what he already is. He is urged not only to learn to read, but to read with proficiency. If he does not, there is a two-way alarm—both at school and at home. He becomes immersed in the values of conformity and the compulsion to use all of his innate ability. If he fails, this failure is more difficult to handle because most of his contemporaries will be moving on.

In the process of becoming what his social-class environment has predisposed him to become, the middle-class child may exhibit problems arising from the pressures of achievement and conformity. In the school setting, he seems to feel that he has never been able to achieve the goals expected of him, that his culture feels are important. He often has a low self-concept. The various demands of his social class sometimes make it necessary for him to give up part of his autonomy—part of himself—to feel safe.

Many of the middle-class child's problems are disguised behind neurotic processes. His anger is rarely overt. He may quite unconsciously resist or fail in school, as a retaliatory maneuver. In this way he can successfully punish his parents, since their anxiety is likely to rise considerably when he does not perform.

Studies have begun to appear on the differing incidence of specific types of emotional difficulties or psychiatric problems in adults in lower- and middle-class environments. Similar studies on children are rare, if not nonexistent. The study by Hollingshead and Redlich (6) on the incidence and type of psychiatric conditions in adults is suggestive. They found that psychiatric disorders that reached the attention of psychiatrists were not randomly distributed in the general population of a New Haven community. The kinds of psychiatric disorders for which people received attention appeared strongly related to social-class position. Furthermore, there was a definite relationship between particular types of social environments and the expression of specific types of psychiatric disorders. Neuroses tended to be concentrated at the upper levels and psychoses at the lower levels of the social-class structure.

While these data may not be entirely conclusive, it seems probable that social-class environment has a significant influence on the types of disorders adults develop. If it can be assumed that such disorders have their roots in childhood, different manifestations of behavior disturbances in children, determined partially on a social-class basis, are very plausible.

Limitations of the Socio-Cultural Environment

Just as a child seems predisposed to different values, attitudes, and behavioral characteristics as a result of his social-class environment, so, for similar reasons, is he predisposed to certain limitations in getting help with his problems. Besides the limitations imposed by the severity of the problem itself, the lower-class child appears to have other influences working against him. In the lower class, families seem to be less intact and more often upset by unpredictable economic circumstances than do middle-class families. One observes in many such settings family instability resulting from broken homes, separation, and divorce. Morever, because of economic circumstances, there is often no money available for adequate outside help when the school cannot provide the necessary psychological assistance.

Providing successful help for children whose problems are deep or severe is predicated upon the active engagement of the parents, as well as the child, in the treatment process. Lower-class parents are often not very receptive to such an approach. As a matter of fact, the lower-class parent is often content to label the child's problems as just "plain old orneriness" or as a product of "his imagination." Such labels serve as barriers in the psychologists' attempts to help the parents gain more useful insight into the true condition. Psychological intervention is often viewed by the lower-class parent with skepticism and, at times, with marked irritation.

When one recognizes the many limitations involved in helping the lower-class child, one begins to assume that it is more feasible to make the school program the primary therapeutic agent—that is, to exercise great care in structuring school programs that are consistent with the socio-cultural, emotional, and academic needs of the child. It is quite possible that, if the school does not develop such programs, the primary source of appropriate help is lost. In the lower-class environment, the store of psychological and psychiatric techniques is quite inadequate. Therefore, it is essential to maximize every school resource if the deviant lower-class child is to be helped.

The middle-class child is much more fortunate in getting the type of help he needs when he experiences behavior problems in the school setting. In the first place, the middle-class school is likely to have services and teachers more oriented toward assisting this child with his problems. Similarly, the middle-class parent is better informed about the importance of healthy personality development in children. The parent has often identified with the role of "the good parent." Moreover, if the child needs intensive therapy, financial resources and parent motivation usually make it possible for him to receive such aid. Within the middle-class group, however, large variations exist.

Perhaps the major difficulty arising from the cultural circumstances of the middle class is the often subtle involvement of the parents in the child's problems. As a general rule, the middle-class parent avoids the extremes in child rearing so characteristic of the lower class; these extreme measures are usually alien to middle-class values. Thus, the child's problems are more complexly woven into his relationships with his parents. Both parent and child tend to disguise their conflicts and feelings by an infinite variety of masks or defenses. For this reason, the middle-class child's problems are not always obvious to the psychologically unsophisticated person. When the child suddenly exhibits a school phobia, the teacher may be surprised, if not alarmed.

It is in the process of uncovering the subtle involvement of parent-child conflict that the stumbling blocks are experienced. In dealing with such problems, the usual prescriptions such as "give the child more love" or "do more things with him" are not very effective. More intensive study and professional examination are frequently required.

It is apparent from what has been said that helping the child with behavior or emotional problems in the school setting is not simple. He is subjected to a host of influences which, like thieves in the night, operate silently and without detection. However, if the therapeutic and growth potential of a school is to be maximized, the major areas of influence must be identified and placed in the service of the child. Only then can the child who is shackled with problems be helped to achieve what are his potential and his right.

References

1. Bovard, E. V. The experimental production of interpersonal affect. *J. abnorm. soc. Psychol.*, 1951, XLVI, 521–528.

2. Bush, R. N. *The teacher-pupil relationship.* Englewood Cliffs, N.J.: Prentice-Hall, 1954.

3. Christensen, C. M. Relationship between pupil achievement, pupil affect-need, teacher warmth and teacher permissiveness. *J. educ. Psychol.*, 1960, LI, 169–174.

4. Getzels, J. W., and Jackson, P. W. The teacher's personality characteristics. In N. L. Gage (ed.), *Handbook of Research on Teaching.* Chicago: Rand McNally, 1963, pp. 506–582.

5. Hedlund, P. A. *Cooperative study to predict effectiveness in secondary school teaching: Third progress report.* Albany: University of State of New York and State Education Department, 1953.

6. Hollingshead, A. B., and Redlich, F. C. Social stratification and psychiatric disorders. In A. Rose (ed.), *Mental health and mental disorders.* New York: W. W. Norton, 1955, pp. 123–135.

7. LaBue, A. C. Personality traits and persistence of interest in teaching as a vocational choice. *J. appl. Psychol.,* 1955, XXXIX, 362–365.

8. Maccoby, Eleanor E., and Gibbs, Patricia K. Methods of child rearing in two social classes. In Celia B. Stendler (ed.), *Readings in child behavior and development.* New York: Harcourt, Brace & World, 1964, pp. 272–287.

9. Ryans, D. G. *Characteristics of teachers.* Washington, D.C.: American Council on Education, 1960.

10. Shaffer, L. F., and Shoben, E. J. *The psychology of adjustment.* Boston: The Riverside Press, 1956.

CHAPTER SEVEN

Management of the Individual and the Group: Prevention and Antisepsis

This chapter will deal with common classroom problems that teachers consistently report. Our purpose is to present methods to help teachers in structuring relationships and developing an environment that is conducive to pupil growth, as well as methods for preventing problems. We will also suggest some approaches for managing common group problem situations. For the most part, the problems that will be identified and discussed are those arising from ineffective techniques in working with a group. They are problems that give beginning teachers an excessive amount of difficulty; however, experienced teachers report them frequently enough to suggest that most teachers can receive some benefit from reading the material.

In a sense, this chapter is a departure from others in the book. To some it may appear too elementary. However, because teachers do consistently report difficulty in these areas, the material seems pertinent for our discussion. Obviously, teachers cannot work very successfully with maladaptive patterns until they have come to grips with the control and management problems posed by a class of twenty-five or more children.

GENERAL PRINCIPLES AND TECHNIQUES

A favorable atmosphere for learning develops from a classroom program that is responsive to the children's maturation levels, interests, emotional compositions, and control systems. Since children respond on the basis of their own endowments and experiences, adequate planning to meet such requirements is essential for every successful teacher.

Adequate Advanced Planning

The teacher can avoid many problems if he plans sufficiently before he meets his group at the beginning of each year. If the teacher wishes to "get off to a good start," organization of instruction and analysis of the group should begin as soon as it is decided which children he will have. Unless the group is vastly different from others, there will probably be two or three children with special problems in each classroom.

The teacher's analysis of his group should start with any information that has already been accumulated on each child. This information should include the child's general intelligence level, the level at which he can successfully achieve, and something about his interests. With such understanding, the teacher is better able to set appropriate goals and select appropriate instructional material for his group. In addition, the teacher needs all the understanding he can muster to decide on approaches to the special problems and to obtain a favorable response from all of the children.

The first week tends to set the tone of the class. What the teacher does, how he relates to the group, and how he organizes instruction, is likely to be prognostic of the future. For instance, in the process of molding the group into a working unit, the teacher, recognizing that much "living" takes place in the classroom, must decide with the group what the ground rules are, how routines are to be handled, and what the operational mechanics of the classroom will be. These decisions are necessary because nothing upsets a child more than not knowing what is expected of him and what he can expect of his teacher.

The initial stages of working out the problems and details are not easy, and teachers often become frustrated, fearing that the children will never learn the routines. When their frustration becomes too great, some teachers resort to power and authoritarian techniques to induce conformity. However, most effective teachers find that, when a sufficient amount of time early in the year is spent in working out these problems, the rest of the year can be used more beneficially. Let us be more specific.

Working Out Routines

Teachers know from experience that much confusion can arise in the classroom when children are changing from one activity to another unless some procedures have been established. The wise teacher begins early to *help children work out* ways or routines for moving from job to job, group to group, or activity to activity. Many children, especially in the primary grades, have difficulty performing routine duties, such as sharpening pencils, moving about the room, using free time, or going to and from special activities outside the classroom, without unnecessary noise and confusion. Furthermore, performance of household duties in the classroom, which can be beneficial to children, can create disturbances unless this activity is appropriately structured. Routines and duties should be carefully discussed and decided at the beginning of the school year, and each child should have an active part in making the decisions. Children enjoy this sharing process, and the standards that are set become their own; they will want to maintain them.

The teacher should not be too surprised, however, to find that, even when standards and procedures have been agreed upon, the children may find it hard to abide by them. As difficulties occur, it is important for the teacher to discuss frankly and honestly with the children what is happening—what has gone wrong. As a matter of fact, in the initial stages the teacher should probably evaluate periodically with the children how things are going. Particularly with first and second grade children, it is helpful to write standards and routines on the blackboard for ready reference and reinforcement. Furthermore, as children progress in their performance, they should be appropriately rewarded.

Even when children have been able to adjust to general routines, they may become overexcited in the anticipation of a special event or activity. This excitement can lead to disorganization and confusion, and when the event finally occurs, the children frequently forget themselves and have lapses in control. Recognizing that there is some predictability in children's reactions to such events, the teacher should be ready for these reactions through some "anticipatory planning." For example, he should prepare the children by a discussion of the event and the behavior that is expected of them. Usually, when children have a chance to consider their own roles and actions, they are able to enjoy more thoroughly the special event (3).

Routines can also be established, depending on the age and maturity of the children, when the teacher helps the children learn to assume leadership. Children who carry out routine duties, such as checking attendance, leading the flag salute, conducting group discussions to arrange a program or solve a classroom problem, can de-velop self-confidence and become motivated to assume responsibility for their own behavior. These arrangements lessen the teacher's need to exercise constantly the authoritative role, and, in addition, the more the teacher is able to help children assume responsibility for their own behavior, the less responsibility *he* must assume.

Establishing Limits

In order to teach effectively, most teachers recognize that definite limits must be placed on the actions of children. As a matter of fact, of all the problems beginning teachers experience, setting appropriate limits probably heads the list. This problem is difficult because one can rarely use the same limits and disciplinary procedures on the same group of children, or individual children within a group, at all times. Limits and disciplinary measures must always be predicated on the maturational level and needs of a child, the nature of the learning activities to which he is exposed, the interpersonal relationships in the home, and the personality of the teacher (2).

This is a knotty problem involving an appropriate balance among freedom, security, and control (2). If one allows too much freedom, it is difficult to organize teaching in meaningful ways, yet too much control can lead to passive dependence and impede the development of initiative and creativity. In part, the answer seems to lie in involving the children. They should be helped to establish limits for themselves through discussion of the necessity and importance of limits.

Most children recognize the need for limits and will participate in their formulation. One way the teacher can encourage participation is to make the classroom situation analogous to the home situation. Each child, as he feels free to express himself, can be asked what his family's rules are, why they are important, how breaches are dealt with, and who does the enforcing. Inevitably the children will express some feelings of irritation when family members interrupt them during an interesting activity. Moreover, they will reveal which rules they believe are necessary, who should enforce them, and their own sensitivities to certain kinds of correction. This information helps the teacher formulate meaningful limits and gives him some insight into the behavior of each child.

Another approach may also be useful. The teacher may indicate to the children that rules or limits are necessary because everyone likes to feel safe. An analogy can be made to adults who feel safe when there are laws and policemen to protect them from dangerous acts on the part of others. Children can readily see the connection between this analogy and their own desire to be safe from harm by others. Furthermore, the teacher can point out that people feel safe when they know what is to be expected and how certain limits will be imposed.

Once the limits have been established, it may be of value (depending on the ages of the children) for the teacher to write them in a specific place for ready reference. It is important that the established rules be maintained consistently. The teacher should teach limits to children with just as much care and skill as he teaches subject matter to them. He must provide for periodic evaluation and modification of the limits as he and the class feel they are desirable. Also, as the class

members make progress in self-control and self-government, it is essential that the teacher commend them.

Changing the Pace

Learning can become a solemn task and produce the monotony that comes from sameness. Boredom and monotony arise in a typical classroom when the activities are too far removed from the interests, motives, and lives of the learners. At other times, boredom may occur when the teacher inadvertently spends too much time in drill, in an attempt to reinforce important learning. The teacher should be alert to these symptoms, when they appear, and change the activity or provide the group with a new focus.

It is important for the teacher to be sensitive to the tone or mood of the class, and his appropriate management of the classroom is greatly dependent upon this perceptiveness. Children who remain unstimulated or overly frustrated for long periods soon express restlessness, and this reaction can become contagious. However, if the teacher is alert to the beginning changes in tone and mood, she can usually prevent the blossoming contagion, but if the changes progress too far, less therapeutic and more high powered tactics may have to be used.

The old cliché "variety is the spice of life" contains a great deal of truth, for newness and change do enhance motivation.

A boring review for an examination can be converted to a popular quiz program. With a little planning, a history review can be structured into a class play, such as the popular television program "You Are There." A teaching unit can be greatly enriched when the teacher assigns to pupils special projects that contribute to the unit but are related to individual hobbies.

A change of pace should not be restricted to a change in the learning activities themselves. A change of pace also means taking the time to have fun —to enjoy things that happen quite spontaneously. If something happens that is funny, the teacher should enjoy it with the children. A hearty laugh with the children indicates that one is human, and children like teachers who relax and show their human qualities.

This principle of changing the focus or nature of the activity of a group is just as useful with individual children. There are always children who are excessively restless, have difficulty in paying attention, and are easily frustrated. The longer these symptoms persist, the more opportunity there is for difficulties to develop. Therefore, the teacher must deal with a child's symptoms in their early stages.

Sometimes the lagging, unresponsive child can be brought back to more concerted effort by adequate interest from the teacher, because friendly interest and personal attention often provide the spark that is needed. At other times the child's behavior may reflect a learning hurdle that a little instruction will help to remedy, or the child may not have understood some directions and is baffled about procedure. In these situations, some remedial help at the right time may quickly correct the problem. Whatever the causes, the important point is that teachers can prevent many problems by being sensitive to children and their troubles immediately; if they are, much grief can be prevented and children can be saved from becoming "discipline problems."

Providing Structure for Expression of Feelings

In spite of a teacher's best efforts to provide an intellectually stimulating and emotionally secure classroom atmosphere, unpredictable things do happen. Neither teachers nor children are always "sweetness and light," and living together in a classroom creates problems in interpersonal relationships. Children, and teachers as well, feel anger, jealousy, depression, and a host of other things that cause unpleasant experiences and leave residues that affect the future.

Such conflicts and unpleasantness affect or sometimes explode in the classroom. Somehow, somewhere, and at some level, they must be dealt with, and certain ways are better than others. Depending on the approaches, feelings can be handled in a way that aids emotional growth, or they can be temporarily suppressed, only to return at another time. Nevertheless, the teacher must deal with a child's problems and must allow the child to express them.

The success of any approach is significantly related to a teacher's personality and ability to tolerate unpleasant feelings in himself. Moreover, the feelings children will be free to discuss are largely determined by the teacher's relationship to the individual and the group. The overly critical teacher will have difficulty entering into the feeling world of a child. Children have to like, trust, and have confidence in the teacher to reveal their feelings to him.

The sensitive teacher has many opportunities to help children express their feelings. Many times things go wrong—the children quarrel among themselves or do not perform classroom assignments, and the teacher can capitalize on the situation by discussing the factors that created the problem and each pupil's feelings about it. He can work with the children toward some solution. The real value is, of course, the freedom the children have in revealing their feelings in problem situations, but they must be assured that their feelings will be accepted and considered confidential.

Certain types of subject matter provide opportunities for children to express their feelings. For example, fictional stories provide numerous situations, people, and events that can be related easily to the lives and feelings of children. The teacher may suggest to the children that they identify the feelings of each character about his experiences, or he may suggest that they "put themselves in the shoes" of the people in the story. In this way, he may gain insight into, and expression of, the children's feelings.

At times the teacher may wish to provide a more definite structure for the expression of feelings, and, depending upon the age and maturity of the children, various techniques can be used. The child who has not yet learned to write can be asked to draw his feelings and later provide a verbal commentary. With older children, theme writing provides an appropriate channel. The theme topics can be related to problem areas of the child or the class. At other times, as problem situations arise that need some discussion or if the children need to vent feelings, the teacher can select films related to the problem area. After the film is shown, the children's feelings about it can be elicited by a free discussion.

Sometimes the nature of the classroom group or the individual problem of a child in the group makes it inappropriate for the teacher to use an overt channel to bring out a child's feeling. In such situations, the teacher should use techniques that allow a child to express conflicted feelings without revealing his identity. For example, the teacher can provide each child with a "secret book" into which entries may be made at any time. No one is permitted access to this book without the child's consent; however, the teacher should indicate that he will discuss the contents privately with any child when he wishes. In this way, confidence is maintained and the individuality of the child is respected.

Other techniques can be used to maintain the anonymity of a child but still provide a useful channel of communication between the teacher and child in the classroom. One such technique is what might be described as a "problem box," "pet peeve box," or "suggestion box." The children are encouraged to write out their problems or conflicted feelings about their work, relationships to classmates, or the teacher's actions that concern or upset them. They are given the choice of signing or not signing their names to the "suggestions" before dropping them in the box. The box is placed in an inconspicuous place in the room, and at regular intervals the teacher opens the box and discusses the problems either with the individual or the group. This technique keeps the teacher "tuned in" to the children's feelings, conflicts, and concerns and helps him to determine what action will prevent problems from growing. Furthermore, the novelty of this technique incites some enthusiasm among the children.

The above techniques are only a few that teachers can use to help children communicate their feelings and that can enrich the mutual understanding between teacher and child. Teachers, with a little imagination and desire, can think of many other techniques. For a more thorough and excellent discussion of feeling-oriented explorations with children, Moustakas' (1) treatment of the subject is recommended.

GROUP PROBLEM SITUATIONS

Research, surveys, and work with teachers over a period of years have revealed to me that teachers experience certain common problems in the teaching, management, and control of classroom groups. These problems are frequently mislabeled "discipline problems," although, in reality, the causes usually are inappropriate methods of teaching, management, and control. The disorganization and confusion that frequently characterize a group are not so much the result of individual disturbances or pathology but of insufficient organization to meet individual and group requirements. Often the teacher is at a loss to know what is going on; thus, he cannot know how to approach a solution.

In the discussion that follows, the assumption is made that most, if not all, children have normal control systems and want to behave when certain normal individual and group needs are met. If the classroom group includes many disturbed children, the approaches to be discussed may not be effective. Certainly, the approaches are not intended as panaceas, but as some steps that a teacher may take when particular problem situations arise. In any situation, however, the teacher must be alert to the origin of the problem in the process of group interaction and take the age and maturational levels of the children into account.

Reaching All Children in Large Classes

This problem is a great dilemma for teachers. The problem arises essentially because the teacher wants and needs to stimulate all children academically, make appropriate arrangements for individual differences, and, still, maintain efficient (or sufficient) classroom control. If the classroom composition is highly diverse, with considerable range in mental ability, the problem becomes even more complicated.

When the teacher is faced with this problem, he may find it useful to:

1. Try to reduce the impact of individual differences by using some form of subject-matter grouping of the children.

2. Stimulate individual and group motivation by actively engaging the children in planning their learning goals, activities, and events.

3. Develop several "interest centers." These might consist of a science center (with materials provided both by teacher and children), a music center (rhythm band instruments, record and record player, and books on composers), a creative dramatics center (cardboard carton for a stage and puppets for characters), a class library (with books appropriate to interest and achievement levels), and an enrichment package center (assortments of puzzles, poetry, stories, and pictures).

4. Create a desire in the pupils to help each other; work out arrangements for the more able pupils to help the less able.

5. Recognize that both the poor learner and the able learner need specific modifications in instruction to meet their particular needs. The poor learner needs shorter periods of concentrated effort, simpler and shorter units, and more frequent activity changes, than does the able learner. A number of enrichment activities should be ready for the able learner.

6. Select for each special group or committee at least one or more capable children.

Organizing Committee Work

Committee work can add zest to learning if it is efficiently organized. However, without proper planning it can deteriorate into confusion and pose management problems for the teacher. Sometimes a few aggressive children will attempt to dominate. The shy child, on the other hand, will stand back and not participate readily. The teacher must be sensitive to the individual personalities of the children and structure the groups so that each child is able to profit from the experience.

The keynote to successful committee work is adequate planning. For instance, the teacher may find it helpful to:

1. Formulate the whole unit with the class before any work proceeds; carefully discuss (with active participation of the children) the major goals, as well as intermediate goals, of each committee or group.

2. Anticipate and plan the intermediate steps each group will take and make certain that the participants in each group have the necessary skills involved. Help the children formulate what they need to know and where to find proper source materials and teach (if necessary) the research skills required.

3. Discuss with each committee the roles each member will play and make a realistic division of labor appropriate to the potential of each child. Structure the activities so that each child can make a contribution.

4. Make certain that the material with which the groups work is of high interest and well within each child's capacity to master.

5. Have frequent "buzz sessions" with each group to ensure that the groups are making progress toward intermediate goals and do not become frustrated from lack of direction.

6. Point to a culminating activity; at the end of the project, carefully evaluate the strong and weak points and commend individual contributions.

Changing Activities without Disorder

Inherent in any change from one activity to another is the possibility of disorder. The younger the child, the more likely activity change will create some confusion. Each group of children varies in its readiness for transitions. The teacher must be alert to these variations and use methods that are appropriate to the particular group. When a teacher encounters this problem, the following suggestions should be considered:

1. Upon completion of one activity and before starting another, give specific instructions to the children indicating exactly what they are to do (how to open books, the appropriate place, and so forth). If the group is too disorderly or overstimulated, have them

rest for a brief period and specify ways to relax.

2. Depending upon the nature of the activity in progress, excuse, if possible, a few children at a time instead of releasing the whole group at once.

3. Allow for participation at the board or introduce subject games, so that children can leave their desks and release tension and energy.

4. If transition creates considerable disorder and other techniques fail, take time from regularly scheduled activities to discuss what went wrong. Relate the problem to previously agreed upon standards and formulate new ones if desirable. Practice the activity changes that cause trouble with a view toward improvement.

5. Be alert to group saturation and frustration points, and initiate breaks or rest periods before these points. Sometimes mid-morning or mid-afternoon breaks are also helpful preventives.

6. Prepare the children for any marked changes in activities by a thorough discussion of the new activity, the group requirements, and possible difficulties that can be avoided.

7. Avoid placing blame or responsibility on individuals for the problems involved. Instead, center any discussion of incidents on problem and solution.

Setting Limits for Students

This can be an individual problem or one related to the whole group. One will occasionally hear a teacher describe his classroom as a group of "chatterboxes." When the class is so labeled, the difficulty becomes a group problem.

In attempting to handle the problem, a teacher should be alert to the fact that excessive talking or restless

hyperactivity can be a symptom of personality or behavior problems. If children with these symptoms are particularly resistant to normal correction, the teacher should solicit special psychological assistance in resolving the problem.

However, in typical classroom groups, composed of "normally healthy" children, this problem usually has four basic causes: (a) lack of adequate teacher preparation, (b) inappropriate or unworkable limits set on behavior at the beginning of the year, (c) inability to respond successfully to the learning situation due to limited intellectual capacity, and (d) individual emotional disturbances. Some diagnostic analyses of the causes usually lead to more effective solutions. When a teacher is faced with these problems, he may approach them diagnostically and attempt to determine individual and group causes; or he may discuss the problem with the individuals involved in order to get their ideas and feelings about it—making sure to keep the discussions "problem centered." If the problem is primarily that of an individual, the teacher may do well to discuss it with him in a private conference, honestly and with acceptance. The following techniques will prove useful:

1. Use established signals, instead of reproach, scolding, and ridicule, to control the child in the early stages.

2. Redirect the child's activity and interest, frequently giving specific suggestions about possible activities.

3. Give some periodic activity assignments to dissipate tension and prevent frustration.

4. Seat the child next to other children who have good work habits and controls and who do not easily suc-

cumb to disruptive behavior. These children may serve as models for the child with the problem.

5. Re-evaluate to make sure that the work assigned is within the child's capacity to grasp.

6. Be quick to show approval at signs of improvement.

7. Provide as many opportunities as possible for the child to be in the limelight.

8. When giving individual attention, use a low, quiet voice.

If the problem is primarily a group one, provide appropriate opportunities for class discussion. In addition, try to set limits early in the year and consistently maintain them. Structure the learning situation so that there are no unnecessary distractions by placing the excessive talkers near the teacher so that control can be exercised immediately as occasions demand; this prevents contagion. Give specific directions for each activity so that excessive questions from the children are unnecessary. Insist that each child must receive permission (and call him by name) before he is allowed to speak, and do not allow others to interrupt. Give directions for classroom activities in a low, quiet voice so that children must be attentive.

Keeping Small Groups Working

This can become a problem as a result of inadequate planning with the children at the beginning of the school year. On the other hand, a problem may arise if the group does not adequately understand the work or tasks involved or if they finish the assigned work prematurely and have "time on their hands" with nothing structured to do.

In attempting to deal effectively with this problem, the teacher may:

1. Give step by step directions to avoid inadequate comprehension of assignments. Put an example on the board and ask individual children (particularly those who have difficulty) to repeat the directions.

2. Begin slowly at the first of the year, using short periods and concrete goals. Evaluate periodically, emphasizing improvements rather than failures.

3. Have material for small groups (and individuals) ready and procedures for them agreed upon in advance. For children who finish their work prematurely, have several choices of additional activities available.

4. Change to another activity if small groups become noisy or uncontrolled. At a later time, discuss the problem with, and reorganize, the group in relation to the knowledge gained.

Loss of Group Control

There are times in any classroom when everything seems to go wrong. The children, for one reason or another, cannot focus their attention or settle down to the learning task, and disorganization pervades the room. When faced with this situation, some teachers attempt to restore order by shouting commands or threats to individual children. Such a technique frequently fails because the whole group, not just a few vocal individuals, are involved in the excitement and chaos. Restoration of order depends upon effective use of techniques that will reorient the entire group.

When faced with this problem situation, the teacher may find it helpful to stop the activity of the entire group and wait until silence prevails. The disorderly activity can be halted by using an established signal, such as a bell or whistle, or some similar technique.

Once the classroom has been brought to some semblance of order or the children have been alerted to an established signal, the teacher may give some specific instructions for them to follow: stand and do an exercise, play a short game that has intrinsic value, or tell a funny story or riddle. After the group is under control and the children have had a chance to relax through some activity, the teacher will find it beneficial to discuss what happened, giving the children an opportunity to discuss their feelings and the standards previously set by the group in an attempt to evolve a plan to prevent future incidents.

This chapter has focused on some classroom problems that teachers often face. Others, not discussed here, will certainly arise. However, if the teacher considers these suggested approaches, he will probably experience success in dealing with many of them. Nevertheless, in applying these principles and techniques, one should recognize that they are not infallible recipes, promising final solutions. They are, rather, aids that, when applied understandingly and skillfully, may be useful. The teacher is, after all, a psychological tactician who must carefully (and constantly) analyze problems, evaluate approaches, and change tactics when the desired results or pupil growth does not take place.

References

1. Moustakas, C. E. *The teacher and the child*. New York: McGraw-Hill, 1956.

2. Olson, W., and Wattenberg, W. The role of the school in mental health. In N. Henry (ed.), *Mental health in education*. Fifty-Fourth Yearbook NSSE, Part II. Chicago: University of Chicago Press, 1955, pp. 99–124.

3. Redl, F., and Wattenberg, W. *Mental hygiene in teaching*. New York: Harcourt, Brace, 1959.

CHAPTER EIGHT

Patterns of Problem Behavior

In this chapter we will consider three major problems that often concern teachers: stealing, brain injury, and overdependency. Each problem will be analyzed in three ways. First, a general description of the problem and its associated behavior, or symptoms, will be given. Second, the underlying dynamics, or causes of the difficulty, will be analyzed. Third, based on the psychodynamics, some approaches to, or methods for, assisting the child who manifests one of the problems will be identified.

STEALING

Simply defined, *stealing* is the act of taking something that belongs to someone else without the expressed consent of the owner. As such, the concept of stealing is not particularly perplexing or mysterious. The objects taken do, of course, vary considerably, depending on the age, motivation, and general life circumstances of the child involved in the act.

Kanner (14) has described several characteristic types of stealing: intelligent and unintelligent stealing, casual stealing, selective stealing, solitary and group stealing, larceny, and robbery. In each situation, the general circumstances and motivations have somewhat different meanings. For example, *intelligent stealing* is the act of taking a desired or needed object so as not to be detected. *Unintelligent stealing* is the act of taking something impulsively, without caution or planning. *Solitary* and *group stealing*, as the descriptive terms imply, are acts of taking things alone or in company of others. *Robbery*, when compared with the other types of stealing, reflects a more serious, aggressive form of behavior, because it is the act of taking something by force or intimidation.

Causes of Stealing

Motivations for stealing, as well as the various acts of stealing, differ in seriousness and in the degree to which they indicate maladaptive or disturbed behavior. Let us consider some common motivations for stealing and the extent to which a particular act of stealing indicates disturbance.

One should realize that not all acts of taking things can be classified as stealing. The term stealing can be applied only when the child who takes something has a concept of property rights and is aware that he is committing an act that is generally unacceptable. Young children (especially those in the first three elementary grades) usually have incomplete concepts of property rights, and when they take something, their behavior may be a result of this immaturity rather than of anti-social or extra-legal intent (14, 19).

An excellent example of such immaturity is the young child who has been indulged and overprotected. To such a child, whose parents have given him material things freely or have not consistently taught him a concept of property rights, the act of taking something is simply a manifestation of his feeling that he may take what he wants. Another example of the same immaturity is the young child from a family that is economically deprived who may be motivated to take something simply because of a strong need arising from the deprivation itself (14).

Furthermore, a child's motivation to take something may be consistent with the moral standards of his family. In this instance, the stealing is simply a reflection of the socio-cultural pattern of the home (6). The motivations underlying specific acts of stealing are often easy to identify if the act and the general circumstances of the child are examined.

Other acts of stealing may be motivated by a desire for recognition, prestige, or status with one's peer group. Motivation in these instances may be less obvious but can be observed in the child who takes money and consistently spends to treat his peers. Or, depending upon the norms of the peer group, a child may conspicuously display his stolen money to demonstrate to his group that he is one of them, that he belongs.

In family settings characterized by strict, rigid controls and little freedom to express feelings, stealing (especially one's first act) may be an act of retaliation or revenge. By stealing and getting caught, a child can embarrass and punish his parents (14). In a sense, the child's stealing is an indirect and unconscious expression of his resentment and hostility toward his parents.

Stealing that occurs in the company of others may have still a different basis. Adolescents, for example, may steal while in a group simply in the spirit of adventure. Members of the adolescent peer group may dare each other to steal to prove their courage or adequacy (14). In such instances, the stealing usually does not persist unless it is part of the code of a particular peer group.

In addition to the relatively obvious instances already mentioned, other acts of stealing have deeper and more unconscious dynamics. That is, the stealing is symbolic of an unconscious psychological need. In many cases it has been demonstrated that stealing represents a child's attempt to compensate for emotional deprivation. In other words, his thefts represent (in a symbolic way), his search for the acceptance and affection that he has been denied (1, 6, 14). As a matter of fact, a child who steals for this reason may feel quite justified because of the great affectional void he has experienced (7).

In this same vein, Fenichel (7) has pointed out that in cases of kleptomania, the stealing may represent one's attempt to gain strength or power to deal with imagined dangers. The dangers that one may unconsciously fear are loss of affection or self-esteem. Also, in a sense, compulsive stealing represents an attempt to "store up" affectional supplies to deal with a past or anticipated loss of love. The behavior of the kleptomaniac is different only in degree from that of the "normal" person who compulsively saves money to deal with some unforeseen eventuality.

To effectively analyze a child's motivation for stealing, one must know what he took and what use he made of the stolen object. For example, is the stolen object valueless, and was it simply hidden away after it was taken? Or is it an item of real value, either to the child who took it or the person who owned it? From whom was the object taken? Perhaps the stealing is a way of punishing the owner. If a child takes money, does he hoard it or use it to buy things for his peers to gain their acceptance? If a child takes food for which he has no real physiological need, his stealing may represent a deep sense of affectional deprivation. Although the clues may sometimes be hidden, the objects taken and the use to which they are put almost always provide some hints to the motivation.

The next step to consider is the degree to which an act of stealing is indicative of a serious problem. This

analysis is necessary if one is to deal effectively with a child who has a stealing problem.

Clues to the Seriousness of the Act

Not all acts of stealing, as we have implied, are equally serious; some may be transitory, while others are symbolic of deeper personality disturbances. In determining the relative seriousness of various acts of stealing, certain clues are especially helpful.

Green and Rothenberg (9) have suggested six major criteria for making this analysis: (a) frequency of the act, (b) value of the stolen object, (c) duration of the stealing, (d) age of the child, (e) amount of punishment the child is willing to accept in order to steal, and (f) his general behavior at home and school.

As we noted in Chapter five, the frequency of a deviant act is a good clue to the seriousness of a child's problems. The same logic applies to stealing. The child who commits an isolated act of stealing probably does not have a problem as serious as does the child who repeatedly steals. In other words, the frequency of the act is a good indication of the strength of the need.

The value of the stolen object is also a useful clue to the seriousness of the stealing, for two basic reasons. First, taking something valuable suggests that a child is willing to take more chances and generally indicates that he has a greater personal need. Second, the value of the object is a crude indication of the severity of the consequences that are likely to follow detection. Naturally, the theft of a nickel is not nearly as serious as the theft of a hundred dollars. Similarly, the theft of a valueless piece of rope is quite different from that of a child's lunch money at school.

However, when children constantly take relatively useless and valueless objects, important symbolic meanings may underlie the thefts. That is, the seriousness of a child's stealing may be evaluated, to some degree, by its duration. A long and continuous history of stealing usually suggests that the pattern is fairly well crystallized and is significant in the personality dynamics of the child.

The age of the child, as noted previously, helps one to evaluate the seriousness of his stealing. Young children frequently take or "borrow" things before they have acquired an adequate concept of property rights. Obviously, such acts cannot be considered as serious. However, when a child steals, yet his age suggests he should have a reasonable concept of property rights, the act is considered more serious.

Furthermore, the extent to which a child will endure punishment for stealing indicates the seriousness of his problem, and an analysis of the child's punishment history is particularly important. It is apparent that the child who is willing to endure repeated and severe punishment has a very prominent need to steal. The compulsive nature of the act, in spite of repeated punishment, conveys the seriousness of the problem.

The final criterion for determining the seriousness of stealing is evaluation of the act in the context of the child's typical behavior at home and school. For example, is the stealing a relatively isolated symptom in a basically healthy child, or is it a symptom in a delinquent or anti-social personality? Stealing by a child who is basically healthy is likely to be an impulsive act, with few anti-social overtones. However, if stealing is simply one of a child's many disturbing psychological symptoms, the problem is more severe and complex and is less responsive to immediate modification. Knowledge of behavior at home and school provides a norm for determining the expected behavior of a particular child. Consequently, when the child deviates from his expected pattern, one can usually assume that the deviation is symptomatic of an abrupt change in his psychological well-being.

Helping the Child Who Steals

Efforts to help a child must be oriented to his motivation for stealing. Therefore, insight into a child's personality and his problem is vital before one can offer real help. Assisting the child who steals is, in general, much like assisting a child with other types of problems. Consequently, it may be helpful to review Chapter five, which deals with problems of changing children's behavior. However, in order to be more explicit, some illustrations of how the dynamics underlying a child's stealing may be used will be briefly presented.

As we have said, the most frequent motivations for stealing in elementary school children are (a) a nonexistent or immature concept of property rights and (b) emotional or affectional deprivation. In the first instance, the problem is an instructional-maturational one. That is, one's task is to help the child develop a concept of ownership, recognizing that such a concept is a product of experience, maturation, and teaching. Therefore, when the teacher must help a child with this problem, his efforts should be toward restoring the missing item without embarrassing, lecturing, or punishing. The child should be given the opportunity to return the object he has taken without having his identity revealed to the class. Other measures that may be advisable depend on the incident, but, in any event, the measures should be carried out in private.

When stealing is a result of affectional deprivation, there is little value in using the incident to "set an example." Since the motivation is usually unconscious and a result of an important psychological need, punishment is not likely to remove the compulsion to steal. In this instance, the teacher should attempt to build a supporting, accepting relationship with the child to provide some of the approval he needs. Furthermore, the parents should be helped to understand why the child steals and encouraged to establish a more rewarding relationship with him. Again, the child should have an opportunity to return whatever he has taken without public censure or knowledge of his identity.

The following case is typical of many acts of stealing in which affectional deprivation is the chief motivation. The boy in the case was seven years old when he was first referred to me for stealing. He had been taking things periodically for about a year. His thefts usually involved money, sweets, soda pop, or other things that were good to eat and drink.

Examination of the child and interviews with his mother revealed the following pertinent information. He had average intelligence and was making normal academic progress in school. He was adjusting well to his peer group and seemed to have no particular difficulty in relating to teachers. Teachers described him as likable, although they were, of course, concerned about his stealing.

The boy was the older of two children. The family appeared stable; however, the mother had been married twice. The child was a product of the first marriage, and it had been a stormy one, leaving the mother with a good deal of resentment toward her first husband. Although the family was basically upper-lower class, there were strong middle-class strivings. The mother, who seemed to dominate the family, had rather rigid standards regarding right and wrong. She was a strict disciplinarian and held high expectations for her children.

Analysis of the test data and the parent-child relationships led to the following conclusions regarding the boy's motivation for stealing. The boy, who had a marked physical similarity to his father, served as a stimulus for the mother's resentment toward her first husband. Therefore, she unconsciously expressed that resentment toward her son. In addition to her displaced resentment, her high standards and strict discipline prevented her from developing an accepting relationship with her son. Under such circumstances, the son could not feel accepted and loved by his mother, nor could he develop a sense of personal worth. His stealing was both a protest (a means of venting his anger) and a bid for affection. The stealing embarrassed his mother and, at the same time, reduced his anxiety which was due to affectional deprivation.

In a series of interviews, the mother gradually gained insight into the dynamics of her son's behavior. As she was able to express her resentment toward her first husband and see the relationship between these feelings and her treatment of her son, she began to develop a closer relationship with him. As a matter of fact, the boy did not steal again when his mother stopped punishing him for the act.

This case illustrates a key principle in dealing with any act of stealing. That is, one cannot successfully help a child who steals until the reasons for the stealing have been correctly analyzed and remedial measures instigated to fit the dynamics. Regardless of an act or the motivation underlying it, permanent modification of a child's behavior rests on one's understanding of the child's need—the reason for his behavior.

BRAIN INJURY

It may seem strange that the brain-injured child is considered in a volume primarily devoted to maladaptive, deviant, or disturbed behavior resulting basically from psychological causes. However, we have included a discussion of brain injury because most brain-injured children exhibit behavior disturbances and because this condition occurs much more frequently than has been realized. Beck (2), for example, has suggested that as high as sixty to seventy percent of all educable mentally handicapped children are brain-injured. Besides the mentally handicapped, there are probably many more "normal" children who experience difficulties in school because of minimal brain damage that is unrecognized. Therefore, the teacher in today's schools should have some knowledge of this condition.

Brain injury is the term applied when an area of the brain is damaged primarily as a result of injury or infection. The most typical or characteristic causes of brain injury are (a) excessively difficult and long births,

(b) RH incompatibility in the parents, (c) German measles in the mother during pregnancy, (d) inflammation resulting from diseases, such as meningitis and encephalitis, (e) extremely high fevers resulting from an illness, (f) circulatory difficulties, and (g) head injuries caused by accidents (5, 20). Some authorities estimate that seventy percent of all brain injuries occur as a result of birth trauma (20).

Characteristics of the Brain-Injured Child

Symptoms or observable characteristics of the brain-injured child vary, depending upon the damaged area, the extent of injury, and the child's personality prior to the onset of this condition (5). However, it is now fairly well established that dysfunction can be identified in four major areas: perception, concept formation or abstraction, language, and emotional behavior (16, 20). Dysfunctions or impairments in these areas lead to specific symptoms that are typical but not always present in brain-injured children (3).

Impairment in perception is characteristic of brain-injured children because they have defective screening or "filtering systems." That is, the child has great difficulty in screening important from unimportant visual and auditory stimuli. He cannot determine essential detail. Thus, he is flooded with irrelevant stimuli, with each stimulus competing for his attention. In a sense, he is compelled to attend to everything at once; consequently, he cannot attend to or structure a dominant stimulus pattern. Figure and ground stimulus relationships (the way in which foreground and background are perceived) do not assume proper organizational patterns—at least as the child experiences them (16, 20). That is, foreground and background may appear alternately and the child may become confused.

As the brain-injured child has difficulty organizing sensations and stimuli (perceiving), one would expect him to have difficulty developing concepts; this development is dependent upon one's capacity to organize perceptions so that similarities and differences in objects are identified, recognized, and remembered. Consequently, when the child is unable to develop concepts, he inadequately classifies objects, qualities, and experiences.

The brain-injured child may also have difficulty in the acquisition and use of language. As we have noted, problems in perception lead to impairments in the formation of concepts, and difficulties in conceptualizing must, of necessity, be reflected in speech and language patterns. For example, a child may have difficulty finding the right words to express a thought or an idea, orally or in writing. That is, he may omit articles, conjunctions, and connective words, or he may reverse letters within words. Furthermore, because his ability to discriminate among sounds is impaired, he may not articulate correctly the words he hears (17, 20).

Disturbances, also, are often evident in the emotional behavior of the brain-injured child. Perhaps the most basic problem in this area is the child's impulsiveness or lack of self-control. He usually does or says what comes to his mind, and he displays marked swings in mood. He may vacillate from elation to despair, and his emotional reaction is usually exaggerated. When he experiences only mild frustration, for example, he may become disorganized and cry easily (4, 20).

The problems of the brain-injured child may be indicated by some specific traits although not all of these traits are characteristic of all brain-injured children. Specific characteristics and symptoms vary, depending upon the child and the type and extent of his brain damage. However, these characteristics or traits are typical enough to have been identified frequently by those who have written about the brain-injured child (3, 4, 8, 17, 20).

Hyperactivity. This trait is typical of most brain-injured children and is expressed by overactivity, restlessness, and general excitement. The child has great difficulty focusing on even a single stimulus, but his reaction to a number of simultaneous stimuli is impulsive and undifferentiated.

Distractibility. The brain-injured child's distractibility is closely related to his hyperactivity. Both occur because of his limited ability to filter selectively the stimuli that bombard his sensory receptors. Distractibility is manifested primarily by the child's inability to stay with a task to its completion. He becomes submerged in a small part of a total act or moves in several directions at once. His attention span is short, and sustained attention is almost impossible.

Perseveration. The tendency to repeat an action or activity is quite characteristic of the brain-injured child. For example, he may laugh continuously for long periods, color an entire page with one color, write the same letter repeatedly, or play for long periods with one toy in a repetitive, mechanical fashion. In doing arithmetic, he may successfully solve the problem of three plus three but continue to give the same answer, six, to different problems such as two plus three or four plus four. He perseverates in this manner because he wants to hold on to situations that he has successfully structured or solutions that he has worked out. He does not readily give up a successful pattern to face once again stimuli that to him are so confused and disorderly.

Impulsivity. Because the brain-injured child has difficulty selectively screening and integrating stimuli, one should expect him to be impulsive. He reacts almost as intensively to one stimulus as to another, since his poor control system does not allow him to discriminate and react appropriately to each stimulus that he experiences. Consequently, he may talk out or act out almost any thought or impulse that presses upon him at the moment.

Impairments in motor coordination. Difficulties in a child's motor coordination may be manifested by peculiarities of movement in walking, skipping, running, jumping, or hopping. Furthermore, because the child has difficulty judging shape, size, distance, and direction, he may be awkward and bump into things, and he will usually be unable to judge quickly right from left. Impairment in visual-motor coordination often becomes apparent when he is asked to copy squares, diamonds, or triangles. When this impairment is present, the child's reproductions reflect angulation difficulties, and the drawings appear somewhat dog-eared.

Difficulties in social adjustment. Considering the many difficulties that the brain-injured child faces, one would expect him to have problems in adapting socially. His impulsivity and low frustration tolerances predispose him

to act aggressively, and aggressiveness does not lead to ready acceptance of him by his peers. His various problems with conceptualizing, following sequences and patterns, and motor functioning make it difficult for him to participate successfully in many games with his peers. Consequently, he is often rejected by and isolated from his peer group.

Intellectual and learning problems. The degree to which a child is intellectually handicapped is intimately related to the exact nature, area, and degree of his brain injury. Severe brain injuries usually cause marked learning and intellectual deficiencies or various degrees of mental retardation. However, even in cases of mild or moderate brain damage, certain specific characteristics occur quite frequently.

For instance, if we recognize that most learning involves the acquisition of concepts, generalizations, and principles, the brain-injured child is obviously handicapped in many areas of the curriculum. Indeed, the levels of abstraction required in learning generalizations and principles may often be unattainable for the child with a brain injury. He approaches learning concretely; therefore, the complexities of symbolic, numerical reasoning are often beyond his grasp. As an example, he will conceptualize numbers by relying excessively on finger counting.

The brain-damaged child will also manifest difficulties in serial or sequential learning. For instance, he may not remember the number that comes after eleven or the letter that follows "f." In reading, he may be unable to follow the sequence of events in a story. Similarly, when a story has a subtle meaning or inference, he may not be able to comprehend it.

In addition, impairment in visual-motor coordination may make it difficult for a child to learn to write. This problem may be especially apparent when the child changes from manuscript to cursive writing. He may be successful in writing letters that do not require retracing ("c," "u") but have difficulty with those letters that do ("i," "t").

Furthermore, since the brain-injured child has difficulty with immediate memory or recall, he may quickly forget something that he has apparently just learned. For example, a word that he has been helped to identify in one paragraph may be unknown to him in the next; learning that he seemed to acquire on Monday may have vanished by Tuesday.

With these indications that reflect intellectual and learning deficiencies in mind, let us consider some illustrative ways of working with the brain-injured child.

Helping the Brain-Injured Child

The teacher who has a brain-injured child in his classroom faces two immediate problems: (a) finding effective methods of instructing the child and (b) handling his confused, disorganized, and often disturbed behavior. The suggestions offered here are directed toward these two problems. They are general guidelines that will hopefully orient the teacher toward more productive work with the child. However, it should be noted that, in addition to the help the teacher may offer in the classroom, the brain-injured child may need special medical attention or referral for complete psychological evaluation.

Since the pathology of the brain-injured child makes it difficult for him to organize his perception, to structure and conceptualize, to inhibit impulses, and to organize the stimuli that impinge upon his senses, how can we help him? Perhaps the first and most basic thing we can do is to provide him with an orderly, structured environment where excessive stimuli are minimized. He performs best in a distraction-free environment with relatively fixed patterns and routines. For instance, in the classroom, he should be seated away from open windows or doors. Sometimes it may even be necessary for the teacher to shade the windows or put a folding screen around the child's desk (16, 20).

Generally, instruction should be oriented to use as many sense modalities as possible. However, there may be times when the elimination of certain sensory stimuli is desirable. For example, if the teacher is helping the child develop skill with auditory or tactile sensations, it may be beneficial to eliminate visual stimuli by having him close his eyes or by giving him a blindfold. With some learning activities, a child may benefit by working in a darkened room or with a projector (20).

Also, the child's complete attention should be secured before the teacher attempts any activity, and when a new activity is instigated, simple but very specific directions should be given. Whenever possible, directions should be demonstrated, with a minimum of verbalization. Once the activity has been initiated, the child should be helped to focus on the main elements of the task. For instance, if he is to color a picture, an outline of it in heavy black lines will be helpful to him (8).

The brain-injured child's problems with conceptualization make it more difficult for him to succeed in learning situations that are highly verbal than in those that are primarily task-oriented. Also, in learning to count and conceptualize numerical relationships, he can be aided in the activity by using disks, sticks, buttons or beans. In the initial stages of reading, this child may be taught more effectively by the "sight-word method" than by the phonic method. He can learn words easier by associating them with appropriate pictures than by blending separate sounds. The phonic method of teaching reading requires facility in discriminating among sounds—a capacity that is limited in the brain-injured child (20).

Since the visual-motor coordination problems of the brain-injured child make learning to print or write difficult, his instruction in this skill requires assistance in guiding motor movements and identifying important cues. For example, the teacher can write the alphabet in large, heavy black letters and encourage the child to trace them. If a child has severe motor impairments, it may be necessary for the teacher to guide his hand until he has learned to trace.

Besides the specific aspects of instruction that require the teacher's careful planning and thought, handling the behavior of the child with a brain injury will pose some problems. Perhaps the guiding principle here is that of systematic pre-planning or prevention. It is worth emphasizing again that the child needs the security of structure, limits, and routines.

Beyond these general considerations, there are specific guidelines. For instance, when a child is excited or in a generally disorganized state, it is of little value to tell him to stop or to issue threats. Instead, the teacher can usually improve the child's behavior by introducing a new focus of activity and giving the child specific directions regarding what he should do and how he may proceed. In some cases, it may be necessary for the teacher to take the child by the hand calmly and move him to a new interest area, or if the child is very disorganized and out of control, the teacher should lead him to a quiet place. This removes him from the scene of excitement and gives him an opportunity to regain control.

The teacher should learn to detect signs of arising disorganization in the child and, at the moment he shows signs of becoming excited, move him quickly and provide a new focus. This procedure is much better and more effective than trying to handle a screaming, unhappy child.

Finally, the child should not be faced with too many decisions, and, when a change from one activity to another is undertaken, a period for the transition should be provided. The teacher should make certain that the child knows what he is to do because structure provides security that the brain-injured child especially needs. Also, when an activity change is to take place, the teacher should make an orienting statement indicating that in a particular length of time the task will be changed (20).

OVERDEPENDENCY

A cursory glance at the child who is excessively dependent may lead one to believe that his problems are not particularly noteworthy. In contrast to many children who exhibit maladaptive reactions, he does not rebel against his environment or behave in ways that may be harmful to others. Instead, he relies greatly upon others for nurture, support, or help in satisfying his needs or achieving his goals (12, 22). He usually needs a great deal of emotional reassurance and assistance from adults in the tasks he undertakes. His behavior reflects a minimum of self-direction and a prominent need to cling to the teacher or solicit his attention. So, even though his problems may be expressed in relatively innocuous forms, the overly dependent child often has difficulty achieving goals set for him at school.

The degree to which this child is a problem to the teacher depends upon the time the teacher has to give him and the teacher's own dependency needs and social-class values. Large classes often make it difficult for the teacher to meet the dependency needs of the child. Also, if the teacher has strong, unconscious dependency needs, the child's needs will conflict with his own, be difficult for him to meet, and become a source of annoyance to him. Furthermore, the problems of the overdependent child may become overwhelming to the teacher who emphasizes the middle-class values of self-reliance and independence, for this child is utterly incapable of meeting such expectations.

Since a cursory glance at the behavior of the overdependent child is unreliable, it is important that we take a deeper look into his dilemma, see how he develops as he does, and learn how the teacher may help him. This examination will necessarily consider the ways in which dependency is acquired and becomes elaborated into excessive dependence.

Development of Dependency

Perhaps the best formulation we can make at the present time is that dependent behavior arises from the infant's state of complete helplessness. Being helpless, the infant must rely entirely upon others for his maintenance and survival. When others (mainly the mother) satisfy his needs by feeding him or keeping him warm, he learns to associate his feelings of well-being (reduction of basic drives and anxiety) with nurturing care. Thus, the child learns to value his mother's presence both for satisfaction of his primary drives and for the affectional care she provides. Affectional care or warmth is eventually sought for its own sake; therefore, we may reiterate that the child seeks his mother as an instrument to satisfy both his survival and his emotional needs (11).

Children who have had emotional warmth from a consistent mother-figure will develop normal dependency needs that are necessary and desirable at early stages of development. For example, normal dependency needs that have been gratified through emotional warmth help a child develop the capacity to seek and give love and affection in later life. If, however, such gratification has been denied, the child will develop excessive dependency needs (always seeking that which he has been denied) and will not develop the capacity for normal love relationships in later life. That young children who have been denied emotional warmth from a consistent mother-figure do not learn to seek and give affection is indicated by Hartup (10), who summarized several studies of children institutionalized during infancy. Nevertheless, once the foundations for normal dependency strivings have been established, subsequent interpersonal relationships and child-rearing practices will still determine future dependency patterns.

Several theories have been postulated to explain the development of excessive dependency. The first, previously discussed in Chapter two, is the psychoanalytic hypothesis which emphasizes the crucial importance of the mother-child relationships during the oral stage of a child's development. If the infant is excessively frustrated or deprived during this period, according to the psychoanalytic theory, he will develop exaggerated oral characteristics. Thus, in later life his personality structure will probably be characterized by marked passivity and dependency.

A second theory suggests that maternal overprotection may cause a child to develop overly dependent behavior. For example, Levy (15) studied the case histories of children of overprotective mothers and found that mothers who are both dominating and overprotective tend to have children who are passive, dependent, and submissive.

Stendler (21) also studied the causes of overdependency in children. She selected twenty six-year-olds who were rated as overdependent and compared them with a control group of twenty children who were not so rated. Careful study of the "infant disciplines" of these children supported the hypotheses that discontinuities in socialization during the critical period of nine months to three years and maternal overprotection lead to excessive dependency.

A third hypothesis is that a child develops overdependency as a result of excessive frustration and punishment. The study most relevant to this relationship is that of Sears, Whiting, Nowlis, and Sears (18). They investigated the antecedents of dependency and aggression in young children by interviews with mothers regarding earlier feeding, weaning, and toilet-training practices. Ratings of dependency were also obtained from nursery school teachers and independent observers. The extent to which dependent behavior was manifest in children of pre-school age was positively correlated with rigidity of feeding in girls but not in boys. However, severity of weaning correlated with dependent (overdependent) behavior in both boys and girls. Thus, it seems reasonable to assume from this study that frustration related to oral satisfaction in infancy and early childhood is likely to lead to overt dependency needs. Hartup (10), after reviewing several studies relating to dependency in early childhood, reaches substantially the same conclusion.

From these studies one might conclude that marked frustration, deprivation, and dominating overprotection are to be avoided if a child is to establish reasonable autonomy and independence. When strong dependency needs become established and are fostered in a child, they tend to persist. Furthermore, any attempt to alter these needs by withdrawing affection through punishment or rejection only strengthens the child's needs (18).

While the overt manifestations of dependency may change in form as the child grows older, the underlying trend toward dependency seems to remain. When this dependency trend (the need for excessive assistance, reassurance, and help in meeting the world) continues at later ages, it is undesirable and may be termed overdependency.

Heathers (11) did a study of twenty two-year-olds and twenty four- and five-year-olds to examine the changes in dependency as children grow older. He found that a child's dependency on adults decreases with age as it is transferred to other children. That is, demands for assistance and reassurance are made more frequently of peers than of adults. He also discovered that physical clinging and overt affection-seeking behavior declined with age as it was manifested in more mature ways of gaining approval.

Kagan and Moss (13) studied the persistence or stability of dependent behavior from childhood through adulthood as part of a longitudinal investigation at Fels Research Institute. Their subjects consisted of twenty-seven males and an equal number of females on whom they had extensive data from birth through adolescence. The results of this study suggest that passive and dependent trends tend to persist in women but are not nearly so well-defined in men. However, men have more conflicts regarding dependent behavior than do women. This result is explained on the basis that there is more social pressure for men to become independent and autonomous, while women are permitted, or even encouraged, to be passive.

Even though overt changes may take place in the way one expresses dependency needs, no real benefit is derived if the dependency remains as inhibited or unconscious needs. Simply changing the mode of expressing needs that are still a significant part of one's unconscious personality does not mean that one's basic needs have changed. Until one gains insight into a problem and desires to change, the problem will continue to influence his behavior.

Helping the
Overdependent Child

Although progress has been made in formulating the basis for overdependency, researchers have given less attention to its modification. However, from the information available, it is apparent that the overly dependent child needs acceptance and approval, and the teacher, if he is to help the child, must be aware of his needs. The more this child is punished, criticized, and lectured for attention- or approval-seeking behavior, the stronger his drive becomes. Any child, especially one whose dependency needs compel him to solicit help or approval from others, functions more adequately with acceptance than with disapproval, even though his basic personality structure does not change.

Therefore, since the overdependent child needs experiences that will help him to acquire feelings of competence, the teacher is in a particularly advantageous position to help him. Heathers (11) has suggested several methods for helping a child develop greater self-assurance. For example, the "threshold method" consists of giving him an opportunity to master a skill or threatening situation by dealing with it part by part, so that his anxiety can be properly handled. Or, if a child requires excessive help or appears especially unsure of himself in performing a skill, the teacher should give him an opportunity to over-learn the skill until he has complete confidence that he can perform it alone. A third approach, according to Heathers, provides the necessary crutches until the child has the confidence to discard them. For example, a child learning to swim is less fearful of the water when he is placed in a life preserver and discovers that it keeps him from sinking. The life preserver is a crutch that he will discard when he learns that he can stay on top of the water as a result of his own movements.

Another approach to the problem of excessive dependency is that of assigning tasks that the child can deal with successfully. This success will usually enhance his self-confidence. Furthermore, success at one level of performance will often give him enough confidence to attempt a slightly more difficult assignment.

Besides working directly with the child to enhance his opportunities for success and to help him develop feelings of competence, adequacy, and personal worth, the teacher may be able to enlist the help of the parents, for little can be accomplished if the parents negate his efforts. The teacher may be able to help the parents gain insight into their child's dependency needs and to offer suggestions that will alter their approach to him. However, work with the parents may not be possible. For example, if a parent has a strong, unconscious need to control or overprotect the child, the teacher may be unable to help him change his basic relationship with the child. When such a situation exists, both parents and child should be referred for professional assistance.

When the parents are receptive and not too deeply involved emotionally in the child's dependency problems, they may respond to specific suggestions from the teacher. For instance, they can reduce the child's frustration by assigning only those tasks or making those demands that the child can perform successfully, by rewarding him verbally or affectionately for signs of independent action, and by helping him (through reassurance) to develop confidence in his ability to handle responsibilities on his own or to attempt something untried. With such parent-teacher cooperation, the child can gradually gain self-confidence from his newly accomplished independent action, which should encourage him toward further independence.

References

1. Adler, A. *The problem child*. New York: Capricorn Books, 1963.

2. Beck, H. S. The incidence of brain injury in public school special classes for the educable mentally handicapped. *J. ment. Defic.*, 1956, LX, 818–822.

3. Benton, A. L. Behavior indices of brain injury in school children. *Child Developm.*, 1962, XXXIII, 199–208.

4. Berkowitz, Pearl H., and Rothman, Esther P. *The disturbed child*. New York: New York University Press, 1960.

5. Chess, Stella. *An introduction to child psychiatry*. New York: Grune & Stratton, 1959.

6. D'Evelyn, Katherine E. *Meeting children's emotional needs*. Englewood Cliffs, New Jersey: Prentice-Hall, 1957.

7. Fenichel, O. *The psychoanalytic theory of neurosis*. New York: W. W. Norton, 1945.

8. Fouracres, M. H. Learning characteristics of brain injured children. *Except. Child.*, 1958, XXIII, 210–212.

9. Green, S. L., and Rothenberg, A. B. A *manual of first aid for mental health*. New York: The Julian Press, 1953.

10. Hartup, W. W. Dependence and independence. In H. W. Stevenson (ed.), *Child psychology*, The Sixty-second Yearbook, NSSE, Part I, 1963, pp. 333–363.

11. Heathers, G. Acquired dependence and independence: A theoretical orientation. *J. genet. Psychol.*, 1955, LXXXVII, 277–291.

12. Heathers, G. Emotional dependence and independence in nursery school play. *J. genet. Psychol.*, 1955, LXXXVII, 37–57.

13. Kagan, J., and Moss, H. A. The stability of passive and dependent behavior from childhood through adulthood. *Child Developm.*, 1960, XXXI, 577–591.

14. Kanner, L. *Child psychiatry*, 2nd ed. Springfield, Ill.: Charles C Thomas, 1948.

15. Levy, D. *Maternal overprotection*. New York: Columbia University Press, 1943.

16. Lewis, R. *The other child*. New York: Grune and Stratton, 1951.

17. Nelson, C. D. Subtle brain damage: Its influence on learning and language. *Element. Sch. J.*, 1961, 317–321.

18. Sears, R. R., Whiting, J. W. M., Nowlis, V., and Sears, Pauline S. Some child rearing antecedents of dependency and aggression in young children. *Genet. Psychol. Monogr.*, 1953, XLVII, 1935–2034.

19. Seaton, J. K. Dr. Seaton discusses the child who takes things. *Instructor*, 1961, LXXI, 34.

20. Siegel, E. *Helping the brain injured child*. New York: Association for Brain Injured Children, 1962.

21. Stendler, Celia Burns. Possible causes of overdependency in young children. *Child Developm.*, 1954, XXV, 125–146.

22. Watson, R. I. *Psychology of the child: Personal, social and disturbed child development*. New York: John Wiley and Sons, 1959.

CHAPTER NINE

Aggressive Behavior

Aggressive behavior in the classroom causes more concern to teachers than any other type of deviant behavior, largely for three reasons. First, aggressive behavior disrupts the learning process in the classroom, primarily because another person is usually the object of the aggression. Second, aggressive behavior produces threat to the teacher's established order or group control. Third, aggression usually cannot be ignored. Some response or action to handle the behavior is required of the teacher, but it is not always easy to determine the type of action that will be appropriate or effective. Furthermore, the action the teacher takes will communicate to the whole class, as well as the aggressor, the approach the teacher will probably take in the future when dealing with similar behavior.

Although aggression is commonly regarded as a form of destruction or physical attack on an object or person, it can be expressed in several other forms. For instance, it is often expressed in verbal form by attacks on a person's pride, adequacy, or status, or it can be expressed subtly through certain forms of humor.

Aggression, when psychologically defined, usually refers to behavior that is hostile in expression and arises from frustration in the attempt to attain personally significant goals. Its intent is typically to inflict physical or psychological discomfort or pain, although such intentions may not be consciously perceived by the aggressor. It should clearly be differentiated from competition or striving, both of which are generally regarded as appropriate in seeking socially acceptable goals. Indeed, competition is strongly sanctioned as desirable in our society and is normal to the extent that it frequently occurs. Therefore, the behavior in which we are particularly interested is aggression that is destructive, hurtful, and thus non-adaptive and unnatural. Aggression in children is frequently expressed by stubbornness, teasing, tattling, and other, less obvious but perhaps more serious, forms of behavior.

All children, at some time and in some way, exhibit aggressive behavior. The consistency and effect of this behavior is very much dependent upon the understanding and training techniques employed by parents and other significant people in the child's life. To understand aggressive behavior in a child, one must understand the child, his relationships with others, and the needs he is attempting to satisfy through aggression.

DEVELOPMENT OF AGGRESSIVE BEHAVIOR

Aggression, according to Sears, Maccoby, and Levin (5), has two basic aspects: (a) the fundamental quality of rage or anger and (b) the desire to hurt or inflict some type of pain. Rage or anger has an instinctive quality, which is characteristic of infants, in response to certain kinds of restraint, discomfort, and frustration. The desire to hurt or inflict pain seems to be learned.

One might assume that the frequency and intensity of an infant's rage, as well as his desire to hurt, are related to the relative satisfaction that the child experiences in his relationship with his parents. If the infant is constantly frustrated by his parents, he is likely to exhibit rage often and experiment with ways to reduce his discomfort. For example, as the child masters physical control, he begins to manipulate his environment, by crying

vehemently when he is hungry and biting, kicking, or screaming when his demands are not met. These elements of behavior may become potentially aggressive weapons. That is, if such behavior produces success for the child, the aggressive behavior will be reinforced.

Aggressive reactions in infants may also serve other purposes. For instance, they may provide relief from discomforting internal tensions. If so, such aggressive reactions may become an end unto themselves, rather than a means of acquiring some other satisfaction.

Aggression and Parent-Child Interaction

Obviously, the nature of parent-child interaction and parental reactions to a child's instinctive rage largely determine the amount of aggression a child will have and the way he will use it. In the process of socialization, Sears, Maccoby, and Levin (5) have suggested that the interaction between child and mother may be viewed in two general ways: as controlling the actions of a child and training him. The mother's control is an attempt to influence the present actions of a child, while her training is an attempt to influence or modify the child's future behavior in specific ways. Socialization requires both control and training. Control only will not help a child grow into a stable, responsible adult; training is necessary to help the child develop standards of conduct and internal controls that do not require continuous external supervision.

Therefore, parents who deal with a child's aggression only through control do not give him appropriate help because aggression usually provokes counter-aggression; furthermore, the aggressive model of the parent may terminate the overt action but not necessarily the aggression of the child. Instead, the child's aggressive impulses usually remain but are expressed in subtle, disguised ways. Also, the aggressive model of the parents often provides a pattern of behavior for the child.

Results of the study (5) previously mentioned indicates that several different influences produce excessive aggression in children. For example, it was found that mothers who are highly permissive, or those who punish severely, generally have aggressive children. On the other hand, mothers who are most permissive but, at the same time, most punitive, also have highly aggressive children. However, mothers with low permissiveness and low punishment have the least aggressive children.

According to this study either extreme (severe punishment or high permissiveness) produces considerable aggression in children. Apparently, children learn to deal better with their aggression when limits are clearly set, when there is appropriate affectional interaction between mother and child, and when severe punishment is not employed to enforce reasonable limits.

Bandura and Walters (1) did a study of aggressive adolescent boys and obtained results somewhat similar to the study previously reported. They found that aggressive boys (in contrast to non-aggressive boys in a control group) are subjected to fewer socialization pressures, particularly from the mothers. For example, the mothers of the aggressive boys placed fewer limits on the boys at home, were not so demanding of obedience, and did not consistently enforce demands. The fathers of the aggressive boys, however, were more demanding of obedience

but were also more hostile and rejecting toward their sons. The aggressive boys were very resentful of such treatment from their fathers and consequently resisted controls.

In analyzing the results of this study, the authors speculated that failure of mothers to exert strong and consistent socialization pressures is instrumental in the aggressive boys' lack of control. They further suggested that there is likely a critical socialization period when the child is most receptive to the development of controls and the acceptance of adult standards, and, if appropriate child-rearing measures are not employed at that time, the child will have difficulty later in the control of aggression.

A mother's pattern of interaction with her young child, the child-rearing methods she employs, and her dynamic personality trends are probably the most crucial factors in determining over-aggressive reactions in children. The mother is, after all, the one who must assume primary responsibility for training and controlling the child. However, the mother's unresolved problems often become involved and influence the process.

As the previous discussion has suggested, there are many factors arising from the child's relationship to his parents that have the potential of producing more than a normal amount of aggression in children. In general, however, it may be stated that aggression arises in children when they feel deprived of affection, are subjected to standards beyond their physical, mental, and emotional maturity, and are the objects of severe and harsh child-rearing measures. Any such treatment creates difficulty for the child in making appropriate identification with his parents, and, as a consequence, his controls cannot be adequately internalized.

Aggression and Socio-Cultural Factors

Although parent-child relationships are probably most basic to the development of excessive aggression in children, the cultural or social-class environment plays a significant role in prohibiting or sanctioning aggression. In an earlier chapter we stated that the lower class allows considerable freedom in impulse expression. Also, parents in the lower class employ more physical punishment and generally act more aggressively toward their children than do parents in the middle class. Because of cultural acceptance and the parental model, the child in the lower class is likely to imitate such aggressive behavior. In the same way, the lower-class child is prone to act out his conflicts in an aggressive manner.

In contrast, the middle-class child tends to inhibit direct expression of aggression. A high premium, culturally, is placed on restraint and control. The middle-class child may have difficulty dealing with his aggression, but his defenses disguise its expression. These disguises may appear in subtle ways, such as resistance to learning, or indulgence in activities to "get back" at the parents. Of course, it is not unusual to find the middle-class child dealing with his aggression by developing various kinds of neurotic symptoms.

The differences in the way children deal with aggression pose problems for the teacher in successfully handling it. For example, the aggressive lower-class child does not have a great deal of guilt related to his own aggressive behavior. Therefore, appeals to his sense of reason or fair play or efforts to arouse guilt may be quite ineffective. The middle-class child is more likely to feel guilt for his aggressive behavior, and, since he holds many of the same cultural values as his teacher, he may be more amenable to change, particularly when a good relationship exists between the teacher and the child. However, regardless of the class membership of the aggressive child, his behavior often creates difficulty for the teacher. In a subsequent section, methods of dealing with it will be discussed.

Aggression and Classroom Influences

Unwholesome parent-child relationships and cultural influences are not the only factors that produce aggressive behavior in children. The manner in which the teacher approaches the group, the way in which he organizes instruction, and the way he attempts to control the group can have much to do with the nature and amount of aggression expressed in the classroom.

In general, anything operating in the classroom that is at great variance with the needs, maturity, and readiness of the children in the group has all the potentialities of fostering aggressive reactions. Children get angry when they are unduly frustrated or when they are thwarted in their attempt to accomplish successfully things that are expected of them. Teachers who have more than a normal amount of aggression in the classroom will do well to consider these factors.

As a first step, the teacher should scrutinize carefully his program to determine whether his academic, behavioral, and physical expectations are realistic for each child. Unless the class is composed of children who are markedly homogeneous in intellectual ability (and this is rare), individual academic adjustments must usually be made for each child. Similarly, behavioral expectations or group control methods that do not permit children a reasonable amount of freedom to enter into social relationships with other children can arouse aggression. Activities in the classroom that are too highly competitive may also pit some children against others and lead to group disharmony and classroom or playground aggression.

Any disparity between the goals of the teacher and those of the children in the group is often revealed by general resistance and uncooperativeness on the part of the children. The children may, for example, have difficulty settling down to work, require an excessive amount of time in changing from one activity to another, or continuously disrupt the classroom. Such behavior can be an expression of group hostility toward the teacher for his failure to take the requirements of the children into account. In such a situation, it is of little value for the teacher to reprimand the children, for they must express their frustrations in some way. A better approach is for the teacher to structure a program that more nearly meets the requirements of the children.

A study by Cunningham and associates (2) is pertinent in suggesting the teacher's influence in fostering particular classroom activity and group climate. In this study, a group of children was observed as it proceeded from teacher to teacher throughout the day. In one classroom the children were quiet and docile; in a second classroom, the same children were noisy and aggressive. In a third classroom situation, these same children involved themselves in constructive activity even before the teacher appeared.

Obviously, children are remarkably responsive to the feeling or emotional tone created by the teacher. This climate is often a product of unconscious, as well as conscious, attempts on the part of the teacher to organize the teaching situation in particular ways, for a person's unconscious personality trends have an interesting way of expressing themselves without one's conscious awareness. Furthermore, if, for reasons not entirely conscious, the teacher is the "punishing for misbehavior type," children may reflect the same attitudes and ways of dealing with situations as the teacher, because children tend to model their behavior after those who are significant to their welfare, and in the school situation, the teacher is the primary influence.

The teacher must be constantly alert to his influences in the classroom situation. If he is not, he may be faced with rather vague pupil resistance to the on-going processes of teaching and learning.

HANDLING CLASSROOM AGGRESSION

It should be apparent from the previous discussion that to deal effectively with it, one must understand classroom aggression and its various causes. That is, one must have some understanding of parent-child relationships, individual personality dynamics, socio-cultural forces, unconscious personality factors, both teacher's and students', and the group dynamics operating in the classroom.

General Considerations

Obviously, if one is to teach effectively, there must be some semblance of order in the classroom and a balance between freedom and control. Unfettered expressions of aggression on the part of one child, or more, are not good for the rest of the children in the group. Also, children who are permitted complete freedom to express aggression rarely develop adequate internal controls, and they often grow up to be egocentric, aggressive, anxious, and unhappy people.

Youngsters need the assurance that some of their defiant, aggressive feelings are acceptable, but they should not be allowed to hurt themselves, injure others, or destroy property. Little is to be gained by force or by extreme measures. One can, of course, inhibit most aggressive behavior by engendering enough fear; however, such tactics may induce defeat and apathy in a child. Furthermore, if extreme measures are consistently used, a child may redirect expression of his hostility through other symptoms, such as fainting spells, asthmatic attacks, and certain allergic illnesses.

Somehow, and in acceptable ways, we must allow the child to express his aggressive feelings. When he is allowed expression of hostility, the child is relieved of inner tensions. Such relief is very helpful to the child as long as his guilt, afterwards, is not too great. One should recognize, however, that only the symptoms, not the cause, of a child's aggression are alleviated through overt expression.

Specific Considerations

The teacher should consider three basic prerequisites to decision making before attempting to handle aggressive behavior or the aggressive child. First, one must attempt to determine the chronicity of the aggression, because the child with a long history of aggression is handled differently from the child whose aggressive behavior ap-

pears suddenly. Children who have long histories of extreme aggressive reactions probably have been subjected to all the usual disciplinary techniques and punishments, and the fact that they continue to be aggressive suggests that previous relationships and methods have not been effective.

Second, some knowledge of the depth of the aggressive child's disturbance is necessary. Aggression may be symptomatic of several emotional disturbances; therefore, this symptom alone gives only a general indication of a child's disturbance. One should be alert to any other symptoms or manifestations of disturbance in the aggressive child, because the nature and degree of his disturbance determine the methods for handling his aggression. For example, aggression in a basically stable child should be handled very differently from aggression in a neurotic or severely disturbed child. Furthermore, the nature and degree of a child's disturbance and the way he uses or expresses his aggression will largely determine the amount of control one can expect from the child.

Third, the age of the child is an important consideration in assisting him with his aggression. Young children, certainly many primary grade children, are still in the process of developing controls over some of their stronger impulses and should not be unduly penalized for an occasional explosion. However, children of this age do need well-chosen and appropriately enforced limits to provide them with security. Aggressive upper-grade children pose greater problems because their aggression may have become more deeply imbedded in their personalities. Approaches to these children must be more systematic, the goals more limited, and the methods more antiseptic.

Let us now consider, in detail, some

methods of handling aggression. For example, a sudden onset of aggressive behavior in some instances indicates that a child is reacting to a situational crisis. If so, his equilibrium is upset, and his anxiety and confusion are being expressed through unusual, for him, aggressive behavior at school. The teacher should first learn something about the crisis and the pressures upon the child before he attempts to handle the child's behavior.

The crises to which a child might react will vary from child to child and with the particular circumstances in which he lives. Some of the more common crises are (a) sudden separation from one or both parents, (b) unexpected hospitalization of a parent to whom the child is very much attached, or (c) a dramatic and provocative conflict between parents, or between parent and child. The more directly the child is involved in the conflict or crisis situation, the more the child will probably react to it. Also, parents will vary in degrees of awareness of the effects a crisis will have on a child. Very often parents are not aware of the intensity of a child's reaction to a crisis and welcome such information from the teacher. This knowledge may help the parents focus on the needs of the child and give him the support that he so urgently needs.

When such a problem exists, the teacher should be supportive and tolerant in his relationship with the child. Any extreme measures on his part to make the child conform not only add to the child's disequilibrium but damage the teacher-pupil relationship. It is reassuring for the teacher to know that, once the crisis has passed, the child usually regains his emotional balance. In addition, if the teacher does give the child emotional support and demonstrates tolerance, he will probably find that the teacher-pupil relationship is strengthened considerably.

On the other hand, if the child who is exhibiting the aggressive behavior is a relatively stable child, firm limits on his behavior will usually help him develop better control. It is essential, however, that the person who applies the limits is one who likes, and is liked by, the child, for firm limits set by a person who has a poor relationship with a child usually fail to yield the desired results. Children will accept prohibitions, demands, and disappointments from people they like, or who like them, but will steadfastly resist demands or controls from those with whom they do not have a good relationship.

Firm, consistent limits are particularly effective with the child that has been reared in an overpermissive home. This child is frequently referred to in popular parlance as the "spoiled child." He tends to be aggressively demanding and egocentric, and his impulse controls are usually weak. Since this child has had few consistent and firm limits set on him at home, he expects (although he may unconsciously not desire) the same treatment at school. However, as a result of conflict between his expectations and the demands of the school and of his social group, the child may become extremely anxious about his inability to exercise appropriate inner control. In this instance, reasonably firm, consistent limits will provide needed security for the child. In the initial stages he may be quite resistant to the controls, but he will learn to accept them.

This principle is perhaps best illustrated by a case. The case is that of a fourth-grade boy whose behavior epitomized the "spoiled child." He was demanding, aggressive, solicitous of attention, and generally hyperactive. He was a most ingenious manipulator and had a good deal of charm. In the classroom he had great difficulty staying in his seat; he hovered around the teacher's desk, made frequent gestures to attract the attention of his classmates, and rarely completed his classroom work at the appropriate time. He had above average intellectual capacity and was quite capable of meeting the academic requirements.

This child had been reared in a lower-middle class home with very permissive parents. He had been indulged with material things by his parents as a result of the guilt caused by their inability to provide adequate affection. The permissiveness and inability of the parents to establish appropriate limits was well illustrated by an anecdote and a question the father raised during a parent interview.

The father reflected concern about his inability to enforce any limits he attempted to impose upon his son. He illustrated his point by indicating that invariably twice a day he purchased ice cream from the "Good Humor Man." This was the exact number of times the ice cream man traveled through the neighborhood each day. The father then asked how he might acceptably refuse such demands from his son and how limits might be enforced. Whereupon, the father was asked: "Have you ever tried uttering a resounding 'no' and meaning it?"

Of course, considerably more than "a resounding no" was needed to help the father deal more effectively with his son. However, setting effective limits on the son's demands was an important first step for the parents, as well as the child's teacher, to take. Unfortunately, both the parents and the teacher had difficulty following through on this important first step.

The boy was subsequently moved to another school where he had an accepting but firm teacher. For four or five days after the transfer to the new teacher, the boy cried almost constantly as a reaction to her firmness. The teacher was very accepting and tolerant of the child's tears but carefully, though nonpunitively, specified and enforced her expectations and limits. For the first few days, the teacher was advised to make minimal academic demands on the child, although there were certain tasks he was absolutely required to complete. Furthermore, the boy was not given an audience for an expressed request until he followed acceptable procedure. During her free periods and spare moments, the teacher spent time talking with the child, reflecting his underlying anger, and she also had him help her. At the beginning of the second week, the boy stopped the constant crying, was much less resistant to the imposed limits, and began to finish most of his school work. Subsequent weeks proved to be the happiest, most productive ones the boy had experienced since he started school.

However, with a child who is more deeply disturbed than the boy in the above illustration, the same methods might prove less effective or even ineffective. More seriously disturbed children tend to have defective egos; they have, therefore, great difficulty tolerating tension and frustration and adequately handling their hostility. Consequently, the wise teacher will attempt to learn and utilize methods that "fit the pathology" of a disturbed child.

Methods Useful with Individuals

The teacher is faced with two problems in dealing with aggression in the classroom. First, he must learn to deal effectively with the aggression problems of individual children. Second, he must handle aggression that is primarily a product of the group dynamics of the classroom. The methods to be discussed in this section are probably most useful with individual children, although some are applicable to group situations.

Before discussing methods and their potential value, a word of caution is indicated. Any method of handling a particular behavior problem is fraught with difficulties, because rarely do any two children react the same way to the same method. Furthermore, the manner in which a method is employed usually varies with the person using it, and the skill and sensitivity of that person are very influential. Therefore, in dealing with a child and his problems, one should more importantly work toward developing a satisfying relationship with the child than toward applying exactly the right method. Methods, by themselves, have no magic.

Punishment. It may seem strange that punishment is selected first as a method for handling the behavior of an aggressive child. The term "punishment" is often shocking to our emotional sensitivities and is a strongly suppressed word in the vocabularies of many "modern" educators and psychologists. However, punishment may modify behavior under some circumstances, even though the direction and significance of the modification may be highly debatable. Because its application is often confused and abused, one should attempt to analyze how and when punishment can be used effectively.

Although punishment is used by adults for a great many reasons (both conscious and unconscious), it is most effective when its use is a planned strategy to influence a child's behavior in a desirable way. Therefore, punishment is a doubtful method when one uses it in the heat of anger or with a child whose controls over impulses and feelings are inadequate. For instance, some aggressive, disturbed children have so little frustration tolerance that the use of such a technique produces disorganization. Punishment breaks down their controls further and greatly increases their existing resentment (4).

Redl and Wattenberg (3) have suggested that punishment can exert a constructive influence on a child when three conditions prevail. *First*, the behavior for which the child is punished should involve some initial conflict. That is, the child should experience some internal struggle between the unacceptable impulse and self-control. The child should recognize that his actions or behavior were not right. *Second*, there should be a positive relationship between the child who is punished and the adult who does the punishing. This means that the child must feel liked by the one who punishes him, and that person should be one upon whom he relies for affection. *Third*, the punishment should be of such a nature that the child feels it is a natural, as well as an understandable, consequence of his actions.

When these three conditions prevail, the anger produced by the punishment tends to be internalized and directed toward that part of the personality responsible for the unacceptable action, and, when his anger is so directed, the child's attention is more likely to be toward standards of conduct that are acceptable. The child is then ready for "post-situational follow-up"—helping the child work through his feelings and learn something from the unpleasant experience (3).

Nevertheless, it can never be assumed that punishment will stop a child's undesirable behavior once and for all, for learning to behave and developing control over impulses is a difficult task. When this learning task is compared with the sometimes arduous task of learning to read, the latter is dwarfed in comparison. There is, however, a distinct tendency for many to believe that one application of punishment should take care of all of a child's future behavior breaches, yet teaching a child to read is the object of systematic instruction throughout most of the elementary school years. Punishment, also, to be effective, should embody the application of the best educational principles.

Let us discuss then, in detail, methods, as well as some of the pitfalls, of using punishment in handling aggressive behavior. Redl and Wattenberg (3) have pointed out that many things can go wrong with punishment. For example, the relationship between the child and the punisher may be so poor that the punishment simply incites more anger and resentment in the child, or the child may not have a sense of wrongdoing so that punishment does not increase his desire to control his behavior. Furthermore, punishment may greatly add to his disturbances or existing emotional burdens when the child is incapable of consciously controlling his actions. Moreover, punishment may inadvertently act as a reward. It may bestow status on the child who dares to rebel against a teacher who is generally disliked by the group.

Before it is used with the aggressive child, the teacher should establish conditions under which punishment has some chance of bringing about favorable educational and behavioral outcomes. If it is not a planned strategy, it should never be used. Certainly, it should never be employed with a child who is so disturbed that he cannot, of his own volition, change his behavior. Moreover, if punishment fails to yield desirable results after a reasonable period of time, it should be stopped.

"Signal interference." This is a technique through which one can communicate to a child who is beginning to misbehave that his behavior is not acceptable. The signal may be a gesture, such as waving a finger or shaking the head, or a verbal command that indicates to the child that the developing behavior should be terminated (4).

There is no magic, of course, in the use of a signal to deal with the behavior of an aggressive child. Its use is based on a sound principle and, if its applications are understood, can be helpful in handling the aggressive child. The principle is that, if the beginning misbehavior or arising disorganization in a child is discovered soon enough, a signal may block or help prevent a full eruption. A signal should indicate to a child that he must be vigilant and prepared to end his misbehavior. Furthermore, once he receives the signal, he should be expected to control his own behavior.

Signals, then, are best used in the beginning stages of misbehavior. In the earlier stages of misconduct, the child is more capable of exercising control over his behavior. Signals are not effective when a child's misbehavior has progressed far enough to mobilize his aggression to a high level. Moreover, signal interference will have little effect when employed by a person who has a poor relationship with the child.

In addition, signal interference may prevent excessive hostility in a child, and any technique that avoids the build-up of hostility is a useful tool. Then too, if something is done to stop the child before his anger explodes, one can avoid other, more severe, methods that may be punitive and damaging to the child.

The teacher can make this technique more effective if he endeavors to learn which situations, activities, and circumstances at school are most frustrating or provocative to the aggressive child. What times during the day does he seem to be most aggressive? What types of incidents set him off? If the teacher is aware of situations that tend to be most provocative, he can be ready with a signal and quickly redirect the child before he is involved in aggressive misconduct.

"Proximity and touch control." Any teacher who has taught children for a period of time has probably observed that his physical nearness to a child helps that child maintain control over his behavior. Perhaps the proximity helps the child avoid certain temptations, enhances his vigilance over his behavior, or gives him added personal strength. Whatever the reason, physical proximity does help a child maintain control. Similarly, a friendly touch or pat from the teacher helps the distraught child maintain balance in a difficult situation (4).

This technique, of course, is not new; most experienced teachers have probably used it with some success. Proximity and touch control work best with young children in situations that are too frustrating or too tempting for their control systems to handle, and there are many such school situations. Consider the difficulty some children have in lining up and walking to the auditorium for some special event.

Some of the more active or aggressive children cannot resist the temptation to push, hit, or shove if left to their own devices, or they may be unable to resist playing or running in the auditorium. In such circumstances, the teacher can help the children control their impulses by utilizing proximity and touch control. For example, he instructs the children who are likely to have the most difficulty to walk with or near him to the auditorium. He might even hold the hands of children who have the least control of their impulses. In the auditorium, he gives these children more support by seating them by or near him throughout the activity.

Skillful teachers also use the technique frequently to deal with some of the routine situations in the classroom. For instance, a teacher may seat a misbehaving child near his desk or place the restless, hyperactive youngster near him in the reading circle; moreover, the teacher may amble back to a pupil's seat and stand for a while until he settles down to a newly assigned lesson.

There are circumstances, however, when the touch-control approach does not apply and the teacher should be cognizant of them. For instance, some children who have had very unfortunate experiences with adults react to the touch of another with great negativism. They resent any physical contact and will go to some length to avoid it. Obviously, under these circumstances, the teacher should not use touch control. Similarly, with children of certain ages and those of the opposite sex, the teacher should be very cautious. For instance, girls in the upper elementary grades and those of high school age may not interpret a friendly pat or squeeze of the hand by a man teacher in the manner it is intended.

The technique of proximity and touch control, like signal interference, has advantages because its use is not likely to lead to secondary complications. That is, contrary to punishment or other high pressure tactics, its use does not ignite poorly controlled hostility or destroy an existing good relationship with a child. Moreover, this technique can be applied without disrupting the on-going class activity of the other children or in other ways involving them.

"Hurdle help." The child with poor control over his aggression is unduly affected by frustrating situations, and a minimum amount of frustration will frequently trigger a very angry, aggressive reaction in the child, regardless of how much he desires not to give vent to his anger.

Schools abound with situations that can provoke aggressive episodes in the more vulnerable child. For instance, there are many rules and regulations that are necessary to the orderly functioning of groups, but the aggressive child may have difficulty conforming to them. Then too, the aggressive, disturbed child often has difficulty with the academic program. He usually cannot focus his attention and interest as long as his "normal" classmates, and long assignments, with little intrinsic interest, have a disconcerting effect on this child. Similarly, competitive challenges and other situations that expose his inadequacies can trigger aggressive actions.

Hurdle help is a technique to prepare a child for or support him in a frustrating situation to prevent his loss of control. For instance, a child may have an arithmetic assignment that is too difficult for his present level of skill, and the more he works on the problems the more frustrated and upset he becomes. If he is left to his own devices and his controls are inadequate, he may quickly respond with anger to the frustration. However, if the teacher is alert to the child's plight and gives him the hurdle help he needs, both child and teacher may be spared a fit of temper (4).

Let us consider another situation. Suppose that an aggressive child prides himself in being one of the best baseball players in the class. He is excited about the prospects of being chosen as a member of the class baseball team. Furthermore, because he feels that he has considerable facility at baseball, he has convinced himself that he is the most likely prospect to be chosen captain of the team. However, since this decision is made by the team members, there is considerable doubt that this boy will be chosen because his aggressive behavior has not made him very popular with the group. The teacher, recognizing from the child's comments that he will be sadly disappointed if he is not made captain, will need to prepare the child for the possibility that he may not be chosen. The teacher may do this by helping the child better appraise the realities involved and, later, by helping him deal with his feelings when he comes face to face with the actual reality of not being chosen.

Giving a child hurdle help does nothing to cure his pre-existing disturbance, but it often helps him face the frustrations arising from specific situations or experiences. Moreover, it is an effective preventive measure, because it helps the child maintain balance and helps the teacher avoid having to deal with the more serious behavior that would arise if this technique were not employed.

"*Antiseptic bouncing.*" With some disturbed children, there are times when most interference techniques fail to produce the desired results. For instance, a child's behavior may become so disturbed and out of control that he may go into a severe temper tantrum. Faced with this behavior, the teacher must act immediately but still maintain control over the situation.

In such a crisis, a useful technique for the teacher to employ is antiseptic bouncing. This technique is simply a means of removing a child from the excitement or the scene of confusion so that he may regain control. The word "antiseptic" implies that removal is not punishment but a planned strategy to help the child regain his composure away from the scene of excitement (4).

This technique is particularly useful when (a) a child's actions may be harmful or injurious to others, (b) his behavior may have a contagious effect on the other children, and (c) it is clearly evident that the child needs an effective demonstration of limits (4).

Since this method is commonly employed in school situations as a last resort measure and in the heat of anger, it is important to emphasize a caution. When the teacher uses the technique, the offender, as well as his classmates, is likely to view the action as ostracism or punishment; consequently, it is not likely to have beneficial effects. The teacher should, instead, communicate to the offender and to the other children in the group that the child is being moved to help him regain his control. Furthermore, it is important for the teacher to reinforce the idea that the child's recovery to more normal functioning requires a period of time in a quiet, less exciting place. Without doing this follow-up, the teacher may find that he has lost rapport with the individual offender as well as the class. Unless these conditions can be met, the technique should not be employed.

"*Restructuring.*" There are times in the classroom when individuals and groups become over-excited, too highly stimulated, or even wild. When this situation arises (either with individuals or the total group), it is a signal to the teacher to go into action before things get out of hand. It is very helpful in this circumstance for the teacher to change quickly the nature of the activity or the focus of the group. Such a procedure is much more effective than focusing on the behavior of a child or the group. In this situation, "talking at children" or verbalizing threats is not likely to perform the controlling function for which it is intended (4).

A change of activity or a new focus helps children to rechannel their energies in more constructive directions. A boring history lesson can be changed to a TV program involving some type of quiz. A mass exodus to the school auditorium for a special event can be better organized by asking the children to pretend they are "soldiers on parade" (3).

This technique can work effectively with individual children also. Some children, because of emotional difficulties, are unable to concentrate or have poor frustration tolerance and cannot focus on class activities very long. They need acceptable motor outlets and activity changes before forbidden activities beckon them too strongly. So, when a teacher notices that a particular child has begun to "bog down," he redirects the child's attention and interest by permitting him to participate in a new activity. This activity may be simply to perform an errand, to walk outside to get a drink of water, or an opportunity to involve himself in one of the interest centers around the room. With a little ingenuity the thoughtful teacher can readily devise other methods of restructuring individual and group activity in ways that are extremely beneficial. Use of this technique, like some of the others discussed, does not create some of the side effects that other high-pressure tactics involve.

"Feeling-Oriented Discussions." Although this technique or therapeutic avenue has been mentioned in other contexts, it is discussed again because it is helpful in dealing with the covert feelings of aggression that can be disruptive to group process. The technique is often referred to in popular parlance as a "gripe session." It has as its objective the draining off of irritations or anger that sooner or later must be reckoned with. This method simply provides a child (or children) an opportunity to discuss openly some submerged feelings that otherwise may appear in undesirable and disruptive behavior. It can be useful as a group procedure or employed with problem children privately.

The stimulus for, or the initiation of, a discussion of this kind can evolve around some classroom problem, films that portray common problems of children, or stories that epitomize problems of children in the class. An example is one situation in a classroom in which a Negro boy had become the object of aggression by several of the other children in the class. I discussed the problem with the teacher and we decided that a film that emphatically portrayed individual differences would help the children gain insight into their own reactions and the feelings of the persecuted Negro boy. Presentation of the film was followed by a "feeling-oriented" discussion. Children saw the similarity between the theme of the film and the classroom problem and offered several things that could be done to improve the classroom problem.

The real value of a discussion of feelings can be realized in a classroom situation only where freedom to express feelings without censure is possible. If a teacher cannot permit such freedom, a discussion of this type should never be initiated. The experiences of teachers who have used this approach often indicate that it is well to have the children confine their discussions to specific problems or situations, rather than permitting the children to discuss all situations about which they have strong feelings. In this way the discussion is better controlled and, to the uninitiated, poses fewer problems.

This same approach works well with individual children who have many "bottled-up" aggressive feelings. As a modification to the approach, the teacher may have periodic, private sessions with a child encouraging him to express the feelings that plague him. One teacher, for example, developed a rather ingenious way of helping children express unacceptable feeling. At the beginning of each school year she passed out a notebook to each child in class and indicated to the group that the book was their "secret book." She discussed with the children that we all have feelings that cause us concern, although it often seems that no one wants to hear or discuss our feelings with us. She then told the children the secret books were provided so that they could write about any such feelings they might have and could request a private conference with the teacher any time they wished. The secret books were kept under lock and key and no one was permitted access to them except the owner. In this way, no child was forced to express his feelings in private or to experience embarrassment by expressing his feelings before the class.

The techniques, approaches, and methods discussed in this chapter, by themselves, offer no magic. However, to the thoughtful, analytical teacher, who works toward better understanding and ways to help children, these approaches may open up new vistas.

References

1. Bandura, A., and Walter, R. *Adolescent aggression.* New York: Ronald Press, 1959.

2. Cunningham, Ruth, and Associates. *Understanding group behavior of boys and girls.* New York: Bureau of Publications, Teachers College, Columbia University, 1951.

3. Redl, F., and Wattenberg, W. *Mental hygiene in teaching,* 2nd ed. New York: Harcourt, Brace & Co., 1959.

4. Redl, F., and Wineman, D. *The aggressive child.* Glencoe: The Free Press, 1957.

5. Sears, R., Maccoby, Eleanor, and Levin, H. *Patterns of child rearing.* Evanston: Row, Peterson & Co., 1957.

6. Shaffer, L., and Shoben, E. *The psychology of adjustment,* 2nd ed. Boston: Houghton Mifflin, 1956.

CHAPTER TEN

Inhibited and Withdrawn Behavior

The inhibited, withdrawn child can be observed in almost every classroom, sitting quietly, often unnoticed, wearing the mask of sameness. He lacks relatedness, stays aloof, and is frequently alone. There is a striking lack of color, spontaneity, and vitality about him. He reluctantly participates in the activities of his peers, if at all, and is generally unenthusiastic. Because he prefers to be unnamed and unnoticed, he fades inconspicuously into the larger group. His individuality is well submerged into the deeper matrix of his personality. Indeed, he has learned, all too well, to inhibit those aspects of himself that his parents and culture have taught him to fear.

Because the inhibited, withdrawn child is often polite and conforming, he is frequently believed to be something he is not. It is true that he is anxious to conform to rules, to do his work, and to perform the things that are expected of him, but these traits are often confused with healthiness or adjustment. However, extreme inhibition, or withdrawal, is not psychologically healthy, although it does represent the best compromise the child is able to make in his environment.

It should be emphasized that all children who exhibit inhibited, shy, or withdrawn behavior are not necessarily maladjusted. Inhibition and withdrawal are typical of most children at times, in certain situations, and at particular stages of development. As is true of any behavior deviation, withdrawn or inhibited behavior becomes maladaptive or serious when one uses it exclusively as a way of meeting life. In analyzing the extent to which it is maladaptive, we must determine the degree to which such behavior prevents one from developing satisfying human relationships and deters one from dealing adequately with his environment.

It is the child whose behavior is consistently and excessively withdrawn and inhibited that we wish to consider in this chapter. We will consider why he develops as he does and what can be done to help him.

DEVELOPMENTAL BACKGROUND

One of the basic problems of the inhibited, withdrawn child is his inability to relate openly and satisfactorily to others. The developmental background of such a problem is usually related to the parents' inability to establish a relationship with the child that is accepting and predictable, and, as we know, a child learns to relate to others on the basis of his relationships with his parents. The child simply transfers the essential patterns of relating which he has learned at home to all relationships outside it.

Parents fail to develop accepting, satisfying relationships with their children for many reasons. While it is not appropriate to explore the subtleties and complexities of the reasons here, it should be noted that the parents' difficulties generally arise from experiences originating in their own childhood, rendering them incapable of loving their child or meeting his needs.

A second cause for a child's developing inhibited, withdrawn behavior may be his parents' tendency to look upon him as an extension of themselves. In this instance, the parents use the child to meet their own important but usually unconscious needs. He is regarded as a possession to be molded and utilized to bring credit and status to the

parents, and in order to meet these parental aspirations, he is urged or forced to become the model child, to embrace academic excellence, or to be exceptional in some other way. The result is that usually the expectations are beyond the child's mental, physical, or emotional capabilities, and the more inappropriate the demands, the more frequently the child fails and the more upset the parents become. Consequently, it is natural for the child to retreat, escape, or withdraw from demands, situations, or activities that endanger success and subsequent loss of love (7).

Since the parental expectations are beyond the child's capacity, he has a chronic fear of failure, and his failures are frequent; this leads to feelings of inadequacy and low self-evaluation. Thus, the child becomes even more inhibited, shy, and withdrawn (1).

A third major reason for inhibited, withdrawn behavior is a pattern of parental discipline that is rigid, harsh, and unreasonable (3). Under these circumstances, the parents demand obedience, conformity, and non-aggression, and the child learns to place rigid controls on his feelings and impulses. Indeed, if he is punished enough, he may decide that all impulses are dangerous. Therefore, the child carries a heavy burden of anxiety and rigidly inhibits all behavior that is socially unacceptable.

There is a variation of this pattern that is probably not so openly harsh or punitive but is none the less devastating. The variation is a pattern of hypercriticalness. This parent may not be punitive in disciplinary methods but is constantly critical, and the child's every action is so critically appraised that his performance never quite measures up to the high expectations of his parents. This strategy is often subtle and may be accompanied by an "enlightened" child-rearing orientation on the part of the parents. However, almost inevitably this parent will first praise the child's action and then nullify the praise by a concluding critical comment.

Another dimension of parent-child relationships that may cause a child to develop inhibited, withdrawn behavior is inconsistency. In this instance, structure in the parent-child relationship is lacking; limits are poorly defined or inconsistent, depending upon the temperament, mood, or impulse of the parent. The child never quite knows what his parents expect of him; therefore, he does not know which impulses he can safely express or which actions they will approve, and in order to deal with the anxiety that this treatment produces, the child inhibits and withdraws.

Parental overanxiousness is a fourth basic condition that is often associated with inhibition and withdrawal in children. Overanxious parents relate to their child, as well as the world, in a very apprehensive way. The child is aware of his parents' apprehension and, through conditioning, becomes apprehensive himself; consequently, the world becomes to him a dangerous place, and he tends to withdraw from it. Furthermore, if a child sees constant apprehension in his parents, he may give up active exploration of many things in his environment and let his parents test reality for him.

Some of the ways in which the inhibited, withdrawn child copes with his environment were mentioned when various causal factors were discussed. In fact, the terms inhibition and withdrawal are, themselves, basic coping modes. Nagelberg et al. (6) found in their analysis of withdrawn children that withdrawal is a defense against an over-stimulating parental environment. For example, children, by withdrawing from close emotional relationships, are better able to control impulses that are tempted by an over-stimulating environment and, therefore, need not act out destructive drives toward their parents.

Furthermore, when a child does not gain emotional satisfaction in his relationships with his parents, he feels that it is simply not rewarding to develop attachments to others, and, being disappointed and ungratified, he retreats into himself. He attempts to seek from himself the satisfactions he has been denied from others; thus, the child may develop an intimate, private world of daydreams, fantasy, or imagination, where he is king, and the pain he has experienced in the real world is absent. Indeed, in his play the child may even treat his toy soldiers as if they were real people, and if his dissatisfactions or disappointments have been extreme, his world of fantasy may even gradually replace reality.

On the other hand, some children who have had these or similar experiences may use slightly different coping methods. For instance, instead of erecting an elaborate fantasy world, a child may withdraw into stubborn self-sufficiency. This child, being ungratified in relationships with his parents, shuts them out completely and attempts to convince himself that he needs no one. The child becomes angry when people try to get close to him because he cannot tolerate the hurt that on-again-off-again love entails.

Typically, the child who has experienced harsh, authoritarian discipline places great reliance on denial, suppression, or repression. He erects an impenetrable defense to keep unacceptable impulses and feelings out of consciousness; his personality and behavior become rigid, and he carefully charts every move, attempting to deliver a flawless performance. This child's adjustment becomes one of extreme compliance, and he inevitably has an excessive amount of hostility stored behind repressive defenses. He is in constant fear that his resentment will be expressed; consequently, he is chronically anxious. Sometimes his hostility is directed against himself, and the child develops various kinds of psychosomatic disorders.

Besides the intrapsychic problems that the inhibited, withdrawn child has, there are others closely related to his school performance and peer adjustment. In his search for certainty, he may show a distinct preference for subjects that are structured and devoid of emotional connotations, such as mathematics. Numbers, unlike words, are not emotionally tinged, and they tend not to stir up repressed thoughts.

Depending upon the exact dynamics of his withdrawal, a child may escape from social and emotional investment by directing his energy into academic overcompensation. He seeks through this medium the acceptance, status, and self-esteem that he has failed to get from warm interpersonal relationships. He becomes a "brain" and patterns his life around intellectualization.

Furthermore, some inhibited, withdrawn children will have difficulty with certain subjects. For example, a child who must shut out or avoid much of his environment in order to feel safe may have difficulty in learning to read or comprehending deeper levels of meaning. In as much as reading is the process of bringing meaning to and getting meaning from printed symbols, a child who avoids or shuts out his world has a restricted amount of experience from which to form concepts and relate to ideas represented in print. Since broad experience is the raw material from which ideas that are symbolized in print are understood, it is understandable why a withdrawn child may have difficulty with this phase of the curriculum.

This child may also be greatly handicapped in his social or interpersonal skill learning that is so much a part of active peer-group participation. He misses out on the role playing so characteristic of children's groups and, as a result, he may be totally unprepared to assume adult-group roles. Unfortunately, his peer-group isolation increases in magnitude with each succeeding year, because the more deficient he is in social skill learning, the more socially isolated he becomes. Moreover, this social isolation makes it difficult for him to integrate himself into the group at a later age.

It can be seen, then, that the difficulties with which the inhibited, withdrawn child must cope are extensive. Depending on his developmental background and his particular psychological dynamics, the child learns to cope in unique, individualized ways. In general, however, his inhibition and withdrawal are often associated with coping measures that are characterized by escape, avoidance, emotional constriction and insulation, a shutting out or distortion of reality, immersion into fantasy and denial, suppression, and repression.

Regardless of the coping methods the child uses, they represent the most effective compromise he can make, considering his environment. Although his coping behavior may prevent him from satisfying some of his basic psychological needs, his defenses help to contain or repress impulses that would jeopardize his safety. Therefore, as long as the child is not subjected to greater stress or deprivation, he may maintain a fairly stable, if not wholesome, adjustment.

Morris, Soroker, and Burrus (5) did a follow-up study of fifty-four withdrawn children who were seen in the Dallas Child Guidance Center sixteen to twenty-seven years before. They were able to obtain fairly adequate follow-up information on thirty-four and less substantial information on twenty. Based on the information acquired on the thirty-four, they classified 64.7 per cent as satisfactorily adjusted, 33 per cent as marginally adjusted, and only one person was considered seriously ill. The investigators found that the subjects had maintained the quiet, inhibited personality features which characterized them earlier. Although the subjects had sought employment that was somewhat sheltered, they were generally stable and self-supporting. They valued job security and did not seek advancement or greater job opportunity. The better adjusted subjects had selected marital partners who were more outgoing and aggressive; consequently, it was possible for them to compensate for their personality difficulties through their spouses.

HELPING THE WITHDRAWN CHILD AT SCHOOL

It should be clear from the discussion of etiological factors that helping the inhibited, withdrawn child requires an understanding of the forces that move him to adapt in his unique way. Insight, then, is needed into the child's stresses and strains or his manner of relating and coping, as he attempts to maintain some type of equilibrium. With this understanding, one is able to individualize the child's program and instigate antiseptic and remedial measures.

Even though treatment should be individualized, certain principles and procedures are useful in working with this deviant behavior pattern. Let us underline the most basic principle first. That is, the degree to which the teacher can be helpful is based primarily on the quality of the teacher-child relationship. Therefore, the teacher's initial step is that of structuring a relationship in which the child can feel safe and comfortable. This is the most basic requirement because the child is not free to make emotional investments, develop social relatedness, or release his impulses and energies until he feels the safety and trust that stem from a predictable relationship.

A predictable relationship is one that is consistent, emotionally even, and dependable. Obviously, to establish such a relationship, one must avoid vacillation in feeling and behavior and consistently deliver on all promises expressed through words, gestures, or feelings. Only in such a relationship can a child feel secure enough to express his deeper self.

The teacher must not rush in and emotionally overwhelm the child, because his trust in emotionally close relationships will develop slowly, and, to a considerable extent, the child must set the pace. Furthermore, the teacher should avoid bringing the child out all at once or giving him the limelight prematurely (6, 7). His recitation before the class should not be forced, and criticism, ridicule, and punishment should be avoided. While the teacher is watching for signs of extroversion in the child, he should be generous with

words of encouragement and acceptance.

On the other hand, the docile, conforming, obedient behavior of the inhibited, withdrawn child should not be
reinforced by lavish praise. Indiscriminate praise tends only to reward the
behavior that the teacher wishes to
modify. Also, if the teacher openly
praises the child's conforming, obedient behavior in front of his classmates, it may be even more difficult
for him to integrate himself into the
classroom or peer group. Instead, he
may be placed in the category of
"teacher's pet" and avoided by other
children. Therefore, the teacher should
use praise to encourage the child whenever he shows any signs of individuality, initiative, or sociability.

Moreover, the teacher may be helpful to the withdrawn child by encouraging him, through any special aptitude
he may have, to be of service to others
(2). Helping others provides the child
with a valid basis for establishing relationships with classmates. The help he
is able to give to others will also ele-
vate the child's self-concept because it
will demonstrate to him that he has
attributes that are valued by his group.

We have already stated that although the inhibited, withdrawn child
is generally eager to do what the teacher
expects, he may encounter problems
with studies because of the dynamics
underlying his maladaptive behavior.
We also know that he searches for order and structure and may be easily
upset if he is uncertain about the
teacher's expectations, the performance of routine duties, and class assignments. Because he is withdrawn
and inhibited, he may not, however,
ask the teacher for clarification, direction, or help. Therefore, it is imperative that the teacher specify exactly

what is expected and make sure the
child understands how to perform assigned duties, studies, and projects. In
addition, it is also important for the
teacher to prepare this child to meet
new or strange situations by pointing
out to him what he might expect (4).

The teacher may also help this child
learn to participate in group work by
starting him in pair relationships or
small groups. Then, when the child
feels comfortable in pair or small-group
relationships, the size of his group can
be gradually increased. Obviously, if he
is placed in a large group without preparation, the inhibited, withdrawn child
is overwhelmed, and he simply retreats
into his familiar withdrawing pattern.
Similarly, the teacher should, in the
beginning, place this child with children that are somewhat like him in
personality composition. Aggressive,
outspoken or dominating group members tend to make the inhibited, withdrawn child even more inactive and
closed to participation (2).

After the withdrawn child has developed confidence and trust in his teacher
and when he feels comfortable in the
group, the teacher can then take more
active steps to increase his participation. One step is helping the child build
self-confidence. As the child begins to
respond with less inhibition to the
group, he needs to experience success
in it. For example, if he expresses a
desire to make a presentation to the
class, the child must thoroughly master
it before he presents it to the group.
Some rehearsal with the child can help
him to master his presentation, and,
at the same time, the teacher can
inspire both confidence and courage
in the child.

Furthermore, the teacher, besides
being sensitive to the inhibited child
and watching for signs of his emotional

readiness to become actively involved in the group, may encourage him in various types of self-expression. The inhibited, withdrawn child, as we have noted, tends to be bottled up emotionally, and he needs outlets for his feelings. There are a number of mediums through which the teacher may help the child express his feelings. For instance, the teacher can encourage the child to express himself through drawing, painting, writing, pantomime, and puppetry. It is important, however, that such expression not be forced and that the child's productions be accepted. Later, when the personal relationship with the child has developed to a point where he feels safe, the teacher may help the child label or verbalize the feelings that his productions symbolize. For example, the teacher may say to the child, "Tell me how the person in your drawing feels today," or "It looks like the boy in the drawing is very angry (sad, etc.) today." By this indirect approach, the teacher avoids interpreting the child's unacceptable feelings or attributing them to him. This approach also allows the child to attribute his unacceptable feelings to the person in his drawing, yet he recognizes that the teacher knows how he feels. This recognition creates a deeper tie between the teacher and child because it makes him aware that the teacher accepts him and his "bad" feelings.

All of these ways of relating to and helping the child provide the opportunity for him to feel better about himself and to move toward a more wholesome adjustment. Nevertheless, the degree to which any teacher can help a child depends, to a great extent, upon the severity of that child's difficulties and the extent to which his parents are able to involve themselves in the helping process. In regard to the parents, therefore, it is essential that the teacher establish a good relationship with them and endeavor to help them understand the child's behavior, as well as more positive ways to help him. If the school has a counselor or psychologist, his assistance can be invaluable and should be utilized, especially in difficult situations.

In as much as the inhibited, withdrawn pattern is often the developmental pattern from which serious disturbance may later develop, careful assessment of the severity of a child's maladjustment is very important. In this regard, the teacher may find help, in evaluating a child's difficulties, from the criteria discussed in Chapter five. Also, if the school staff includes a psychologist, he is well qualified to perform such evaluations.

A CASE ILLUSTRATION

The following case helps to illustrate some of the background factors and personality dynamics that are often associated with the inhibited, withdrawn child. The case is that of a nine-year-old, fourth-grade girl who was referred to the school psychologist by her teacher, who was concerned about the girl's general adjustment and school progress. For purposes of reference, the subject will be referred to as Jane.

When Jane first appeared for psychological examination, she seemed somewhat frightened and very inhibited in behavior and speech. She maintained a rigid posture, did not smile throughout the examination, and was most reluctant to volunteer anything about her general life circumstances.

She responded only to direct questions and her answers were always unelaborated and to the point.

Jane's teacher had described her as follows:

She is very shy, dependent, and afraid of responsibility. She never volunteers in class. She is dependent on adults for almost all decisions. While she is attentive in class, she is afraid to participate in class discussions. She is accepted by two of the eight girls in class but remains a follower even in this limited relationship. At the present time she is under-achieving. She is very careful not to make mistakes.

Jane's school records and earlier test results indicated that she was having difficulty with academic work. On the Stanford Achievement Test at the beginning of the current year, she obtained a median grade-placement score of 3.2. Her scores on the Otis Intelligence Test, administered in February of the previous year, gave her a mental age of 8–4 and an IQ of 97. On the Wechsler Intelligence Scale for Children she obtained the following scores: Verbal Scale IQ, 90; Performance Scale IQ, 99; Full Scale IQ, 93. Her performance on the subtests indicated that her greatest difficulty was with the Comprehension and Similarities sections.

An interview with the mother revealed several factors that were intimately related to Jane's present difficulties. She was the first of two adopted children, both of whom were girls. The mother indicated that Jane had always been a somewhat inhibited, shy child. Her physical development had not been particularly unusual, although the mother did report that Jane had asthma attacks dating back to early infancy and that she developed an ulcer at five years

of age. She walked, talked, and developed bladder and bowel control at the ages when these controls are usually expected. Because Jane's natural mother was reported to have had some difficulty in delivery, the possibility of brain damage was suggested by the family physician. However, a neurological evaluation, including an EEG, did not reveal any abnormalities.

The relatively severe asthma attacks had restricted Jane's activity with other children. The family doctor had advised the parents to restrict her from vigorous, active play. As a matter of fact, during the early months of her life, the family physician had cautioned the mother not to let Jane out of her sight.

Both parents seemed to have a sincere regard for the child, and because they had been unable to have children of their own, they felt that it was an exceptional privilege to be granted the right to adopt children. In a sense, it would be accurate to say that the mother was overly devoted to the care of Jane and her sister.

The parents' general child-rearing orientation can be described as rigid and strict, if not authoritarian. Jane was expected to obey all restrictions and directives issued by the parents. She was immediately punished for talking back or deviating from parental expectations, and their expectations appeared to be extremely high in almost all areas of behavior and performance.

With this background material, let us analyze Jane's problems. Several factors stand out immediately. The history of asthma and an ulcer at a young age are especially noteworthy. One may speculate on the degree to which physical or psychological factors contributed to the development of Jane's physical problems; the projective tests (Bender Visual Motor Gestalt, TAT, and Draw-A-Person), however, indicated a substantial psychological basis. The child seemed to rely on denial, repression, and projection as psychological defenses. Impulses were carefully controlled and the child placed an extremely high premium on being obedient and "good"; however, at a deeper level, she had a considerable amount of hostility which was carefully contained behind repressive defenses.

Jane's marked inhibition and tendency to withdraw from others seems related to her overly strict, confining environment. Of course, her physical confinement, as a result of asthma, further restricted Jane's attempts to deal with her physical and social environment. The rigid and strict parental controls also contributed to Jane's fear of her environment, her marked dependency, feelings of inadequacy, and inability to accept responsibility. Furthermore, the parental expectations and control methods caused Jane to question her parents' acceptance of her; consequently, she could not entirely trust relationships with others. Inhibition and withdrawal from close relationships provided a fair degree of safety for Jane and were the adaptive modes that were most workable for her.

However, besides her obvious withdrawal, inhibition, and physical problems, Jane was handicapped in other ways. For instance, she was unable to utilize her intellectual resources to perform acceptable academic pursuits. Her achievement test results indicated academic retardation of approximately one year. The subtest scores on the individual intelligence test revealed that Jane lacked the ability to make adequate judgments, abstractions, or concept for-

mations. Because her defensive structure (particularly the use of repression) prevented her from utilizing past experiences, it naturally followed that she would have difficulty in developing concepts, in reasoning, and in making adequate judgments. Her limited experience also contributed to these deficiencies. Feelings of inadequacy caused her to anticipate failure in most of the tasks she undertook; therefore, she could not respond to school work with confidence. In view of all these pressures upon her, Jane's behavior and coping methods were understandably necessary to her survival.

Some of the crucial aspects of the parents' contributions to Jane's problems have already been noted. However, it is necessary to consider why the parents may have used the child-rearing methods they did, for one must understand and evaluate the reasons for the parents' attitudes and methods in order to help them help the child. Evaluation revealed that both parents were rigid, authoritarian personalities with strict controls over their own impulses. They had very rigid moral and religious philosophies regarding good and evil, right and wrong, and these attitudes reflected rather tyrannical superego structures in the personalities of both parents. Their methods of dealing with the world and their own impulses were readily applied to their child-rearing methods with Jane. Consequently, Jane had to incorporate her parents' standards of behavior in order to avoid more anxiety in her parents and the threat of losing their love.

The parents' inability to have children (which may have been psychologically based) created attitudes, especially in the mother, that were also detrimental to Jane. First, because she felt that her privilege to adopt a child had been sanctioned by higher authority, the mother was especially sensitive to the importance of raising a "good" child. Therefore, from the very beginning Jane was over-valued, carefully trained, and ushered into strict socialization procedures. Second, the mother had a great deal of anxiety in relation to the care and training of Jane, which was evident in her manner of protecting, supervising, and controlling the child. Also, because of her own emotional needs, the mother went to extremes to make certain that nothing happened to Jane. Consequently, the mother's pattern of over-protection, mixed with anxiety, undoubtedly contributed to the early development of Jane's problems. It is obvious, then, that the problems of the parents entered into their relationships with Jane to create her problems.

In view of these dynamics, what was done to help the child? First, it was necessary to help the parents gain some understanding of their own problems, particularly those problems which affected their relationships with Jane. In addition, the parents were helped to understand some of the child's needs. For example, efforts were made to help the parents realize that their extreme controls and demands created and fostered Jane's dependency and anxiety, thus robbing her of the opportunity to develop self-direction. It was explained also that Jane could not feel adequate unless she was helped to develop the confidence to utilize her own capacities. Consequently, the parents were encouraged to relax some of their controls and demands. They were also encouraged to help Jane develop social skills by allowing her to invite a friend to their home on weekends, and, later, when she felt more secure, the parents should encourage Jane to go to her friends' homes for short visits or weekends.

In addition, it was suggested that the parents allow Jane more opportunity to express, without censure, some of her negative, angry feelings when she was thwarted or frustrated. It was also recommended that the parents make a special effort to reward Jane for small accomplishments and to avoid criticism or disapproval for her failures. This recommendation was an important one to help Jane build a more adequate self-concept and was strongly emphasized to the parents.

Jane's background and the reasons for her behavior were interpreted to her teacher, who was asked to arrange a school program for Jane in which she could not fail. Jane was also to be given' more opportunity to work on classroom activities with the two girls who liked her and whom she liked. In addition, the teacher was asked to give Jane a few status responsibilities, some to be done after school. This was to provide both the teacher and the child an opportunity to develop a closer relationship. However, Jane was to be allowed to set the pace, and the teacher was advised not to overwhelm her with "affection" until Jane was ready to develop a closer relationship.

Jane did make progress in coming out of her shell, interacting with her peers, and relating to others in a healthier manner. However, the parents experienced difficulty in changing their strict, controlling ways. Even so, Jane was a healthier child at the end of the year than she was at the beginning.

If the most desirable treatment plan could have been implemented, both the parents and the child would have been placed in psychotherapy. However, for personal and financial reasons, the parents were unable to accept psychotherapy. Therefore, an alternate plan that was possible, considering the time, resources, and insight of the people involved, had to be implemented.

The case of Jane is illustrative of thousands of other children in classrooms throughout the country. They are children with deep conflicts that are not always recognized or understood. Yet, before these children can realize their potentialities, they need assistance in learning to handle their anxieties, fears, and inhibitions.

References

1. Bonney, M. E. *Mental health in education.* Boston: Allyn and Bacon, 1960.

2. Detjen, E. W., and Detjen, Mary F. *Elementary school guidance.* New York: McGraw-Hill, 1952.

3. Hymes, J. L. *Teacher listen child speak.* New York: New York Commission on Mental Hygiene, 1949, pp. 1–44.

4. McHugh, G. *Developing your child's personality.* New York: Appleton-Century-Crofts, 1947.

5. Morris, D. F., Soroker, Eleanor, and Burrus, Genette. Follow-up studies of shy, withdrawn children: Evaluation of later adjustment. *Amer. J. Orthopsychiat.*, 1954, XXIV, 743–754.

6. Nagelberg, L., Spotnitz, H., and Feldman, Yonata. The attempt at healthy insulation in a withdrawn child. *Amer. J. Orthopsychiat.*, 1953, XXIII, 238–252.

7. Ross, Helen. *The shy child.* New York: Public Affairs pamphlet, 1956, No. 239.

CHAPTER ELEVEN

School Phobia

School phobia is defined as a child's excessive fear of going to school. This phobia is different from the young child's reluctance to go to school, because it is not uncommon for some children who are beginning school for the first time to be resistant or reluctant. Such reluctance is usually due to a child's difficulty in adjusting to a new and strange situation, as well as leaving the security of home. Normally such a child will respond to gentle firmness, and, in a short period of time (usually a week or two), the child will make the adjustment and be quite willing to attend school.

School phobia is a much more serious problem, and, as evidenced by the fact that the term "school phobia" first appeared in professional literature in 1941, the concept is relatively recent in origin (3). This phobia is not limited to the young but is seen clinically in children from five to seventeen years of age, and the condition is much more complex than a simple reluctance to go to school. Rather, it is characterized by extreme fear and sometimes even panic. Although the symptoms may vary with a particular child, the symptomatology is relatively standard. Symptoms often appear rather dramatically in children whom teachers describe as "well adjusted." For example, a child with school phobia may suddenly become very resistant to the prospect of leaving home. When he approaches the classroom, he may exhibit a pronounced fear reaction, by trembling or verbalizing various physical complaints such as nausea, headache, or sore throat. Breathing may be labored, and the child may exhibit a strong need to take flight.

Besides a strong fear of school, a child may manifest other fears or phobias, such as fear of dogs, the toilet, the school lunchroom, noises, and adult strangers. Although a particular child usually does not have all of these fears, he may exhibit some of them in various combinations. These associated fears, as well as the phobic reaction to school, indicate that a child is reacting to something more than school.

Unfortunately, those who do not understand or recognize school phobia in a child often regard the behavior as the antics of a spoiled child. It is true that some children who are resistant to school do not have school phobia; however, one should always consider such a possibility when a child is fearful of school. The problems of school phobia are very complex, and lack of understanding often leads one to very inappropriate handling of the child with this problem. For example, when the assumption is made that the child with school phobia is simply spoiled, he is often forced to conform to behavior that is impossible for him and detrimental to his psychological well being. The child's symptoms are very real and reflect considerable anxiety and suffering; therefore, he needs a great deal more help than talk or discipline.

PHOBIAS AND PARENT-CHILD RELATIONSHIPS

As is typical of most behavior deviations in children, school phobia has its roots in past parent-child relationships. Understanding this child's relationship to his mother is particularly essential if one is to gain insight into his problem. Some clinicians who have studied this reaction consider it to be a phobia in which a child's anxiety becomes detached from his earlier life situations and is displaced onto school as a neurotic fear (4). According to those clini-

cians, the child is not fearful of going to school or of some special aspect of school but is fearful of separation from his mother. The term school phobia, according to them, is in reality a misnomer because the child's real fear is of letting his mother out of sight.

There is considerable agreement among those who have studied school phobia regarding the nature of the mother-child relationship. One of the more comprehensive studies, done by Waldfogel, Collidge, and Hahn (5), has elucidated these relationships particularly well. This analysis suggests, as have others, that mothers of children with school phobia make strong identifications and affectional attachments to them as an attempt to gain vicarious satisfactions, which the mothers have been unable to attain in past or present relationships. For instance, a child is often used as an object for disguised (unconscious) erotic or sexual gratifications, and this appears to be particularly true if the child is of the opposite sex. Consequently, the mother is overprotective and controlling as a means of dealing with her own resulting anxiety. She is also solicitous of the child's welfare, is subservient to him and his desires, and generally allows him to experience little deprivation. The mother, in other words, overcompensates by protecting the child from frustration, shock, and pain, because she feels inadequate in her maternal role.

Furthermore, mothers of children with school phobia vacillate in their approach to child rearing. For example, a mother may be strict one minute and lenient the next, or she may be affectionate one minute and scolding the next. Furthermore, when the mother's attempts to reason with the child fail, she resorts to pleading or nagging, and when she uses physical punishment the mother destroys any possible effectiveness of the punishment.

Apparently, the basic disturbance in the mother-child relationship is due to the mother's own unresolved problems. Many mothers of children with school phobia have experienced, in their own childhood, similar phobic reactions. Moreover, it is fairly common to find that these mothers have a history of unresolved dependency conflicts involving their own mothers, so that they too had a problem in emancipating themselves from their mothers.

The father of a child with school phobia is less directly involved in the child's difficulty. He may, however, express the same anxious concern about the child and often attempt to prove to his wife that he is more adequate than she to handle the child, and his attitudes, incidentally, further undermine the mother's confidence and security in her role. In addition, the father, like the mother, vacillates in handling and rearing the child, and his paternal position, as well as his sex identification, is frequently ill-defined. Both parents appear to have strong dependency needs, and their sexual adjustment may be unsatisfactory. In fact, in a large percentage of cases, the total marital relationship is generally unsatisfactory.

THE DYNAMICS OF SCHOOL PHOBIA

It should be restated, for emphasis, that the unresolved conflicts and problems of the parents are projected and interwoven into the parent-child relationship and the phobic reactions of the child with school phobia. The child's emotional development is seriously hampered because the relationship between the mother and himself has made him markedly dependent upon her. The mother's constant solicitousness toward the child makes him self-centered, demanding, and omnipotent. Yet, the child's extreme dependency upon the mother causes him to feel that he is helpless and alone without her, which seriously restricts the child's autonomy and makes him feel incomplete without his mother.

The child's numerous demands upon the mother further emphasize her own inadequacies, which create ambivalence and resentment in her. Her ambivalence is revealed in her vacillation in handling the child. The mother's ambivalence and resentment perpetuate anger and hostility in the child, because he senses, without understanding, his mother's difficulty in accepting him and his demands. Unfortunately, the child cannot directly express his hostility because of fear of losing his mother completely and, thus, of being alone and helpless. The child resolves his dilemma by displacing his hostile wishes toward the mother onto some other person or object. Thus, the school becomes the phobic object.

Why is the child fearful of leaving his mother or letting her out of his sight? Great anxiety is created in the child if he does not stay close to his mother to reassure himself that his hostile wishes toward her will not come true. Also, his clinging communicates to his mother how indispensable she is to him and reassures her against her own inadequacy. Thus, the dependency-resentment relationship between mother and child is reinforced, and a vicious circle is perpetuated. Both mother and child are tightly bound together in a conflict that neither can resolve because it is largely unconscious.

Unconscious resentment and hostility is often dramatically revealed in children with school phobia. A nine-year-old boy who presented all of the classical symptoms serves as an excellent illustration. The acute symptoms of the child's difficulty appeared suddenly, as is often typical, one Monday morning as he approached the classroom. He complained to his teacher that he was unable to enter the classroom and felt very much afraid. His breathing was labored, and he seemed on the verge of an asthmatic attack. No amount of coaxing or pleading could entice him into the classroom. He subsequently went to the principal's office, where he was interviewed.

The boy found it exceedingly difficult to verbalize his reactions, but it was apparent that he was very much ashamed of his inability to remain in school. He was, however, able to express some feelings that clearly revealed his phobia to school. He indicated that he had a vague feeling that something would happen to his mother in his absence from home. He also expressed the fear that his pet, a young male hamster, would kill the mother hamster if he left them together without his careful supervision. The concern about his hamsters rather dramatically symbolized the child's own hostility and resulting anxiety about his mother; however, the child obviously had no insight or understanding of these unconscious connections.

An interview with the father revealed several interesting facts. For instance, the boy first experienced phobic reactions to school when he entered kindergarten, two weeks before the birth of his sister. At that time he expressed fears about his mother's hospitalization, cried hysterically, and could not be persuaded to go to school for three weeks. The boy was described as an especially good child who tried very hard to please. He was also considered very studious, preferred reading to other activities, and had few friends among boys his age. He had many fears, generally lacked self-confidence, was overly conscientious, and apparently struggled valiantly to meet the high expectations of his parents.

The child's relationships with both parents were conflicted. His mother protected and dominated him, while his father maintained a rather distant relationship with him. Also, the child and his mother were involved in a dependency-resentment relationship which neither could break. The parents' relationships with each other were also conflicted, and the child's problems had been interwoven into the parental conflicts because of his dependency ties to his mother. He felt rejected by his parents, less loved than his sisters, and had great hostility toward his mother.

Although the school was successful in getting the child back periodically, he could not tolerate long periods in the classroom. His attendance record became increasingly worse, and his parents became more impatient, angry, and embarrassed by the child's inability to remain in school. Both parents had resisted the prospects of intensive psychotherapy for their son during this interim. Recognizing that the problem would get worse and that the parents' motivation to place their son in therapy would improve as the problem increased, the school psychologist simply waited until the propitious moment arrived. However, during this time, contact between the child and the school was maintained. The child was required to complete school-work assignments at home, and the teacher and classmates were encouraged to write letters to convey their desire to have him back in school.

The parents finally consented to psychotherapy for themselves and the child. They received therapeutic help for three months, although the child was re-entered in school six weeks after therapy began. At first, he could stay in school only for short periods of time. However, his time in school gradually increased, and at the end of two months he had made the adjustment completely. Even such a short period of therapy helped the child come to grips with some of his deeper problems. For example, his unconscious anger toward his mother was well revealed in his play therapy sessions—he burned her at the stake no less than ten times! This opportunity to act out his hostility in therapy helped the child to relieve his hostility and guilt, thereby relieving him of some of his anxiety.

HELPING THE
PHOBIC CHILD

How much the child with school phobia can be helped is very much dependent upon the seriousness of his disturbance. Furthermore, the basic personality composition of the child will determine the relative success of environmental manipulation in helping the child, and Chess (1) has indicated that school phobia may arise in a variety of personality structures. For instance, school phobia may be part of a primary behavior disorder, a character disorder, a psychoneurosis, a psychosis, or mental retardation. The results of several studies (2, 5) indicate that a large percentage of these children will need psychotherapy before they can re-

solve their school phobias. However, when the problem is less severe and the child's symptomatology has not crystallized, it is possible to keep him in school for a time.

The child whose problem is less severe can be helped to stay in school if his parents are able to take a firm stand on the necessity of his staying in school. Typically, however, the mother is unable to be firm, and it is the father who must assume the primary responsibility of taking the child to school. Once the child has been delivered to school, the teacher must be prepared to be supporting but firm with the child. Invariably the child will shed many tears and attempt to manipulate the situation. It is at this point that many teachers become upset and concede to the child's demands or attempt to force the child to cease his disturbing behavior. Neither way of dealing with the situation is helpful to the child.

If this child is to remain in school, he needs the security of firm limits. He needs to feel the warm acceptance and approval of the teacher as well, but the teacher must be one he can count on to maintain certain limits. It is sometimes helpful for the teacher to reassure the child that his mother will be all right during his absence from home. At other times it is reassuring to the child if he is permitted to phone home and talk with his mother. However, when this is done, it is wise to make certain that the mother will be home to receive his call. Otherwise, he may feel that something actually has happened to her.

Some situations are more complex. For example, there are times when neither parent can be firm enough with the child to get him to, and keep him in, school. In such instances, it is often helpful to ask the attendance officer or the school nurse to transport the child to school. However, this is done only when the child seems sufficiently able to handle his anxiety and fear without panic. This brings up the question of physical coercion. If the child is so resistant and fearful as to require physical coercion, he is obviously too disturbed to be in school.

When a child with school phobia can be kept in school (through the assistance of an attendance officer or nurse), it is often beneficial to the child for someone to help him verbalize his feelings. A daily interview or supportive session often provides enough support to help the child remain in school.

At this point, a logical question arises: "How does one know whether a child should be required to attend school or permitted to stay at home?" This is a question that is best answered by a psychiatrist, psychologist, or social worker. However, such a person is not always available for consultation. In the absence of such assistance, the most important factors one should consider are the intensity with which the child reacts and the degree to which he is able to handle his anxiety while he is at school. If the child is able to settle down after he reaches school, and can participate in regular activities without becoming very upset, he can probably deal sufficiently well with his anxiety to remain in school. However, if the child is considerably upset for long periods, or if his phobic or fear reactions extend to other objects, situations, or relationships, pressure should not be used to keep the child in school.

Many children, whose symptoms are not well crystallized and who tend to be highly manipulative, often adjust after the initial anxiety of separation from their mothers. For instance, after his mother has left the school grounds and the teacher has firmly set the limits, a child may settle down and enter into the classroom activities with considerable composure. Also, if a program is followed that is fairly consistent, one is often able to help such a child continue in school.

Once a child presents the classical symptoms of school phobia, one may reasonably question how much can be gained by the use of various environmental maneuvers and tactics in an effort to keep that child in school. Furthermore, there is a pronounced tendency for children who present the classical symptoms of school phobia at one time to present the symptoms at another time. This is true even when the first onset of symptoms appears to have been handled successfully without therapy. The parents, therefore, should be encouraged to seek therapy for the child at the first onset of the symptoms.

In actual practice one finds that parents of children with school phobia are quite resistant to therapy when it is first suggested. Their resistance may arise because the parents have assessed the child's past conforming behavior as indicative of a "good" adjustment and cannot accept the actual need for therapy. Also, the child's real problems have generally been disguised behind a network of defenses without other overt symptoms that are disturbing to the parents. Then, too, the separation is just as difficult for the mother as it is for the child; therefore, the mother's unconscious needs enter into her resistance to therapy. Furthermore, the parents may resist therapy to avoid facing their own contributions to, and resulting guilt for, the child's problem. It is sometimes wise, therefore, to allow the parents to try out their own strategy for getting the child back in school. Eventually, the parents usually recognize that their efforts are inadequate and something else must be done. When their attempts fail, the parents' motivation for therapy is enhanced, and the child may then be able to receive the assistance that is essential for his future welfare.

The school's role in helping the child does not end when the child is placed in therapy. The therapist and school must carefully coordinate their approaches when attempts are made to reinstate the child in school. Moreover, *it is absolutely essential that the child be returned to school as soon as possible, and contact should be maintained between the child and school all the time he is out.* This contact is important for three major reasons. First, it prevents the crystallization of symptoms and any resulting impediments to therapy. Second, it diminishes the secondary gains obtained from staying home. Third, as Chess (1) has pointed out, successful treatment is partially dependent upon a child's maintaining contact with the anxiety-provoking situation.

The child should be required to do at home as much of the classwork as possible, while he is in therapy, as part of the continuing contact with the school. It might be advisable for the child to be instructed in a neutral setting (one to which the child does not react with fear or phobia) if his academic performance warrants it, so that this will not be an obstacle to his return to school. It is generally unwise for a visiting teacher or homebound teacher to instruct the child at home.

This increases the child's isolation and withdrawal and diminishes his motivation to return to school.

It is often wise to require the child to do as much of the classwork at home as is possible. This is important for two reasons. First, if the child gets behind in his studies he is all the more reluctant to return to school. Second, when some contact with the school is not maintained it is easier for him to withdraw from the situation completely and he is less motivated to handle his problem in therapy.

When therapy indicates that the child should return to school, he should be permitted to re-enter on any basis that is considered therapeutically advisable. This may mean that the child attends for only a portion of the day. Then, as the child begins to handle his problem more effectively, the length of time at school can be extended gradually. The child's initial readjustment to school is a crucial one. The teacher's general attitude and approach can help the child to continue in school. Since the child may feel guilty about his absence from school and concerned about his classmates' attitudes toward him, it is sometimes helpful for the class to compose a letter to the child indicating that they want him back. The teacher's tolerance and acceptance of the child upon his return will also help to provide him with emotional support. One should recognize that the child will be somewhat fearful during his initial return to school. He will not, and should not be expected to, have the same zest and interest in all school activities as the other children. However, as his anxieties decrease and he successfully handles his problem, his school performance is usually better than it was previous to the manifestation of his difficulty.

References

1. Chess, Stella. School phobia. In M. B. Gottsegen and G. B. Gottsegen (eds.), *Professional school psychology*. New York: Grune and Stratton, 1960.

2. D'Evelyn, Katherine E. *Meeting children's emotional needs*. Englewood Cliffs, New Jersey: Prentice-Hall, 1957.

3. Kahn, J. H., and Nursten, Jean P. School refusal: A comprehensive view of school phobia and other failures of school attendance. *Amer. J. Orthopsychiat.*, 1962, XXXII, 707–718.

4. Suttenfield, V. School phobia: a study of five cases. *Amer. J. Orthopsychiat.*, 1962, XXXII, 707–718.

5. Waldfogel, S., Collidge, J., and Hahn, P. The development, meaning, and management of school phobia. *Amer. J. Orthopsychiat.*, 1957, XXVII, 754–780.

CHAPTER TWELVE

Summing Up

We have covered a great deal of material in the past eleven chapters. It is appropriate, therefore, that we reflect on some of the key ideas and concepts in those chapters as a way of summarizing and emphasizing the material.

We began by conceptualizing the infant as a helpless, dependent organism dominated by primary drives which must be satisfied to insure his survival. An infant is an egocentric creature, preoccupied with his survival, and when his needs are not properly satisfied, he experiences tension which to him is frightening. So, very early, tension is a threat to survival, and the infant attempts to rid himself of it. Fortunately, he inherits an organism endowed with homeostatic mechanisms that help him cope automatically with unpleasant tension. These homeostatic mechanisms operate, not only to signal his distress to others but also to maintain the infant's own biological equilibrium. His dependency status and his distress signals place him in interaction with others. And, depending upon how well others administer to his needs, the infant's tension level is reduced or increased, and he feels secure or unsafe. Furthermore, when his needs are satisfied and his tension is reduced, the infant begins to develop an awareness of others and to attach significance to them. Thus, he begins to value the presence of others and the care they give, and it is here that the rudiments of giving and seeking love begin. So, a long period of socialization begins.

The id, or primary drives, characterized as they are by the pleasure-seeking principle, soon launch the child into the forbidding territory of societal prohibitions. He has hardly reached the age of one year when he begins to experience restraints, inhibitions, and punishment for his uncontrolled pleasure seeking. Consequently, the child is forced to evaluate reality more carefully, to find acceptable sources of satisfaction, and to inhibit those of his urges that bring disapproval and loss of love. Therefore, as he matures and experiences conflict between his own impulses and parentally imposed frustrations and rules, the child's ego functions (reality) arise to mediate between the id and superego. The conflict between urges and prohibitions creates anxiety which warns the ego that impulse expression must proceed cautiously, if at all. Threats to the self are dealt with by various coping mechanisms to avoid the consequences of reality and the guilt originating from the superego. Moreover, once the child's superego is established (as a result of identification with parental standards), any loss of his self-esteem is comparable to, and almost as devastating as, the loss of parental love.

Unfortunately, the child's rearing (and the frustrations and discipline imposed in the process) creates in him the need to deny, inhibit, or repress many of his impulses, needs, or thoughts to an unconscious realm. However, unconscious impulses and their ideational representations do not vanish. Instead, they continue to seek discharge, and they determine in subtle ways a child's behavior that may become disturbed or maladaptive.

Unconscious impulses (those that the individual has felt are dangerous) seek many substitute routes. For example, a person who has a great deal of unconscious hostility may provoke situations that allow him to "justifiably" express it. He may appear to others as a person with a "chip on his shoulder." When someone challenges him, he becomes excessively angry and readily justifies his own behavior, which to him is a result of the other person's reactions. Yet, in reality his own unconscious hostility invites the challenge in the first place.

Anxiety, arising from impulse temptations or personal threats, also instigates a variety of coping or defensive methods. The goal of such coping measures is to reduce one's anxiety to comfortable levels and, ultimately, to keep forbidden thoughts, wishes, and feelings out of his consciousness. Thus, it is apparent that one ego function is to implement coping behavior that changes a person's ways of perceiving, orienting himself to reality, and making judgments about everyday affairs.

PSYCHOSOCIAL GROWTH

The culture in which a child is reared and the socialization processes to which he is subjected affect him in many important ways. Cultural patterns, transmitted primarily through the family, determine the extent to which a child is able to actualize his genic or hereditary potential. That is, depending upon the goals and value orientations of a culture, child-rearing measures that are consistent with the attainment of these goals are generally implemented. Consequently, certain attributes or behaviors are differentially singled out, rewarded, or punished while other behaviors are relatively neglected. That is, not all attributes that have potentiality are nurtured to the extent that they are actualized.

Furthermore, as different aspects of a child's behavior and development are singled out for emphasis, training, and reinforcement, the child acquires specific needs which become active motivators of his behavior. Thus, he learns to seek certain socially approved goals and to avoid others. In this way he learns to react to his drives or impulses as pleasant or unpleasant, as desirable or dangerous. If the socialization practices and goals of his family and culture are beyond his capacity or ability, it is more difficult for the child to adapt; therefore, deviations or disturbances must inevitably arise.

There are a number of ways in which socialization may be conceptualized. The psychoanalytic conception elaborated by Erikson was our basic model for discussion. While the discussion will not be repeated here, certain aspects of it are worth underlining. One may usefully conceptualize socialization and development as consisting of specific stages or critical points which an individual must successfully achieve to attain adult maturity. If he encounters excessive frustration, deprivation, or stress at any stage or crisis point, he approaches the next step in his development without the full power of his forces working for him. That is, his energies become bound or fixated at the points of excessive frustration and are not completely available for participation in the later stages of development. For example, difficulties experienced during the oral stage lead a child to an uncertain coping or mastery of tasks at the anal stage. Or, stated in another way, difficulties experienced in developing a sense of trust or safety predispose a person to difficulties in developing a sense of autonomy and affectional security. Similarly, problems at later levels of development may be encountered if earlier developmental stages have been fraught with difficulties.

It should also be noted that a child's experiences during the earlier stages establish for him certain models for relating to and viewing the world, simply because his early learning is in-timately related to his survival needs and, as such, is not readily unlearned. New learning, then, is cast into the existing structure or mold. That is, a child's way of reacting to his own impulses and the external realities that arise early, and are continuously used, is highly resistant to change. Therefore, fixations at the oral stage (when the child is faced with the crisis of trust vs. mistrust), predispose a child to meet problems at later ages from an orientation that is oral, dependent, passive, and distrusting. Such a consequence is not entirely inevitable if later ages and stages of a child's development provide new orientations and a more secure environment; however, given the environmental patterns of nurture and child rearing that are presently in vogue, the outlook is not often optimistic.

PARENTAL INFLUENCES AND THE CHILD

The extent to which a child experiences difficulties at different stages is largely determined by his relationships with his parents. Being the child's cultural representatives of the larger society, his parents have the responsibility of influencing him to become the type of human being that is considered desirable. Parents are more or less free to do so, depending upon their own unconscious need systems and personality structures. That is, when they are not excessively preoccupied with their own conflicts or unconsciously moved to use the child for their own need satisfactions, parents are able to create an environment that is facilitating to the child's development.

An over-all pattern or child-rearing style can usually be discerned in the way parents perform their roles. Concerning this, four major dimensions relative to parental attitudes are helpful in conceptualizing parent-child relationships and child-rearing patterns: (a) emotional responsiveness and acceptance of the child, (b) type of control and training methods, (c) valuation of the child and (d) level of aspiration and expectations. When these dimensions are carefully studied and analyzed, one can often predict the kinds of difficulties a particular child is likely to experience. A more complete summary of this discussion may be found at the end of Chapter three.

Perhaps our major generalization regarding child-rearing patterns and parent-child relationships is that the parental influences which affect the child most are ones that are often disguised in their expressions. For instance, parent-child relationships (especially the devastating ones) are more influenced by the parents' unconscious needs, conflicts, fears, problems, and aspirations than by rational choice. Although many parents may go through the external motions of being "good parents," their deeper unconscious trends have the most pronounced and lasting effect on the developing child. This is why simply knowing the "right practices" or methods does not necessarily help parents to develop healthy, stable children. Indeed, well-meaning, "good" families often produce neurotic children.

UNDERSTANDING THE CHILD

One cannot discover what a child needs or understand the external manifestations of his problems unless one can analyze the forces that move him. Therefore, since the way a child responds and the goals for which he strives are so much a product of the relationships he has experienced with his parents, one must understand these relationships to be of any real help to the child. Furthermore, from these relationships the child forms reality and his ethical (superego) and fantasy attitudes from which he forges his own self-evaluations. The composite of these self-attitudes, moreover, provides an operational center from which he orients himself to the world. Consequently, how the child behaves is generally consistent with his self-evaluation and his inner feelings.

However, the real person (the self-attitudes and feelings) is often hidden behind an intricate network of psychological defenses, because a child in our society is permitted the luxury to be himself only for a short time. He is pushed, pulled, and molded from the early years to be the kind of person his society feels he must become. Therefore, it is not surprising that the symptoms that express his stress, the mechanisms with which he adapts, are only indirect manifestations of a child's conflicts and problems. The symptoms are merely indicative of the motivations that instigate the child's behavior. Consequently, from his behavior one must trace the sources of his difficulties and develop a strategy for helping the deviant child—with the realization, however, that permanent change comes only from modification of the inner core of the personality.

While it may be difficult to understand the meaning of symptoms as signals to deeper motivations, the task is essential for any hope of success. It is a dubious victory for one to suppress an annoying symptom only to find that another takes its place. The second manifestation of the conflict may be more serious than the first and more difficult to modify satisfactorily.

It is imperative, therefore, that the teacher acquire techniques to gain complete data about a child in order to get at the roots of his problems. Of course, the teacher cannot, and should not, be expected to be competent with the arsenal of analytic techniques of the psychologist or psychiatrist. However, the teacher can learn a great deal by watching, listening, and observing the child as he interacts with people at school and uses the materials to which he is exposed. This behavior yields some of the same data that psychological tests yield, since one purpose of the tests is to provide a systematic opportunity to observe the reactions of the child.

Perhaps the teacher's primary difficulty is that of learning to use the information that is available, to seek out the proper data sources, and to systematically organize the data into a meaningful picture of the child. Essentially, this learning involves looking for cause and effect relationships. A good developmental history of a child, for instance, aids the teacher's understanding of what will or will not motivate that child or what facilitates his desirable or undesirable behavior. Teachers must also be sensitive to a child's reactions to change, as strategies are implemented to help the child, because unless the teacher learns to watch for feedback, to see what facilitates and what disturbs him, very little progress can be made in understanding or helping the child.

THE FACILITATING POTENTIAL OF A SCHOOL

By the time the child enters school, his basic orientation and personality structure have been established; however, what the child is and his potential are significantly affected by his experiences at school. If the school captures the essence of what he is, his growth is facilitated; if it does not, the child's potential for healthy growth is narrowed and restricted.

Nevertheless, schools cannot always do what is healthy or desirable for children. In the first place, the broader community may not support what the school is attempting to do, even though it may be in the best interest of the children. The public has the ultimate sanction, the final veto power, which is effectively exercised in the dollars they are willing to spend for education. So, the final result is often an unhappy compromise.

However, despite the limits under which the school must operate, certain other factors converge and jointly influence the impact a school has. For instance, the educational and administrative philosophy of a school determines how the school is organized, the type of curriculum that is developed, and the kinds of persons that are employed to do the teaching job. Consequently, schools that have insight into the needs and development of children reflect their insight in the teachers they hire, the curriculum they build, the interpersonal relationships they sanction and foster, and the commitments they make to and the respect they have for children. In such schools a child's development has an opportunity to flourish, and his potential is maximized. Schools with this quality also have a great impact on the mental health of a child.

In general, the quality of the relationships among school personnel significantly influences teaching effects. The administrator sets the tone, establishes a climate, and provides the model that filters down to the lower echelon; therefore, when he is able to build healthy relationships with and among his staff, the teachers usually build similar relationships with children.

Nevertheless, teachers have an impact that is independent of the school policies and administrative sanctions. They are people in their own right. They have needs, hopes, aspirations, and conflicts from the past that inevitably become involved in their teaching techniques and relationships with children. By and large, those whose needs are met satisfactorily outside the school situation and whose psychological defense systems can control excessive anxiety, guilt, and impulsivity do not need to involve children in unhealthy ways. Nor are they unreasonable in their expectations.

Furthermore, the impact of the school on the child is differentially influenced by social-class membership. Schools are predominantly middle-class in their philosophy, organization, and value orientation. As a result, the middle-class child is simply urged to be more of what he already is. The values of self-reliance and restraint, achievement, and keeping an eye on the future, are further emphasized and reinforced. Therefore, this child does not usually experience a great clash between his own goals and the goals of the school. The stresses and strains that he does experience arise from his urgent pursuit of recognition through achievement. Thus, his problems often originate from too rapid engagement in competition, status seeking, and social-ladder climbing. It is little wonder, then, that the middle-class child often exhibits problems centering around neurotic conflicts.

On the other hand, the lower-class child comes from a background that makes him feel like an alien when he comes to school. This child's background is such that he is inclined to give freer rein to impulse and to have little persistence in the face of long-range goals. Verbal abstractions and middle-class morals and manners have little capacity to capture him. He is often irregular in his school attendance and, therefore, becomes academically retarded, and he shows his disenchantment with school by various types of misconduct.

Any school that positively affects a child captures the child's uniqueness—regardless of the environment from which he comes—and translates this uniqueness into experiences and relationships that enhance his potential. Such a school also helps the child to feel safe and to gain continuing dimensions of the world around him without his having to use defense mechanisms that cripple his intellectual functioning. In addition, this school does not allow the child's background or value orientation to pre-determine failure or conflict for him because he is different. Furthermore, this school encourages divergence rather than narrowness; it encourages openness to experience rather than restriction of perception. Finally, the enhancing school responds to the child as an individual who is constantly striving to discover his own unfolding resources.

THE DEVIANT CHILD: SOME GENERALIZATIONS

As we reflect about the types of deviant behavior that have been considered in this book and consider ways to help the child, certain strategies are central. In this final section we wish to state them explicitly for clarity and emphasis.

The enlightened school anticipates and plans for deviant children, since in every classroom in today's schools there are at least three or four children whose behavior deviates sufficiently to require special planning and assistance. In addition to this number, there are usually five to ten more children whose difficulties are serious enough to also require some additional help. It is not sufficient for a school simply to administer "discipline" or use various forms of ingenious punishment. Instead, a school must develop a philosophy and implement programs that consider the nature of disturbed behavior. Whatever program is conceived must be accepted by the whole staff. Psychologists, counselors, administrators, or teachers cannot work in isolation. There must be unity of purpose and planning at all levels. Otherwise, gains made by a few will be jeopardized or lost by those who believe in a different philosophy or plan of action.

Beyond this obvious generalization about the need for unity of planning and action, there are methods of thinking about and working with the deviant or disturbed child that have utility. In the interest of brevity, these generalizations will be listed.

A strategy for helping any deviant child must be based on a reasonable understanding of his dynamics and an accurate assessment of the severity of his disturbance. A child's symptoms, by themselves, may provide clues for the use of certain emergency or antiseptic measures, but permanent change in a child's behavior requires a strategy that is planned around his deeper dynamics. Furthermore, if a child's disturbed behavior is deeply entrenched, a day-to-day program that fits his pathology must be planned. For example, the teacher cannot hope to "cure" the

deeply troubled child. In this instance, the teacher should set up more limited goals and work toward helping the child receive from experts the assistance he needs.

Deviant behavior that has a sudden onset and is atypical of a child's past behavior is often indicative of a situational crisis. Nevertheless, even though the child's behavior may be disruptive, strong measures to inhibit or stop the behavior are usually a mistake. Such behavior is often a signal that a child's equilibrium has been temporarily upset; he usually regains composure when the crisis passes. Therefore, the child needs a friendly, supporting relationship while he is regaining his stability.

One can maximize the possibility of favorably changing a child's behavior by enlisting the cooperation and help of those who have intimate contact with the child, because teachers, principals, psychologists, and counselors have great difficulty helping a child when they work in isolation. For instance, one teacher can undermine the efforts of another, or the parents can jeopardize the work of a specialist, if the goals are not commonly shared and understood. Therefore, helping a child requires a planned strategy that is commonly agreed upon by those who are attempting to assist the deviant child toward a better adjustment to his environment. Consequently, every school should have a carefully specified philosophy and strategy for dealing with "discipline cases" or deviant children.

Any person who is working with a child should recognize that his own behavior is vitally important in his attempts to help the child. For instance, when a teacher's behavior toward a child is negative, regardless of whether it is conscious or unconscious, the deviant child detects the negativism and is influenced by it. If a teacher has negative feelings toward a child and is unable to change, the child should be placed elsewhere for a better chance of being helped. It is not a disgrace; in fact, it is very desirable for a teacher to recognize the need and make such a recommendation.

Regardless of the type of disturbance a child has, one should not wait for the disturbance to blossom before taking some action. One must learn to look for signs of disturbance and, when they appear, change the child's activity, move him out of an overstimulating situation, or give him immediate situational assistance. In other words, it is more efficient to anticipate and give help to a child when his symptoms first appear than when he is, for example, in the midst of a severe temper tantrum. Once the child has disrupted a situation, one is inclined to employ measures that may permanently damage rapport with the child and make it difficult to restore any prior gains.

Punishment, even under the most favorable circumstances, is a relatively ineffective method for bringing about permanent and desirable behavior changes. Punishment may serve to inhibit certain undesirable behavior, but it does not help the child to substitute more desirable behavior. Furthermore, while punishment may cause the child to avoid the behavior to which it is directed, he may generalize his avoidance to include also the teacher, school, and academic work.

Nevertheless, teachers do sometimes resort to punishment, as we all do when our feelings run away with us. At such times, teachers should recognize that the punishment does produce negative, resentful feelings in children. Therefore, after the pun-

ishment, the teacher should help the youngster deal with his angry feelings in order to reestablish and maintain the relationship which is so important to the child.

In working with the disturbed child on a day-to-day basis, the teacher should be problem-centered and nonjudgmental. When judgments are made about his "badness," a child's concern is focused on defensive or self-protective measures rather than on problem solving. Furthermore, the disturbed child can accept his problems and their consequences better when he is not faced with rejecting attitudes and negative self-evaluations.

It is also helpful in working with the disturbed child for the teacher to have frequent private conferences with him. These conferences should provide an opportunity for the child to verbalize his conflicted feelings, and it is quite acceptable for the teacher to discuss the child's problems with him; however, the emphasis in the conferences should focus on goals which the child can attain. Little is to be gained if the conference is used to censure the child or list for him all of the things that he has done wrong. These conferences, in addition, can provide the teacher with an opportunity to develop a sympathetic and positive relationship with the child as well as an opportunity to gain additional insight into his problems.

A child may be able to change his maladaptive behavior patterns when a helping person establishes a relationship with him that is accepting, predictable, safe, and need-satisfying. Such a relationship helps a child to feel less threatened; as a result, his feelings of anxiety and guilt are reduced, and he is able to feel greater self-esteem. In other words, as threat, anxiety, and guilt are reduced, a child's defensive need to attack or withdraw from his environment is lessened, and he begins to feel more positive self-regard. Consequently, much of the energy that the child has spent to deal with his conflicts becomes available to him for more productive pursuits. Therefore, he can feel hopeful, expect success, and use his resources to be competent in the face of his environment. As he feels this success and is rewarded for his positive efforts, the child is more likely to give up his defeating patterns and move toward solutions that are more adaptive.

Index